NONE
OF THE
ABOVE

NONE
OF THE
ABOVE

Why Presidents Fail—And
What Can Be Done About It

BY
ROBERT SHOGAN

NAL BOOKS
NEW AMERICAN LIBRARY
TIMES MIRROR
NEW YORK AND SCARBOROUGH, ONTARIO

For Ellen, Cynthia and Amelia

 NAL BOOKS TRADEMARK REG. U.S. PAT. OFF. AND FOREIGN COUNTRIES
REGISTERED TRADEMARK—MARCA REGISTRADA
HECHO EN HARRISONBURG, VA., U.S.A.

SIGNET, SIGNET CLASSICS, MENTOR, PLUME, MERIDIAN AND NAL BOOKS
are published *in the United States* by
The New American Library, Inc.,
1633 Broadway, New York, New York 10019,
in Canada by The New American Library of Canada Limited,
81 Mack Avenue, Scarborough, Ontario M1L 1M8

Library of Congress Cataloging in Publication Data

Shogan, Robert.
None of the above.

Bibliography: p.
Includes index.
1. Presidents—United States.   I. Title.
JK516.S46   1982   353.03'1   82-8293
ISBN 0-453-00426-1

Designed by Leonard Telesca

First Printing, October, 1982

1 2 3 4 5 6 7 8 9

PRINTED IN THE UNITED STATES OF AMERICA

Contents

Author's Note

This book was written during the first year of Ronald Reagan's presidency, in the midst of heated debate about the meaning of his election and the wisdom of his policies. Its underlying premise is that Reagan's administration, and the future of presidential politics for the rest of this century, can only be understood by looking back, particularly at the past twenty years.

The scholarship and journalism covering this period are ample and I have used these resources freely, as evidenced by the source list and reference notes at the end of the book. But the judgments entered here are my own. They have been shaped mainly by the values formed during twenty-five years as a reporter and editor, most of them spent dealing with politics and government from City Hall to the White House. This experience, like every other, has had its own advantages and limitations. The chief lesson I have drawn from it is the importance of asking the right questions, which is what I have tried to do in these pages.

Though the responsibility is mine alone, the book owes a great deal to a great many people. The initial debt is to the editors of the *Los Angeles Times* for their encouragement and cooperation in arranging my work schedule. I particularly want to thank John Foley, assistant managing editor; Dennis Britton, national editor; Jack Nelson, Washington bureau chief; and Richard Cooper, deputy bureau chief.

Tom Allen, Lawrence Baskier, Curtis Gans, and Gaylord Shaw read portions of the manuscript and provided constructive criticism. Ellen Hume, David Keene, Ben Palumbo, William Schneider and John Stacks also gave help and advice when they were much needed.

Among those who were generous in sharing their own work and ideas were Josiah Lee Auspitz, Kenneth H. Bode, David S. Broder, Carol Casey, Charles Hardin, Everett Carll Ladd, Charles Mohr, Martin Plissner, Robert D. Novak, Richard M. Scammon, Richard Wirthlin, and Jules Witcover.

For their extra trouble in helping me get access to research material I am grateful to Gloria Doyle, Diana Moore, and Barclay Howarth of the *Los Angeles Times* Washington Bureau; Diane Dewhirst of the Democratic National Committee; Heather David of the American Enterprise Institute; Karlyn H. Keene, managing editor of the AEI publication *Public Opinion;* Anne Reingold of CBS News; Thomas E. Mann, executive director of the American Political Science Association; and Sunday Orme, of the *New York Times* Washington Bureau.

Final thanks are due to those closest to the book from its inception to its conclusion: my agent, Carl Brandt, and my editor, Arnold Dolin, for their confidence in me; my neighbor, Anita Mitchell, for her swiftness and accuracy in typing this manuscript; and my wife, Ellen, and our daughters, Cynthia and Amelia, for their boundless patience and support.

CHAPTER ONE

The Gap

In the warm Florida sun the men wore short-sleeved shirts and many of the women were in shorts. Some sprawled on blankets but most stood patiently near the speaker's stand. It was October 1976, the presidential campaign was nearing its culmination, and these citizens were waiting in a park in Tampa to hear Jimmy Carter, the Democratic candidate.

On this day Carter at least seemed to have the elements on his side. The balmy weather had helped attract a good-sized crowd, perhaps a thousand persons. But Carter, as he took off his coat and tie and greeted the audience, knew that he could not count on the weather to help him on election day, just three weeks off. Carter was under pressure. He had launched his challenge to the incumbent Republican, Gerald Ford, with a formidable lead. But as the campaign lengthened, the polls showed that Carter's advantage was dwindling. The polls also showed that all across the land Americans were disillusioned and apathetic about politics and government. The Democratic nominee feared that, rain or shine, a good many people would simply not bother to vote in November. And he realized that for him, as for most candidates of his party, a small turnout threatened defeat.

Hoping to overcome the alienation of the electorate, Carter had early on stressed his faith in the American system of politics and government as one of the major themes of his campaign. Carter maintained that the system remained sound and vital, despite upheaval and scandal. He made this point incessantly, and so emphatically that he sometimes invited mockery, as he did this day in Tampa.

"Richard Nixon didn't hurt our system of government," I heard Carter tell the crowd in the park, as I had heard him tell voters around the country.

"Watergate didn't hurt your system of government," he said, and I noticed that some of his listeners looked puzzled and skeptical.

"The CIA revelations didn't hurt our system of government," Carter continued with his customary litany.

At this point a young man standing near me in the crowd lost patience. "It didn't help," he shouted, and those around him laughed.

But Carter plunged ahead with his peroration. "Our system of government is still the basis that doesn't change, that gives us a way to correct our mistakes, to answer difficult questions, to bind ourselves together in a spirit of equity and look at the future with confidence."

Carter had good reason to speak favorably of the system, for he had learned to use it to his advantage as a candidate. Moreover, the faith that he espoused in the system complemented his oft-repeated campaign promise to restore trust and efficiency to government through his own integrity and competence. He believed that it was not the system itself but the flaws of his predecessors which were responsible for dissatisfaction with the presidency. His confidence in his own ability to do better was symbolized by the question he raised early in his candidacy, which became the credo of his campaign. The question was "Why not the best?" and Carter brashly presented himself to the country as the answer.

In view of Carter's fretful stewardship of the nation, and his subsequent rejection at the polls, the question and the answer may now seem like a bad joke. But if it is any kind of joke, the laugh is on all of us. For Carter was only the latest in a succession of presidents whose performances fell far short of the expectations they created. Their twenty-year record of frustration and failure, which is the focus of this book, gives cause for alarm and reason for reappraisal of the presidency, and of the entire system of government and politics which Carter defended so fulsomely.

Not since Dwight Eisenhower has a chief executive served out two full terms in office. The subsequent story of the presidency is dominated by upheaval and distress, producing erratic swings in political fortunes. Kennedy's death left his major promises unkept. Johnson won a landslide victory, then was forced to retire. Nixon, another landslide winner, was obliged to resign in disgrace. Then came the successive defeats of incumbents Ford and Carter, the last by electoral landslide, and the succession of Reagan, whose presidency before long began to show signs of the same stresses and strains that had marred the tenure of his predecessors during two decades.

Our most recent six presidents, three of them Democrats and three Republicans, brought a variety of credentials and backgrounds to the White House. The last two had been governors, three others had been senators, four had served in the House and three had been vice-presidents. They came to the Oval Office from every section of the country—the West Coast, the Southwest, the deep South, the Midwest and New England. They differed markedly in temperament and philosophy and each initially had his own approach to meeting the responsibilities of the presidency. Yet ultimately, as an examination of their performances will show, all of them created many of the same problems for themselves and responded in many of the same ways.

Their combined experience suggests that the chronic failings of the presidency overshadow differences in the characteristics of our presidents. The White House is gripped by a syndrome whose symptoms are manifest in the record of the past twenty years. They are evidence of an affliction which has less to do with features of personality, upon which so much attention is lavished and upon which Carter placed so much stress, and more to do with the political and governing system to which presidents must respond.

Bearing out this diagnosis is a series of other signs of ill health in the political system which have coincided with the troubles of the presidency. Voter turnout has dropped steadily in congressional as well as presidential elections. Public opinion polls show that trust in political institutions and faith in their ability to deal with national problems have also diminished. Allegiance to political parties has ebbed, so much so that the two-party system is in danger of disintegrating into a "no-party system."

The political outlook is all the more disturbing because it has darkened in the midst of a period of dramatic change aimed at making the system more open and more equitable. The franchise was extended by constitutional amendment to eighteen-year-olds, and by congressional action to black citizens in the South who for a century had been denied free access to the polling booths. Supreme Court decisions brought an end to the grossest distortions of malapportionment and established the principle of one man, one vote as the rule of law.

Regulation of campaign financing was greatly strengthened, establishing limits on spending and contributions, requiring broad public disclosure of both, and providing federal subsidies for presidential candidates. Agitation mainly within the Democratic Party led to an overhaul of presidential nomination procedures for both parties, spurring proliferation of direct primaries and a quantum increase in the number of voters directly participating in the selection of candidates for the White House.

The fact that these changes of the past two decades have failed to overcome the problems of the political system, and in some ways have aggravated them, has added to the general sense of disillusionment. This disappointment has generated criticism of the reforms and stimulated what amounts to a wave of counter-reform.

Most of the criticism focuses on the presidential nominating process, where faults are easy to find. Campaigns have become prolonged endurance contests in which candidates compete against each other, but none is measured against the actual challenge of governing. Some of the legal restrictions on campaign financing have proven to be unrealistic and overly burdensome. The revisionists are proposing, among other remedies, to shorten the campaign by rescheduling primaries, to give extra weight in the presidential selection process to elected officials and to ease the financing regulations.

But in pressing for these kinds of changes the counter-reformers are following in the footsteps of the reformers down a much traveled dead-end street. The new revisionists, like their predecessors, are concentrating on jiggering and rejiggering political machinery. Their proposals leave untouched the relationship between politics and government, which suffers from fundamental defects and which requires fundamental change.

At the heart of the problem is what amounts to a gap between politics and government. The gap was not created by recent presidents, or by modern reforms. Instead, as the next chapter will show, the gap is imbedded in our laws and sustained by our customs. Its origins are in the constitutional impediments to the healthy development of political parties and the abiding public suspicion of both parties and politics.

The purpose of politics is to express the often conflicting concerns of the voters. The role of government is to resolve these concerns equitably. To put it in simplest terms, politics defines what people want; government decides what they get. For democracy to work, government must respond to politics.

This is where political parties come in. They are the best means available to us for connecting politics and government, for making politics relevant by providing voters with meaningful choices between policies and candidates, and for holding government accountable to the electorate.

Obviously this arrangement can never work perfectly. There are too many conflicting demands, too many unanticipated and uncontrollable events and too many opportunities for error. So any judgment of the parties, and the political system, must be relative. What standard should be used? One possibility is the performance of other governments. But the great variance of conditions in other countries from ours restricts the usefulness of this guide.

Our own history provides a more valid basis for comparison. And a good many modern politicians and scholars are convinced that the parties functioned better in the past than they do today. But these judgments need to be qualified. If the parties used to do a better job, this was in large measure because less was demanded of them. Politics was more stable, government less ridden by crisis. On the great public challenges that divided the nation the parties did not distinguish themselves by their leadership, for some of the same reasons they are in trouble today.

But there is another criterion, and that is the sum of our own expectations. This standard, while it may be subjective, is not arbitrary. It is an outgrowth of the American Creed, soundly based in the Declaration of Independence's assertion that government's powers are derived from the consent of the governed and in the Constitution, which, as John Marshall read it, created "emphatically and truly a government of the people. In form and substance it emanates from them, its powers are granted by them, and are to be directly exercised on them, and for their benefit." This theme of government accountability has been echoed through the decades by public officials and private citizens, in countless statutes, judicial rulings, newspaper editorials and soapbox orations until, as Clarence L. Ver Steeg observed, it "pervades every convolution of the national mind."

"Politics ain't beanbag" is a well-worn expression among the ranks of contemporary political professionals, intended to make the point that their occupation is no gentle pastime, but rather a harsh competition for public office and power. But "politics ain't beanbag" for the mass of private citizens either. Their government has the authority to reach into every nook and cranny of their existence. They are obliged to obey its laws, pay its taxes and, on occasion, risk their lives for it. They cannot reasonably expect the government not to err in its policies. But they pay dearly for mistakes—when farm prices drop, interest rates soar, jobs dwindle, neighborhoods are destroyed or the country is plunged into war.

Political leaders like to stress the virtues of pragmatism and the value of compromise. But too often, as voters have discovered, pragmatism serves as a rationale for expediency while compromise results not from hard and legitimate bargaining but rather from the evasion of controversy.

Since they entered the first grade, voters have been led to believe that they are entitled to a voice in the process of making the decisions which can produce these outcomes, the chance to register their preferences beforehand or, at the least, their reactions after the fact. Certainly they have a right not to be bamboozled. But nearly every sign and portent of the opinion and behavior of voters today tell us that they have concluded, and with good reason, that the system of politics and government has failed to meet this standard. This failure can be traced to the inability of parties to provide the essential link between politics and government, which is the underlying cause of irrelevance in politics, of unaccountability in government, and of the current crisis in presidential leadership.

The parties were born to fail. To succeed they must be able to win support from the electorate and deliver results in government. But the Constitution makes no provision for the functioning of parties; it does not even mention them. Indeed, the Constitution makes the task of parties difficult, if not impossible, by ordaining a permanent antagonism between the executive and the legislature which transcends party allegiance. By curbing the authority of parties in government, the Constitution undermines the influence of parties in politics and in effect institutionalizes the gap between politics and government.

The gap has been with us from the beginning of the Republic, resisting various efforts at reform. Every president since George Washington has been frustrated and has also been condemned with varying degrees of justification. The values and practices of political campaigns have always been suspect. In the late nineteenth century, the British scholar James Bryce devoted a chapter of *The American Commonwealth* to discussing "Why Great Men Are Not Chosen President," and concluded that party leaders usually decided that the most outstanding prospects were too controversial to get elected.

But in recent years the gap has widened dangerously. There are three principal reasons: the electorate, on one side of the gap, has been going through a period of turmoil and devisiveness; the government, on the other side, has had to deal with growing demands and rising expectations; and the parties, which ought to serve as the connecting institution, have been steadily debilitated.

The parties, and the entire system, have been transformed by a combination of interlocking events and circumstances in which nearly every factor seems to be both cause and consequence of nearly every other factor.

Sweeping social and economic changes have eroded old political loyalties. Sociologist Morris Janowitz has described the pervasive impact of what he labels the "disarticulation" of society: the splintering of traditional constituency groups into a magnitude of fragments, making it increasingly difficult for individual citizens to discern their political interests and for political leaders to establish reliable coalitions.

Take the case of George Jones. He is a hypothetical example, but his predicament is real enough. Jones is a skilled auto worker who earns more than $25,000 a year. His union endorsed Carter in the 1980 election, but Jones was fed up with inflation, for which he blamed Carter, so he voted for Reagan. When unemployment climbed after Reagan was elected, Jones started worrying about his job and wondered if he had made a mistake.

Jones has other job worries, too. He knows that government pollution standards add to his company's production costs and cut into his own paycheck. On the other hand, though, Jones likes to fish, and one weekend he discovered that the lake he usually goes to had been poisoned by chemical waste. So Jones is uncertain about whether he is for or against strict environment regulation.

Jones does not see much use in political parties. He likes to hunt and he belongs to a rifle club. Recently he sent the club ten dollars to help lobby against gun control, which is more than he has ever contributed to a political party. All told, the Gallup Poll estimates, about twenty million Americans like Jones belong to special-interest organizations and an additional twenty million give money to such groups, far more than contribute to the two political parties. These citizens are walking concatenations of conflicts of self-interest and it has become increasingly difficult for political parties to gain their support.

Against this backdrop of social and economic cross-pressures, innovations in technology and refinements in political techniques have undercut the parties' own influence. The preeminent technological force is, of course, television, which with its capacity to reach mass audiences has spurred competing media to expand their own markets and thus intensify their impact on society. "Men . . . still talk to each other," Joseph Bensman and Bernard Rosenberg write in "Mass Media and Mass Culture." But they add, ". . . what we say to each other is very often no more than an extension of facts and feelings relayed to us by the mass media. . . . As such the mass media are *impersonal agencies of socialization.*"

By the same token the media are also agencies of politicization. Just as the media have overwhelmed the old channels of social communication, they have swamped the traditional routes of political contact relied on by political parties. Measure the audience for Carter's speech in Tampa, for example, against the audience that could have seen excerpts or analyses of the speech on their television sets.

The media have also enhanced the impact of polling, just as this branch of political science, thanks to computers, was coming of age technologically. No pollster has ever asked George Jones his opinion about anything. But every week Jones hears about some public opinion survey on television or in the press and these results shape his views about what the majority of Americans believe, and sometimes incline him to think the same way. Just as importantly, the polls influence the views of politicians about what Jones and most of his fellow citizens believe. The old-time politician, who used to take the pulse of his constituents in conversations on Main Street, is no match for the scientific sample and its massive reinforcement.

While the public pollsters, like Gallup and Harris, have been increasing their indirect influence on politics and government, private pollsters, armed with their computers, have been playing a greater direct role in the strategies of the politicians whom they serve. In 1980, Richard Wirthlin, Ronald Reagan's chief pollster, combined the latest opinion survey figures with data on past voting patterns to periodically simulate the election contest between Carter and Reagan and to advise Reagan on the consequences of specific tactical decisions—whether he should defend his own record or attack Carter's, stress an issue or ignore it, spend a day less in one city and a day more in another.

Computers also have helped to change the nature of political fund raising, once again to the disadvantage of parties. Time was when the major source of campaign financing was a relatively small group of "fat cats," wealthy contributors who were carefully cultivated and appropriately rewarded by party leaders. But the computers made possible a surge in solicitation of funds through the mail to millions of small contributors, who, like George Jones, had no special loyalty to a party but were concerned about one particular issue or another. During one recent year Richard Viguerie, an ambitious conservative who revolutionized political fund raising, and in the process made himself wealthy, estimated that his computers fired off fifty million letters on behalf of the various right-wing causes and candidates who were his clients. They yielded $15 to $20 million, about equal to the total revenues of the Republican and Democratic national committees put together.

The combined impact of the new technology and the social and economic ferment on the party system has been devastating. Together they have helped to make it impossible for the parties to keep up with George Jones and all the other Joneses of America.

Out of these circumstances has emerged a new breed of candidates for the White House, and for other offices as well, who manage to get elected without much help from their parties. Not surprisingly, once in power they tend to maintain their distance and their independence.

Parties have never had an effective official means for contributing to the development of public policy. The platforms dutifully adopted at every national convention are famous for their grandiose generalities and unkept promises. Whatever weight parties used to carry in government depended on informal pressures brought to bear on behalf of constituencies they claimed to represent. But nowadays such claims are hard to substantiate, as are the corollary pledges of support at the next election.

Modern presidents do not need party leaders to get their messages across to the electorate. They reach voters en masse through television, they test the reaction with their own pollsters and they maintain their own specialists for dealing with the various interest groups.

The availability of these resources has fostered one of the major phenomena of the gap between politics and government, the personalization of the presidency. Unable or unwilling to depend on their parties, presidents have increasingly charted their own courses, relied on their own instincts and tried to fulfill their own ambitions. In the process they have inevitably made their office less accountable and less responsive to the electorate.

These presidential tendencies have been accentuated in response to the mounting burdens on the chief executive and the federal government in general. The expansion of Washington's role in our lives, which began in the 1930s, has been spurred by events of the past two decades. The perennial national problems of economic and foreign policy have become more complex and more urgent. Meanwhile, new dilemmas such as energy and the environment are demanding national attention. The sobering onset of the era of limits on national wealth and power has called traditional values into question and forced the establishment of different priorities. Here at home, as the economic engine runs low on resources long taken for granted, Americans accustomed to pushing ahead toward broader and brighter horizons now worry mostly about protecting what they already have. Abroad, American prestige and influence are under mounting pressure from Soviet militarism, Japanese industrialism and Third World nationalism.

All this has led to a substantial enlargement of presidential responsibility, both explicit and implied, but without a corresponding increase in presidential power. Responsibility and power are sometimes confused. The power of the federal government has expanded in recent years, as reflected in the proliferation of programs and agencies. This has increased the president's responsibilities, his duties and obligations. But the president's power to manage and direct the government apparatus, which depends mainly on his relations with Congress, has not been appreciably enhanced. In dealing with the Congress the president remains what he always has been, a more or less coequal adversary.

The difficulties of this relationship for the president are of course most evident when a majority of Congress belongs to the opposition party. The president is expected to lead, but the opposition is expected to obstruct him and usually does. This is not to argue, of course, that the president is right all the time, or even most of the time. Rather the point is that this state of institutional belligerency makes it next to impossible, except during extraordinary periods, such as wartime or the immediate aftermath of a landslide presidential election, for either institution, the executive or the legislature, to establish policy goals and reach them. The potential for this deadlock is as old as the Constitution. But the weakening of the political parties has made such divided governments more frequent occurrences. In recent years voters have increasingly based their choices for president, House, and

Senate on characteristics of individual candidates instead of party allegiance. The Republicans who won three of the last six presidential elections have each had to confront a Congress in which at least one house was controlled by the opposition party.

After a prolonged fiscal dispute with the Democratic-controlled House led to a temporary shutdown of the government in late 1981, Ronald Reagan complained: "That is no way to run a railroad and it's even less of a way to run a country," a feeling which many of his predecessors have undoubtedly shared.

But even when a majority of the Congress owes nominal allegiance to the same party as the president, the separate constituencies and divergent interests of the legislators make it difficult for the president to rely on them for support. "No member of that majority has the constitutional duty or the practical political need to vote for each element of the president's program," Lloyd Cutler points out from bitter firsthand experience as President Carter's former counsel. "Neither the President nor the leaders of the legislative majority have the means to punish him if he does not. In the famous phrase of Joe Jacobs, the fight manager, 'It's every man for theirself.' " Once again, an old problem has been aggravated by party deterioration. In the past, intervals of party harmony between the president and the Congress have been achieved not through formal sanctions but by what James L. Sundquist of the Brookings Institution describes as "voluntary discipline," the recognition of mutual self-interest by the president and members of his own party in the Congress. But as Sundquist notes, the weakening of party ties has been reflected in "the rise of individualism" in the Congress and has made it harder for the president to find common ground with the legislators.

The problems of institutional rivalry faced by the president have not been eased by the dramatic expansion of the executive branch in recent years. Although the proliferation of agencies creates an outward appearance of enhancement of presidential power, these agencies, like the president, are ultimately answerable to the Congress. Their growth has made it that much harder for the president to ensure that this multitude of bureaucracies takes direction from him and not from the legislators who control their funding or the interest groups who rely on their services.

Seeking help, presidents have increased the number of White House aides. These functionaries serve the president directly, and are more responsive to his commands than are the hierarchs of the agencies. But they are subject to the same limitations as the president himself in dealing with the other institutions of government. Moreover, the clustering of personal staff around the president tends to isolate and ultimately to weaken him.

Technology, not politics, has contributed the one significant addition to the president's powers in recent years, his authority to touch off a nuclear holocaust. But this prerogative is too apocalyptic to be helpful. As Lyndon Johnson remarked: "The only power I have is nuclear, and I can't use that."

Similar grievances have been heard from earlier presidents. "I sit here all day trying to persuade people to do the things they ought to have sense enough to do without my persuading them," Harry Truman grumbled during his early days in the White House. "That's all the powers of the President amount to."

Characteristically, Truman overstated the case, but not by much. Moreover, Truman's successors have had even greater reason to complain as the demands upon them have grown and their political support systems in their parties have atrophied. Presidents suffer the most conspicuously from the gap between politics and government. The citizenry expects the president to lead, to manage the nation's affairs efficiently, to cope with foreign threats, to preserve the peace, to ensure domestic tranquility and to arrange for prosperity. If the president is to satisfy these broad expectations, or even come close, he must make and gain support for a range of complex decisions and choices which would mean that some values and groups would gain while others lose.

But the condition of our political process discourages efforts to argue out these issues and gain public commitments for them in the campaign. The parties, which ought to serve as rallying points for different groups with common interests, lack the vitality and credibility to serve this purpose. Presidential campaigns begin with lengthy intraparty contests for the nomination which often sharpen party divisions and thus leave the party weaker than before.

The successful nominee then has time only for superficial repairs during the relatively brief general election campaign. And the winner of that hectic and disjointed competition typically enters office without party backing he can consistently command, and without a clear mandate for the hard choices he must make, because he has offered none to the voters.

But if presidents are victims of the gap between politics and government, they also help to perpetuate and widen it. Examples of willful and domineering behavior, of unaccountability and irresponsible leadership can be found all through the history of the presidency. But these symptoms of the personalized presidency have become more manifest and more frequent in recent years as chief executives have struggled to fill the enlarged role they have helped to create for themselves.

During the past two decades, presidents, striving to gain support, have made promises they could not keep and have lived to regret. To win attention they have made style a matter of state. Impatient with their parties, they have ignored them except as instruments to assure renomination. Stalemated at home, they have sought prestige by thrusting themselves into the drama of foreign affairs.

Providing the life force for the personalized presidency is the power of the mass media. Presidents have always enjoyed general prestige and respect, but in the past they were regarded from a distance, as abstract representations of their office and their actions. The modern media, particularly television, have thrust them into our family rooms, and inflated their personas out of all proportion.

The ability to transmit his personality into the gap parties once were expected to fill greatly enhances the president's powers of persuasion that Truman mentioned. In the early months of his presidency, Ronald Reagan demonstrated, as have some of his predecessors, that a skillful media performer can use that skill to turn aside challenges to his programs.

But the personality of the president cannot effectively link politics and government because a genuine understanding of issues is clouded by the focus on superficialities and irrelevancies. In our celebrity-centered culture the president has become the preeminent celebrity. Public fascination with his whims, moods, and incidental behavior, which the media stimulate and which the president generally encourages, fosters a pervasive mystique which further confuses values and judgments in an already distorted system.

After he was wounded by a would-be assassin early in his presidency, Reagan's approval rating soared in the opinion polls, reflecting admiration for the good-humored grace with which he handled himself. This was a natural reaction from a duly concerned and sympathetic public. But it was a measure of the force of the personalized presidency that the positive public response spilled over into the totally unrelated debate over Reagan's economic policies, where it further handicapped the president's already demoralized Democratic opponents in trying to challenge his proposals.

Reagan is uncommonly skilled at projecting his personality to the public in a favorable light. But the media's absorption with the White House has been evidenced during the tenure of chief executives much less gifted in this regard.

During the first fourteen days of Gerald Ford's presidency, Barbara Tuchman noted, the *New York Times* ran Ford's picture on its front page twelve times. "Why?" Mrs. Tuchman asked. "We all know what he looks like. . . . By packing our craving for father-worship into the same person who makes and executes policy—a system no other country uses—we have given too much greatness to the Presidency."

The distractions and irrelevancies evidenced in presidential governance are fostered by and mirrored in presidential campaigning. Unable to provide consistent support on policy questions facing the government, the parties are in a poor position to organize reasoned debate on substantive issues in politics. Candidates stress imagery and illusions built around their personalities. Instead of presenting choices on controversial questions, they offer evasions and equivocations. The meaning of the outcome is often obscured by the confusion of the contest.

The campaign for votes in the Iowa precinct caucuses in January 1980 typified the vacuousness of competition for the presidential nomination. Iowa was the first state to select delegates to the national conventions, and the press and politicians had billed the campaign there as an event of great consequence in the struggle for the presidency. Candidates in both parties spent hundreds of thousands of dollars on television commercials. Vice-President Mondale, barnstorming on President Carter's behalf, declared: "The whole world is watching this state."

But the contest in neither party offered voters much to see, or to hear, that would help them in choosing their president. On the Democratic side debate was muffled because President Carter chose to run as commander in chief. He stayed in the White House, claiming the hostage crisis in Iran and the Soviet invasion of Afghanistan prevented him from campaigning. This left his principal challenger, Edward Kennedy, to plod grimly around the state like a man shouting into an echo chamber until he stumbled to defeat.

Among Republicans the give and take was no more enlightening. Ronald Reagan, perceived as the front-runner, decided to protect his advantage by avoiding the principal event of the campaign, a televised debate among all Republican candidates. Reagan contended that the debate would have a divisive effect on the GOP.

He need not have worried about that. Most of Reagan's rivals who did show up for the debate found little to disagree about among themselves. Their only serious quarrel with Reagan was over his failure to join the debate.

"There are no issues here," Richard Bond*, who was managing George Bush's campaign in the state, told me. "This is a test of a candidate's ability to run." As it turned out, Bush passed the test in Iowa, finishing ahead of the Republican field, including Reagan. But as Bond indicated, the result did not mean that the voters preferred Bush's proposals for coping with inflation and the energy crisis to those of his rivals, or considered him better able to deal with the Soviet Union. Such points were drowned out by the din of the thirty-second cam-

* In 1982 Bond, who had been an aide in Bush's vice-presidential office, became deputy-chairman of the Republican National Committee.

paign commercials which became a regular staple of Iowa's broadcasting fare. The caucus triumph merely showed that Bush had the time and common sense to launch his campaign in Iowa early, and then worked more diligently and energetically than any of his competitors. Yet this victory established Bush as the Republican front-runner for a time. And ultimately it helped him to become Reagan's vice-president and thus put him near the head of the line for the Republican presidential nomination when Reagan's turn is done.

One night late in the campaign I stopped off in Indianola, a farming town about twenty miles south of Des Moines, and spent an hour talking to the patrons of Flash's saloon about their choices for president. Most of the customers in the bar had no interest in the campaign, and only two out of a dozen intended to vote.

"The last time I voted was for Jack Kennedy in 1960," said the proprietor, Ronald White. "Has there been anybody worth voting for since?"

"I voted once. That was for Richard Nixon and that was enough," said Jeff McCoy, a truck driver.

"Nixon was a crook," Jean Wilson, a secretary, said. "But at least he knew what he was doing. I'm afraid whoever gets elected is going to make the mess we're in even worse."

In the world outside Flash's, the constant blare of commercials caught the attention of some Iowans who might not otherwise have voted. So did the presence in the state of so many prominent journalists, especially the network luminaries who were more familiar than some of the candidates. "I saw that Walter Cronkite was in town, so I thought there must be something interesting going on," said the Des Moines Ford dealer who had rented me a car. He had decided to attend a Republican caucus at the last minute, but had trouble remembering for whom he had voted. At any rate, the media barrage helped produce a record turnout for the caucuses. On the day after the voting, local party leaders congratulated themselves on the fact that about 20 percent of the state's registered voters showed up at the caucuses. They chose not to think of the turnout the other way: despite the unprecedented hoopla, some 80 percent of the voters, like most of the patrons of Flash's saloon, chose to stay home, a reflection of the emptiness of the campaign.

Voter cynicism was not limited to Iowa, of course. In Philadelphia, during the Pennsylvania primary, Albert Smalley, an unemployed truck driver and registered Democrat, told me that Adlai Stevenson was the last presidential candidate worthy of the office. Carter, he said, just could not handle the job. As for Kennedy, Smalley complained that the Senator "wanted to do too much for black people."

Did he think Reagan would do too much for black people?

"No," Smalley said. "But he wouldn't do much for white people, either."

These comments from voters, which I heard around the country during the campaign, matched the statistics I had seen on declining voter turnout and also the polling studies of increasing voter alienation. Having heard the same cynicism and indifference expressed by voters in every recent presidential campaign, I have come to realize that they have a right to their disenchantment. They have simply reached the conclusion that political campaigns have little bearing on the actions of government that actually influence their lives.

From 1960 to the present there have been six presidential campaigns and six presidents. A good deal has been written about each election and about each administration. But history is cumulative. The circumstances of each quadrennial have piled on the next, melding the past into the present and outlining the shape of the future.

This book explores the period as a continuum, seeking

to trace causes and effects in the major forces that tie the quadrennials together. A brief glance at the ground to be covered shows that in trying to deal with the consequences of the gap between politics and government presidents have sometimes achieved short-term success and personal popularity, but usually at the long-run cost of increasing the burdens on themselves and their successors.

Though his career was tragically foreshortened, John Kennedy had enduring impact on the forms of politics and government. He irrevocably personalized presidential campaigning and the presidency itself, creating a mystique around himself, while subordinating party and issues. He aroused unrealized expectations for the presidency which added to the pressures on those who followed him in office.

Trying to live up to the Kennedy legacy, and his own grandiose pledge of a Great Society, Lyndon Johnson sought to create a consensus built around his own goals and ambitions, not a party coalition of groups committed to common interests. By sheer force of will he tried to override disagreement and to avoid debate on his policies. His prestige and his consensus became casualties of the war in Vietnam and the protest against it at home.

Richard Nixon gained the White House by catering to the resentments created by Johnson, and relied on this negativism to govern. But opposition to his policies intensified, and in trying to deal with his critics Nixon abused his authority and destroyed his presidency.

Confronting a Congress made militant by the excesses of Nixon and Johnson, Ford sought to win support by distinguishing himself from Nixon. But he undercut his own efforts and added to general public cynicism by arbitrarily pardoning Nixon.

Jimmy Carter's election represented a rejection of the traditional political leadership which Carter had in effect campaigned against. But Carter's adversary relationship with the Washington establishment, and with his own party, contributed to his inability to develop coherent policies.

Carter's failure elected Ronald Reagan. Reagan's effectiveness in exploiting his personal popularity and the weakness of his opposition allowed him to make drastic changes in economic policy in his first months in the White House. But the hasty and haphazard machinations to which he resorted produced policies at war with each other. Before Reagan had completed his first year as president, the contradiction between his rosy promises and the gloomy economic realities was already apparent.

"Put not your trust in princes," the Bible says, an admonition which sums up one of the main lessons of the past six quadrennials. Indeed, the flaws of our president-princes are all too clear in retrospect. But the brunt of the blame for the misuses and abuses of public trust committed by the leaders we have chosen should be placed not on them but on the process of politics and the system of government whose frustrations and disorders threaten the national welfare.

How can we achieve relevance in politics and accountability in government? The answer, it is generally agreed, is through strong and dynamic political parties. But opinions differ widely on how the party system can be bolstered, or even whether this can be accomplished at all.

This book will argue that the record of the past twenty years demonstrates that if the parties are to be brought to life the Constitution must be changed. The restraints which have crippled party development should be removed and replaced with machinery that grants the parties expanded responsibility and the authority to match.

The various ways this can be accomplished—through constitutional amendment, acts of Congress, and changes

in party rules and practices—require study and debate.
The final chapter discusses some of the possible ends and
means, including measures to make more likely one-party
control of both the executive and legislative branches, to
strengthen the commitment of the president and the
Congress to party platforms, and to permit special elections when the majority party is unable to lead the country. Whatever the mechanics of the plan, the ultimate
objective should be to shift the burden of national leadership from the personality of the president to the collective authority of the executive and the legislature, bound
together by clear policy goals and a vigorous majority
party. Moreover, in the process of strengthening the
majority party, the minority party should also be made
into a vehicle for responsible opposition and preparation
for the eventual assumption of power.

Defenders of the status quo contend that such a constitutional transformation would create more problems than
it would solve. They point to the difficulties confronting
Great Britain and the democracies of Western Europe,
where parties are not hindered by the separation of
executive and legislative powers.

An analysis of the parliamentary systems in other
countries is beyond the scope of this book. Obviously a
good deal can be learned from studying the strengths and
weaknesses of such governments. But the application of
their experience is limited by the economic, cultural and
other distinctions between those countries and the
United States. This country should remodel its government in keeping with its own past and to meet the needs
of its own future.

The critics of constitutional revision maintain that getting approval for significant changes would be a long and
difficult task. That cannot be denied. But it is also true
that as dissatisfaction with the present system increases,
the possibilities improve for rallying support for change.

Even now there is considerable evidence that voters, while they are uncertain about the causes and are confused about possible solutions, are more and more aware that something is seriously wrong with politics, government and political parties.

Just as the drop in voter turnout—in every presidential election since 1960, and every off-year congressional election since 1966—points to alienation from the political system in general, opinion polls testify to the corresponding disenchantment with parties in particular. In the 1950s and early 1960s, the proportion of voters identifying themselves with either of the two parties stood at about 80 percent; in a 1981 survey by CBS News, the figure dropped to 60 percent. Until the 1960s, 60 to 70 percent of Americans usually voted a straight ticket. Then there was a dramatic change. In 1980, as in other recent elections, a Gallup survey showed that more than 60 percent of the voters split their tickets, choosing from candidates in both parties.

University of Michigan surveys showed that in 1964 two out of five voters believed that parties do "a good deal" to make government responsive; by 1978 the proportion had dropped to one out of five. Only about half the voters surveyed by CBS in 1981 saw "important differences between what the Democratic and Republican Parties stand for."

The decline in party allegiance is also reflected in the volatile pattern of voting behavior in the presidential elections since 1960. Of these six elections, each party has won three. Even more striking than this equal division is the transient impact of the landslide elections of 1964 and 1972. Previous landslides, such as the Republican victory in 1896 and the Democratic triumph in 1936, presaged or confirmed massive and enduring shifts in voter support from one party to another. But Lyndon Johnson's lopsided consensus in 1964 was demolished by dissatisfaction with the conduct of the war in Vietnam and with urban unrest; Nixon's New Republican Majority of 1972 crumbled in the face of Watergate and economic distress.

As for Reagan's victory in 1980, it was really a landslide only in the electoral college, where he won 489 votes to 49 for Carter. In the popular vote tally Reagan received 51 percent against Carter and John Anderson, barely more than a majority. Moreover, most analysts of campaign and election day polls agreed that Reagan's triumph was more of a negative verdict on his opponent than a reflection of confidence in Reagan's policies and his party.

During the past twenty years one unfortunate quadrennial has seemed to lead to another, in an inevitable progression. But an understanding of this progression, and a search for a formula to reverse it, must begin much earlier in our history. In a sense, the parties, presidents and the entire system of politics and government have been operating in a time warp. Contemporary events have altered some aspects of the system. But its fundamental features, which define the gap between politics and government, are much the same today as they were when they were fashioned at the birth of the Republic.

CHAPTER TWO

"If Men Were Angels"

Shortly before his inauguration, Ronald Reagan called his cabinet nominees together for their first working session, and told these advisers that during his presidency he wanted them to feel free to speak their minds on every subject but one. "The only no-no that I'll tell you for discussion, is I don't want anyone to even bring up the political ramifications of an act," he said. The decisions of his administration, the president-elect stressed, "should be based on what's good for the nation, not what's politically beneficial."

The reaction of the cabinet members is not recorded. Some may have taken the point with a few grains of salt, others at face value. At any rate, Reagan attached enough importance to his instructions so that he saw to it that his press secretary made them known to the public.

The new president was playing an old and familiar game. He was trying, none too subtly, to demonstrate his dedication to the national interest, whatever he might conceive that to be, as opposed to the self-interest of himself and his party. Apart from the obvious element of cant inherent in such self-serving declarations, Reagan's remarks reflect an underlying insensitivity not uncommon in the presidency. Certainly any chief executive has to rely in part on his own judgment about "what's good for the nation." But if a president is to be accountable, then his judgment should be shaped by the concerns and expectations of the voters who chose him for the White House. And that is another way of looking at what Reagan dismissed as "the political ramifications of an act."

However, Reagan would be exceptional indeed if he held that view of the presidency and the political process. Distinguishing between politics and the national interest —along with disparaging politics and the political parties, which are the central institutions of politics—is a time-honored American tradition that transcends party lines. Reagan's words might just as easily have been uttered by his Democratic predecessor, Jimmy Carter, who liked to stress his personal aversion to politics, and who, after he was voted out of office, complained that the party which nominated him, and looked to him for leadership, had been "an albatross wrapped around my neck."

The precedent was established by George Washington, who, in his Farewell Address, warned the citizens of the infant nation against "the common and continual mischiefs of the spirit of party," which, he said, "are sufficient to make it the interest and duty of a wise people to discourage and restrain it." The disdain of politics and parties has been carried forward ever since as a dominant theme in the American ethos.

"When today's politicians are not denying their business, they seem to be knocking it," Mark Shields, a veteran of contemporary Democratic Party politics, wrote in the *Washington Post*. "Some first certify their own ignorance of all things political and then censure their opponents as 'politicians' who will provide nothing more than 'politics as usual.' "

Like their modern counterparts, the leaders of the Republic at its birth did not readily admit to being politicians. They regarded government itself as a necessary evil and considered political parties to be even more evil and not even necessary. Parties were viewed as agents for aggravating discord, fostering anarchy or tyranny or both, and promoting selfish parochial interests against the common good.

This attitude contributed to the dilemmas confronting the framers of the Constitution when they gathered in Philadelphia in 1787. Though wary of government, they felt obliged to strengthen the existing feeble regime. Committed to the principle of popular sovereignty, they mistrusted human nature and doubted the wisdom of the populace. Fearful of monarchy and dictatorship, they also dreaded the tyranny of the majority.

Madison, the chief architect of the Constitution, best defined the conundrum facing its framers. "If men were angels, no government would be necessary," he wrote in No. 51 of the *Federalist Papers*. "If angels were to govern men, neither external nor internal controls on government would be necessary."

Since divine assistance was beyond reach, Madison designed the structure of government in a way that would convert the human frailty which worried him and his colleagues into a self-generated restraint on power. To curb the will of the majority, which might come to dominate some part of the government, Madison gave the Congress and the president separate constituencies and armed each with power to check and balance the other. One house of Congress could reject legislation approved by the other house; even if both passed a bill, the president could veto it. The president had the power to nominate high officials, but the Senate could refuse to confirm his choices. The inevitable clash of personal rivalries, Madison believed, would make these restrictions work. "Ambition must be made to counter-act ambition," he wrote. "The interest of the man must be connected with the Constitutional rights of the place."

"The key to Madison's thinking," James MacGregor Burns wrote in *The Deadlock of Democracy*, "is his central aim to stop people from turning easily to government for help." To accomplish this, Madison helped create through his checks and balances the gap between politics and government which has endured from that day to this.

Madison himself was among the early presidents to be hamstrung by the clash of authority and ambition he had ordained. A rebellious Congress would not let him shape his own cabinet and he complained to his old collaborator, Jefferson, that the Congress had become "unhinged." A century and a half later, Lyndon Johnson, in the wake of a great personal triumph at the polls, would warn his staff: "I've never seen a Congress that didn't eventually take the measure of the President it was dealing with."

The same determination to restrict the impact of the political process on government guided Madison and his fellow framers in developing a procedure for selecting the president. But the task of squeezing the presidency, with all its inherent potential for power, into their design of checks and balances strained the ingenuity of the constitutional draftsmen.

In their apprehension about the will of the majority, they first considered having the Congress select the chief executive. But this would have made the president dependent on the Congress, produced something like the British parliamentary system, and undermined the carefully contrived restraints. So, instead, the electoral college was invented to serve as a barrier between the public and the choice of the president. But this cumbersome device was destined before long to be circumvented by a development for which the Constitution's drafters did not provide, and which many of them hoped to avoid—the emergence of national political parties.

The failure to make a place for political parties in the Constitution was no accident. Like Madison's checks and balances, the omission of a role for parties was linked to the goal of a benignly neutral and relatively passive government that would rule by relying on a consensus. The faith in consensus was fostered by the contrasts between the social and economic environment of the Old World and the New. The infant nation had never known feudalism and so it was free from its legacy of class distinctions. Unlike the crowded countries across the Atlantic, there was plenty of land to go around, offering a favorable prospect for proliferation of a yeomanry who would never need to bow or scrape to an aristocracy and, once assured of their individual political liberties, would prefer to be left alone by government. These conditions were so evident, and considered so significant, that the strictures and traditions they shaped persisted long after strife and turbulence intruded on the tranquility of the early setting.

But under the circumstances of the nation's founding, it is easy to understand why government was regarded as a potential nuisance, or worse, not only by conservatives, but also by radicals. Both regarded individualism as the highest value, and considered the greatest threat to this principle to be government, whose role most thought should be limited to guarding against foreign enemies and lawless elements at home. "Every man wishes to pursue his occupation and to enjoy the fruits of his labor and the produce of his property in peace and safety," wrote the radical agitator for democracy, Tom Paine. "When these things are accomplished, all the objects for which government ought to be established are answered."

Surveying their new country, the Founding Fathers not surprisingly saw what they wanted to see, the potential for apparently infinite harmony. "With slight shades of difference you have the same religion, habits, manners and political principles," Washington told his fellow citizens on leaving office. He condemned political parties as a threat to this accord, likely to foster a spirit which "agitates the community with ill founded jealousies and

false alarms; kindles the animosity of one part against
another; foments occasionally riot and insurrection" and
also "opens the door to foreign influence and corruption."
Washington's view was supported on all sides. Hamilton warned that the spirit of "faction," a term then used
interchangeably with party, "is apt to mingle its poison
in the deliberations of all bodies of men." Hamilton's
bitter adversary, Jefferson, declared: "If I could not go
to heaven but with a party, I would not go at all."

So much for heaven. Right here on earth, Hamilton,
Jefferson and most of their colleagues soon became fierce
partisans who organized political parties to achieve their
strongly held beliefs about government policies. The explanation for this contradiction goes back to their belief
in consensus and their aversion to political conflict, both
attitudes which are still strong today. Those early American critics of parties were really opposed to the idea of
an *opposition party*. They believed, as Richard Hofstadter explains, that their particular party would eliminate
the need for all others, thus assuring eternal nonpartisan
harmony. "In their eyes the only true justification of any
party would be its promise of ultimately eliminating all
parties." Thus in 1816 when Jefferson's and Madison's
Democratic-Republican Party, the forerunner of the
modern Democratic Party, was at the peak of its power,
no less a Democratic partisan than Andrew Jackson jubi-
lantly declared: "Now is the time to exterminate the
monster called party spirit."

But in one form or another, of course, the party spirit
has survived, fueled by controversies the Founding
Fathers could not foresee, and spurred by the force of individual ambitions no system could obliterate. Meanwhile, the powers of government and the demands upon
it expanded beyond anything imagined by Madison and
his colleagues. But their eighteenth-century legacy has
lingered on, in the strictures of the Constitution and the

antipathy of the citizenry, to warp the body and the spirit of the political system.

Lacking constitutional status and broad public approval, unable to enforce discipline on their candidates and office holders, the parties from their inception found it hard to develop and promote consistent policies for dealing with pressing national issues. They served instead mainly as agencies for collecting votes, distributing patronage and filling offices. Although they competed against each other for national power in the Congress and the White House, they were really only loose federations of organizations based in the states, to which Congress had entrusted the regulation of elections.

Though a party might happen to be in the majority, theoretically controlling the Congress and the presidency, all too often it could not provide unified leadership. Just as harmful to the system, when a party was in the minority, it generally could not provide responsible opposition.

The conditions that stunted the growth of parties also distorted the role of presidents as party leaders. Confronted by opposition in their own parties, presidents had to reach outside for support for their programs, further weakening their parties in the process.

Since the Constitution made no provision for ordering the role of parties in selecting presidents, makeshift arrangements were adopted, then revised or replaced by new schemes. But each successive reform suffered from being part of a patchwork scheme which failed to address the constitutional barriers between politics and government and which ultimately contributed to the already negative view of parties and politics held by the public.

At first the parties relied on caucuses of their members in Congress to nominate presidential candidates. This was convenient and practical. The caucuses were ready-made assemblages of elected officials who had firsthand knowledge of the potential candidates and the issues that would confront them.

But the defects of this system soon became evident. It gave excessive influence to Congress over the presidency. Moreover, exercise of the presidential nominating process by a relatively insular group of office holders smacked of elitism, which became hard to defend politically as the frontier opened up, immigrants poured in and states dropped their property qualifications for voting.

With the rise of Jacksonian Democracy, King Caucus was forced to abdicate. It was replaced in the 1830s by the first major reform in the presidential selection process, the national nominating convention, which in modified form still functions today. Delegates to the national convention were selected by delegates at state conventions and so on down the line.

This innovation, by seeming to give every voter a voice in selecting presidential nominees, as well as other candidates, held out the promise of fulfilling the principles of self-government. But the progenitors of the convention system, like generations of reformers yet to come, were soon disappointed in their creation. John C. Calhoun, who had joined with Andrew Jackson in overturning the Congressional Caucus because it was considered "liable to be acted upon and influenced by the patronage of government," later ruefully concluded that this same objection was "far more applicable" to the convention system.

That was putting it mildly. Under the convention system patronage was the oil that turned the wheels of the party machinery. The opportunity to disburse government jobs, and other favors, allowed local bosses "down even to the pot house politician and the common thief," as one nineteenth-century critic put it, to maintain effective control of the political process. On paper a party's national convention, and its national committee, sat on top of an organizational pyramid which was based in the wards and precincts of every state. But in fact the national convention and the national committee were removed from the party's day-to-day operations. The real power rested at the state level, where the local leaders who made it their full-time business to run the party organization operated as they saw fit. It was next to impossible for the average voter to penetrate this Byzantine apparatus. Most Americans, raised to take a dim view of parties and of politics, and preoccupied with their own concerns, lacked the time or inclination even to try.

The stagnation of the system at its base was reflected at the top by the failure of party leadership to find a peaceful resolution of the slavery issue. Perhaps, as William Seward, fire-eating abolitionist of New York, declared, armed conflict between North and South was "irrepressible." Yet the fact remained that by 1850, opposition to slavery, based not only on moral grounds but also, and more significantly, on economic self-interest, was steadily growing stronger and broader. This created the potential for an alliance of Northern businessmen and wage earners, Western farming interests and perhaps small Southern freeholders committed to the prohibition of slavery in the new territories and its ultimate abolition in the South, packaged with a plan for economic compensation for slaveowners and tariff concessions to the South. Such a coalition could have dominated national politics and presented the plantation owners who ruled the South with an offer they could not afford to refuse. But this would have required a party system which focused on issues, not personal advantage, and in which the majority party's legislators were committed to the same goals as its president.

Instead, as the crisis deepened, the Whigs and Democrats temporized. Both parties were weakened by sectional conflicts and by squabbles between their Congressional leaders and their presidents. The Whigs, after running a series of elderly generals for the White House, collapsed and were supplanted by the Republican Party in 1856. The Democrats, under the irresolute stewardship of Presidents Franklin Pierce and James Buchanan, watched the country drift into the Civil War and then saw their presidential candidates repudiated for the next twenty years.

After the war, the swift growth of industry and of the cities presented unprecedented opportunities for graft and corruption. The great tycoons of the Gilded Age, determined to promote their burgeoning enterprises, were all too willing to reward the bosses of either party, whichever happened to be in charge, for special favors. This practical bipartisanship was summed up by Jay Gould, who controlled, among other things, the Erie Railroad: "In a Republican district I was a Republican, in a Democratic district I was a Democrat," Gould recalled of his political dealings. "In a doubtful district I was doubtful, but I was always Erie."

At the national level, from the late nineteenth century through the opening decades of the twentieth, the Republican Party generally became identified with the interests of business and the policy of restraint in government. The Democrats, their Southern base sheltered by their support for white supremacy, just as generally claimed to speak for the less privileged and for activism in government. But with a few exceptions—the Republicans championed the protective tariff and the gold standard while the Democrats advocated free trade and, for a while, free coinage of silver—party differences were manifested more in rhetoric than in specific proposals that divided the electorate. Conflicts between the parties were frequently overshadowed by clashes between presidents and their own parties and the Congress.

Despite brief flurries of reforming zeal, neither party when it controlled the presidency was able to muster consistent support for programs to deal with the inequities of industrialization and the power of the economic oligarchs. When they were in opposition, rather than offering significant policy alternatives for public debate, each party depended upon the presidential party being overwhelmed by calamities or its own blunders. Thus the financial panic of 1893 during the administration of Democrat Grover Cleveland, and his party's nomination of William Jennings Bryan in 1896, led to the Presidency of William McKinley and sixteen years of Republican rule.

In and out of power, both parties tended to drift toward what their leaders described as the center, where they believed most of the voters were located. But the center was an illusion. Rather than being the midpoint of controversy, established in open debate, it represented an ideological vacuum, and the locus of inaction and indifference.

Party leaders dominated the nominating process, aided, in the case of the Democrats, by a rule that required a two-thirds vote of the convention rather than just a simple majority for the presidential nomination. The leaders preferred candidates who they believed would not cause undue controversy, as Lord Bryce observed, and whom they could influence, if not totally control.

Candidates of independent bent had difficulty, and when such a candidate did get nominated and elected, as the experience of Theodore Roosevelt illustrated, the limitations of the system ultimately pitted him against his own party. Fed up with Roosevelt's freewheeling reformism as governor of New York, the state's Republican boss, Tom Platt, arranged for him to become McKinley's running mate in 1900. He ignored the misgivings of the party's national chairman, Mark Hanna, who presciently warned that Roosevelt's elevation to the vice-presidency would mean "that there's only one life between that madman and the White House."

Once in power after McKinley's assassination, Roosevelt avoided open conflict with the Republican hierarchy while building his own support. After his election in 1904 by a huge margin, he was emboldened to take the offensive, but the broad economic reforms he promoted antagonized his party's leaders, who blocked most of his proposals. Weary of the battle, Roosevelt relinquished the 1908 presidential nomination to Taft, who had neither the drive nor the inclination to press Roosevelt's programs.

Returning to the struggle with the Republican Old Guard in 1912, Roosevelt challenged Taft for the presidential nomination. He lost, and his subsequent third-party candidacy assured the election of Woodrow Wilson and left the Progressive forces locked out of the GOP.

Roosevelt's dramatic confrontation with Taft at the Republican convention had another effect on presidential politics. It provided impetus for the drive to adopt a new approach to presidential nominations—the direct primary.

The primary idea was one of a series of reforms aimed at curbing the abuses of the late nineteenth-century party system. The merit system sought to weaken political machines by denying them control over public employment. The secret ballot, by protecting the privacy of the voter's decision, was intended to shield him from machine pressure. With the direct primary, the reformers set their sights on the White House. The machine-dominated party caucuses, which controlled the selection of delegates to presidential nominating conventions, would be stripped of their power; instead, the people themselves would make the choice at the polling place.

The idea found support around the country. In the West, leaders of the Progressive movement saw the primary as a weapon for smashing the oppressive alliance between the big railroads and mining trusts and political bosses. In the South, where domination by the Democratic Party had made the general election in November a meaningless formality, the primary at least offered the chance for a genuine contest within the Democratic Party. To Eastern reformers the primaries were an antidote to the poison of the big-city machine whose corruption had been exposed by muckraking journalists. By 1912 twelve states had adopted presidential primaries. After Roosevelt won nine of these contests but was still denied the nomination by the GOP leaders, the frustrated reformers pressed their drive for primaries even harder. The Progressive Party, formed as a vehicle for TR's candidacy, called for a national presidential primary, as did Woodrow Wilson, the victorious Democratic candidate, in his first message to Congress.

Nothing came of that idea. But on the state level the primaries spread swiftly until by 1916 twenty-six states had adopted one form of primary or another. The forms, though, were significantly different. While in some states voters could choose directly between presidential candidates or delegates pledged to them, in others the primaries were merely advisory; the actual selection of delegates was left to some other means, usually a party convention or caucus. In still other states, delegates could run uncommitted to any candidate and often were controlled by the regular party organizations.

As a result of this mixture of methods, the bulk of delegates to the nominating conventions remained under the thumbs of state and local party bosses. Presidential candidates responded accordingly, giving the primaries secondary consideration to the cultivation of the local leadership. Candidates with substantial organization backing did not need to worry about the outcome of primaries. And those challenging the organization properly feared its power in the primaries. In the 1912 Illinois primary, Woodrow Wilson, the candidate of reform, was trounced by Champ Clark of Missouri, the favorite of the regulars, by a margin of three to one, though Wilson ultimately did manage to win his party's nomination.

Candidates with strong organizational backing frequently allowed their names to be entered on a primary ballot as a spur to their local supporters, but avoided risking their prestige by personal campaigning. In 1928 Al Smith was entered in seven primaries and Herbert Hoover in eight, though neither campaigned in those states. Similarly, Franklin Roosevelt was on the ballot in eleven primaries in 1932, but he also was an absentee candidate.

This arm's-length treatment robbed the primaries of much of their impact and significance. If the candidates stayed away from the hustings, the voters had little incentive to go to the polls. In the 1920s only one additional state, Alabama, adopted a primary law and its sole purpose was to guarantee that the state's favorite son, Senator Oscar W. Underwood, could control the delegation to the 1924 Democratic presidential convention. The Alabama contingent remained faithful to their senator for 103 ballots and sixteen days. And for millions of Americans in the radio audience, the automatic roll-call response of "Al-a-bam-ah-h-h casts twenty-fo-ah votes for Oscar W. Underwood" became the hallmark of that stormy conclave.

As public interest waned, a number of states concluded that primaries were not worth the expense and discarded them. After the 1928 Republican presidential primary a North Dakota study commission noted that none of the candidates on the ballot had substantial support and concluded that "the election was a farce which cost the taxpayers of the state $133,635."

Actually, the primaries had been oversold at any price. The attempt at reform was afflicted by one of the major ailments that debilitated the system it sought to improve. The lack of national party control allowed individual state parties to conduct primaries each in its own fashion, confusing the voters and diminishing the overall impact of the primaries. Like most reforms, the primary was only a superficial remedy which did not attempt to cure the basic defects in the relationship between politics and government.

A far greater force for political change than the primaries were the nation's underlying economic problems, which produced the Great Depression and led to the aggrandizement of federal power under Franklin Roosevelt. In his twelve years in the White House Roosevelt exploited to the fullest the possibilities for presidential leadership under the pressure of twentieth-century crises. But he also experienced the limitations imposed by eighteenth-century strictures.

An awareness of those limitations seemed to condition Roosevelt's initial approach to presidential politics. He was not nearly as prepossessing a figure when the Democrats first nominated him in 1932 as he later turned out to be. His campaign against Herbert Hoover gave no indication of the bold programs he would recommend, if indeed Roosevelt had yet thought them through himself.

In a major address in Pittsburgh, the Democratic nominee made a widely heralded pledge to slash government spending. When Roosevelt returned to speak in Pittsburgh in 1936 as a president seeking reelection, after four years of record government outlays, he asked one of his advisers, Samuel Rosenman, to draft an explanation of the earlier speech. "The only thing you can say about the 1932 speech is to deny categorically that you ever made it," Rosenman told him.

Even as he fashioned the dramatic innovations of the New Deal, Roosevelt displayed a traditional American politician's reluctance to commit himself ideologically. His programs lacked coherent design; he relied on instinct more than intellect, and liked to play off ideas and advisers against each other.

Nor was he very different from his predecessors in his relationship with his party. Though he brought the Democrats the greatest victories in their history, he was never fully at ease with their congressional leaders, nor they with him. In his first term, Roosevelt tried to cast himself above mere party concerns. He installed liberal Republicans in his cabinet, urged Democrats to invite Republicans to their Jefferson Day dinners and gave his unofficial but public support to Progressive Senator Robert La Follette of Wisconsin against his Democratic challenger. "If we have the right kind of people, the party label does not mean so very much," he explained.

The Democrats gained ground in the 1934 election but Roosevelt continued to grope toward a new coalition focused on economic issues and centered on himself. His climactic speech of the 1936 campaign epitomized that goal. "I should like to have it said of my first Administration that in it the forces of selfishness and of lust for power met their match," he declared. "I should like to have it said of my second Administration that in it they met their master."

The coalition he forged carried Roosevelt to an enormous victory in 1936. But the election's aftermath demonstrated the limited impact of presidential success on the will of Congress. Roosevelt's presidential reach exceeded his political grasp. The defeat of his scheme to overcome Supreme Court resistance to his policies by enlarging the court's membership was the first in a series of setbacks at the hands of an increasingly intransigent Congress, where the Democratic leadership was dominated by conservative Southerners. After the president tried and failed to purge some Democratic opponents before the 1938 elections, the voters added to his injuries that November by giving the Republicans substantial gains in Congress. Roosevelt was in retreat on the domestic front when the start of World War II led him to announce the replacement of "Dr. New Deal" by "Dr. Win the War," thus sparing himself further embarrassment.

During his unprecedented four terms Roosevelt sharpened the distinction between Democrats and Republicans to the GOP's disadvantage and engineered a stunning expansion of federal involvement in the everyday lives of the citizenry. For a time his achievements spanned the gap between politics and government. But only for a time.

What were the reasons for his successes, and for his ultimate frustrations? FDR was a deft maneuverer and was blessed with a buoyant temperament. Perhaps more significant, in terms of the style he set for his successors, Roosevelt had a theatrical flair and a resonant voice superbly suited to the contemporary mass-media innovations of radio and newsreels.

But it does not diminish Roosevelt's personal attributes to question how far these assets would have taken him without the crises that shaped his presidency. He came to office in the midst of the most shattering national experience since the Civil War. The Great Depression at first rallied every element in the nation behind the new president, and the mood of desperate anxiety disarmed the institutional forces that normally obstruct governmental response to political needs. With little difficulty Roosevelt was able to push through a series of measures designed to stamp out the worst brush fires of the Depression and prevent their recurrence.

But once the immediate threat to the nation's institutions subsided, business leaders and other conservative interests deserted Roosevelt's banner and made their opposition felt in the Congress. Meanwhile, the Depression continued, with its impact falling most severely on the least advantaged economic groups. This situation allowed Roosevelt to build a coalition in the cities of the North and the rural areas of the South based more closely along class lines than any the nation had ever seen. The coalition helped Roosevelt gain approval for such lasting monuments as the Wagner Act and social security and gave him his huge margin of victory in

1936. But the coalition bogged down in the institutional obstacle course created by the Constitution. And in the face of bipartisan conservative opposition in the Congress, the New Deal ran out of steam before it could get at the underlying causes of the Depression.

The threat of war, and then its onset, provided another crisis which unified support for the president personally, though not for his domestic programs. It remained for the economic impact of the war effort to finally end the Depression that Dr. New Deal had been unable to cure. The wartime boom improved the lot of the voters who made up the New Deal coalition but at the same time it eased the pressures that had bound them together. Nothing in the system in which he had been reared inclined Roosevelt to provide his allies with a unifying, long-range agenda. There was only the symbolic force of his personality. No wonder, then, that the coalition began to crumble after his death and that his successors have been struggling either to preserve it or to replace it ever since.

CHAPTER THREE

1960

1. The Politics of Personality

In 1960, as John Kennedy closed in on the Democratic presidential nomination, Harry Truman raised his voice to protest that the time was not right for Kennedy. "Senator, are you certain that you are quite ready for the country, or that the country is ready for you in the role of President?" Truman asked pointedly. "May I urge you to be patient."

Truman had in mind Kennedy's youth, and his Catholicism, both of which he and other Democratic elders regarded as serious and probably fatal obstacles to the success of a Democratic ticket headed by Kennedy. The testy old campaigner had a point, yet his criticism missed the mark. In ways that did not occur to most of his fellow Democrats, Kennedy's timing could not have been better. Hindsight makes clear that his background and inclinations were closely tuned to the mood of the country and the political climate. Because he came to realize this, and to take advantage of it, Kennedy was able to overcome considerable handicaps, capture the nomination of his party and regain the White House for the Democrats after eight Republican years.

In the process, John Kennedy helped to change the nature of presidential politics. By demonstrating the ebbing of the old order, he accelerated its demise and led the way into a new era that would be marked by the domination of personality and technology, the self-selection of candidates and the self-promotion of candidacies, the increase in demands and expectations on the presidency, the fragmentation of constituencies, the shifting of voter loyalties, and perhaps most important of all, the steep decline in the influence of the two major political parties.

All this did not take place at once, of course. It was a metamorphic process that had its roots in the economic and social transformation of postwar America which preceded Kennedy's candidacy and which continued well beyond his thousand-day presidency, spurred by the upheavals of the sixties.

The most significant consequence for the political system of the array of postwar changes was the undermining of the authority and influence of political parties and their established leadership. ". . . In each major party some 50 to 100 men—state leaders, local bosses, elder statesmen, big contributors—decided nominations," presidential scholar Richard E. Neustadt wrote of the way the parties generally chose their standard-bearers before Kennedy's time. "These party barons actually controlled and could deliver delegates at national conventions. . . ."

The ultimate basis of this power had been the ability of party leaders and their underlings to get voters to the polls to support their candidates. But the conditions they had counted on to build and maintain their constituencies —economic demarcations, family ties, regional traditions and needs—were being rapidly altered, with unpredictable and unfathomable results.

The cleavages between the Republicans and Democrats produced by the Depression, which Franklin Roosevelt had brilliantly dramatized, were being eroded by the spread of economic well-being. And the onset of affluence for most of the population set off a chain reaction across the demographic landscape. Americans were a nation on the move, in several directions at once—upward in educational as well as economic status, outward from the cities to the suburbs, inward from the small towns and small farms to the burgeoning metropolitan areas.

Some statistics outline this transformation of the national condition during the postwar era. Between 1940 and 1960 the population increased by 47 million, from 132 million to 179 million. Nearly all of this increase was registered in the metropolitan areas, which showed a jump to 112 million from 70 million. During the same twenty-year period the gross national product increased fivefold, from $100 billion to more than $500 billion.

Also striking were the gains in family income from 1950 to 1960. At the beginning of the decade 10 percent of American families earned under $2,500 measured in 1978 dollars; by 1960 only 5 percent were below that level. And while in 1950 just under 50 percent of American families had incomes in excess of $10,000, again measured in 1978 buying power, by 1960 that figure had climbed to nearly 68 percent.

Educational levels were improving, too. In 1940, only 35 percent of the population had completed four years of high school or more. By 1960 that figure had jumped to 41 percent, and college graduates in the population had increased from 4.6 percent to 7.7 percent.

As they confronted changing constituencies with increasingly complex interests, the party leaders found it harder to define and dominate political debate. Voters were more independent. Increasing income and leisure had fostered the emergence of an influential class of intellectuals—in the media, the foundations and academia—who generated and manipulated political information and who found a growing audience for their output.

And then there was television. The magic box had become a pervasive and intrusive force, at once enlightening and confusing, informing and distracting. Between 1950 and 1960 the number of American families owning television sets had increased tenfold, to more than 45 million, or nearly 90 percent of the population. The medium's capacity for instant projection of ideas and personalities into living rooms everywhere created a voice that drowned out the traditional political chain of command.

Party leaders clung to their old titles and struggled to preserve their traditional influence. But they were fighting a losing battle.

The erosion of party strength was hastened by the presence in the White House of Dwight Eisenhower, who had an abiding disinterest in partisanship. Eisenhower was such a neutral figure that some Democrats had sought to nominate him as their standard bearer in 1948. Not until shortly before he became a candidate in 1952 did he publicly acknowledge that he considered himself a Republican.

The breadth of Eisenhower's personal appeal had helped to blur the fierce partisan loyalties of the New Deal era. "From the Eisenhower electoral maps the proverbial visitor from Mars would never know that Franklin Roosevelt had lived," the political analyst Samuel Lubell observed after Eisenhower's sweeping victory in 1952. And Eisenhower's reelection margin in 1956, despite two serious illnesses and his advanced age, was even bigger and broader.

But Eisenhower made no sustained effort to use his personal popularity to strengthen his party or to promote significant changes in the national agenda. Like a modern George Washington, the hero president held himself aloof from the political arena.

On the issues that mattered most to him, such as foreign aid and coexistence with the Soviet Union, Eisenhower seemed to work more easily with the moderate Democratic congressional leadership than with right-wing forces in his own party. The latter still resented Ike's defeat of their champion, Senator Robert A. Taft of Ohio, in the struggle for the 1952 nomination. The Democratic leadership for the most part conformed to the placid politics of the Eisenhower era. Though their party's twenty-year hold on the White House had been broken in 1952, they regained control of Congress in the 1954 elections and maintained it for the rest of Eisenhower's tenure as president. However, the two Texans who ruled the congressional Democrats, Speaker Sam Rayburn in the House and Majority Leader Lyndon Johnson in the Senate, had little trouble finding grounds for accommodation with Eisenhower. Their conciliatory approach derived from their respect for Eisenhower's popularity and their concern that conflict might jeopardize their own authority. Moreover, neither Rayburn nor Johnson had serious objections to Eisenhower's moderate policies, an attitude that angered many liberal Democrats. In 1959, when the Democrats held big majorities in both the House and Senate, Americans for Democratic Action charged that the party's congressional leaders "made divided government work by the simple expedient of surrendering to the President."

On some broad questions the two parties and their supporters looked at the world differently. Democrats, for example, tended to favor a more active role for government in social welfare than Republicans did. But as V. O. Key wrote of the period: "Few public issues attract the opposition of most Democrats and the support of most Republicans and vice versa." The differences that did exist, Key added, "were muted by the large numbers of both Democrats and Republicans who thought the government was doing 'about right.' "

Now and then untoward events intruded on the bipartisan complacency of the national mood. Periodic recessions took their toll, reviving somber memories of the 1930s and indicating that all was not well with the economy. Sputnik's thrust into space called attention to the challenge of Soviet power. Supreme Court decisions and a flurry of black sit-ins at Southern lunch counters served as reminders of the still unresolved racial dilemma. But most Americans, while they took note of these episodes, did not dwell on them. The nation was at peace, its institutions seemed strong and stable, and the members of the greatly enlarged middle class were preoccupied with taking advantage of the unprecedented opportunities for affluence. Certainly, as the decade of the 1950s drew to an end, most of the nation's political leaders did not perceive any ground swell for drastic change in the status quo.

To the contrary. As he analyzed the national mood from his vantage point as Senate majority leader, Lyndon Johnson, whom John Kennedy considered his most serious rival for their party's nomination, complained about the zeal of some of his liberal Democratic colleagues in pressing for programs designed as remedies for the nation's ills. "The country doesn't want this," Johnson grumbled. "The country wants to be comfortable. It doesn't want to be stirred up."

It was John Kennedy's intention to get the country "stirred up," but not in the way that Lyndon Johnson complained about. Kennedy's emphasis was on style, rather than on controversial policies, and on his own personality, rather than on the fading strength of his party. In the climate that prevailed in the country as he launched his drive for the White House, even his presumed handicaps—his age, for example—offered advantages. As Eisenhower's second term drew to an end, some Americans were growing bored with the bland passivity of the seventy-year-old general. For those who sought a change of pace, the forty-three-year-old senator projected an intriguing sense of vigor and dash. Norman Mailer wrote of Kennedy's candidacy as representing the adventurous side of the national psyche and wondered whether the nation would be "brave enough to enlist the romantic dream of itself" and "vote for the image of the mirror of its unconscious."

The attraction Kennedy held for romantic intellectuals was only one aspect of the fundamental strength that informed his candidacy and then his presidency. This was his ability to rally support through his personal resources rather than relying on the appeal of his party or of any ideology. He had acquired and sharpened his skill over the years. For the same forces that created the new political age of the 1960s—the decline of party and the ascendancy of personality—had shaped Kennedy's career from its beginning.

Kennedy owed his success in his first political race, for a congressional seat in 1946, to personal advantages—the fortune amassed by his father, Joseph P. Kennedy, the celebrity of his family name in Boston, and his own renown as a war hero. Without party ties or allies in the district where he sought the Democratic nomination, he launched his campaign months before his rivals. Then he imported a small army of school friends and wartime comrades who toiled on his behalf under the guidance of seasoned professionals retained by his father. His victory in the primary guaranteed his election in November in the solidly Democratic district.

Though he continued to run, and to win, on the Democratic ticket, first as a congressman, then as a senator, he kept his distance from the regular party organization. He once described the sort of men who controlled the party machinery as "tarnished holdovers from another era," who, he said, "keep busy by attending meetings, filing gloomy forecasts and complaints and fighting zealously to hold on to their positions."

Unfettered by obligations to the party hierarchy, he felt free to pursue his own predilections, which were difficult for him or anyone else to define. Not long after

Kennedy arrived in Washington as a new congressman, he granted an interview to a Harvard *Crimson* reporter who wrote critically of Kennedy's failure to take specific positions and reported that Kennedy "feigns an ignorance of much in the affairs of government and tells you to look at his record in two years to see what he stands for."

Though Kennedy soon became more familiar with government affairs, questions about what he stood for remained difficult to answer. During the Truman presidency he was generally faithful in backing Truman's Fair Deal domestic policies. But he kept himself apart from the liberalism which was the dominant creed of the Democratic Party outside the South. He could not bring himself to criticize Senator Joseph McCarthy, who had been his brother Robert's employer and his father's friend. In private he scorned those he called the "real liberals" and did not involve himself with such concerns of the Left as civil rights and civil liberties. When he chose to define his views he preferred such neutral descriptions as "a northern Democrat with some sense of restraint" or "a moderate Democrat who seeks to follow the national interest as his conscience directs him to see it."

This lack of commitment proved to be an advantage when Kennedy challenged moderate Republican Henry Cabot Lodge for Lodge's Senate seat in 1952. Lodge and Kennedy differed so little that Kennedy's strategists argued among themselves about whether Kennedy should attack him as too liberal or too conservative. As it turned out, he did both.

Just as important as this ideological sleight-of-hand, though, were Kennedy's organization and his personal appeal. "Convinced that Democratic Party regulars weren't going to do anything for Jack Kennedy," Lawrence O'Brien, the campaign's director of organization, established a statewide network of Kennedy campaign workers who operated independently of the party. And he arranged for the candidate's mother and sisters to host a series of receptions, calculating that the family's patrician background would help offset the "snob appeal" of the old-line Yankee Republican leaders. Kennedy's friends and his family helped give him victory over Lodge by a narrow margin, which seemed more impressive because Eisenhower swept the state.

Even before the victory over Lodge, Kennedy's father was privately predicting that his son would someday sit in the Oval Office. "Jack is a man of destiny," Joseph Kennedy told O'Brien.

And so it seemed. Even his defeat by Estes Kefauver at the 1956 convention in a contest to be Adlai Stevenson's running mate turned out to Kennedy's advantage. The dramatic floor fight gained Kennedy national attention on television, and the outcome saved him from sharing the blame for Stevenson's second successive defeat by Eisenhower.

Immediately after the 1956 election, Kennedy began making plans to pursue the destiny his father foresaw for him. Once again, as when he first ran for the House, and then the Senate, he could not count on significant support from the leadership of his own party. By and large, Democratic Party professionals regarded Kennedy as an upstart who carried the special liability of his Catholic faith—an attitude shared with only a few exceptions by Catholic leaders. They all still remembered the disaster suffered by the Democrats when Catholic Al Smith had been their presidential candidate in 1928. The leadership felt more comfortable with Majority Leader Johnson or Senator Stuart Symington of Missouri. Liberals still had a strong sentimental allegiance to Stevenson, and considered Minnesota senator Hubert Humphrey as the likely heir to the liberal legacy. All of these potential rivals appeared to have more organizational or ideological support in the party than did Kennedy.

But alone among them, Kennedy seemed to comprehend the changed realities of presidential politics. The issues that had defined presidential politics during the New Deal era were losing their relevance, and for some of the same reasons the Democratic Party hierarchy was losing its influence. The way to the White House was open to an independent political entrepreneur. Like an ambitious businessman establishing a new venture, the political entrepreneur needed to build his own organization, raise his own capital, develop his own clientele and establish his own goals. Just as for the business entrepreneur, success for the political entrepreneur required hard work and the skillful use of the latest techniques of the trade.

It was also important, as Kennedy had learned in his first race for Congress, to get an early start on the competition. And so Kennedy began running for the 1960 presidential nomination in 1957, and never stopped. Week after week he crisscrossed the country, speaking in union halls and pool halls, schools and restaurants, wherever he could get a hearing. Reserving only the time and energy required to assure his Senate reelection in 1958 by an imposing margin, skimping on his Senate duties, Kennedy committed himself fully to laying the groundwork for his candidacy, while his potential rivals pondered their future in the comfort of their homes.

Kennedy's efforts won him promises of support and taught him about local political conditions. The attention he gained helped raise his standing in the public opinion polls, which early on showed him as the leader in the contest for the nomination. But Kennedy knew that these advantages could not be relied on for long. Their potential had to be developed, and this he soon concluded could only be done effectively through the presidential primaries.

This was a course strewn with obstacles. A full-scale primary campaign required substantial investments of time, money and prestige. In the past the main impact of primaries had been to eliminate some potential nominees; never had the primaries themselves brought victory at the convention. The most recent example was provided by Senator Estes Kefauver of Tennessee, who had campaigned vigorously and with some success in the primaries in 1952 and 1956 but both times had fallen short of the nomination. Kennedy, however, had advantages Kefauver did not possess, most particularly almost unlimited financial resources. The party leaders who had frustrated Kefauver in the 1950s were weaker in 1960. Besides, Kennedy had no choice but to enter the primaries. Only by competing and succeeding in these contests, he believed, could he answer the misgivings about his Catholicism.

Kennedy's main objective in the primaries was not to win delegates; only a small number were at stake in the contests he entered. He was really conducting an exercise in political symbolism. In effect, it was a challenge to the party leadership, but Kennedy sought to avoid direct confrontation. He stayed out of primaries in such big states as Pennsylvania and California to avoid antagonizing local leaders. And he counted as allies a few key bosses, notably Mayor Richard Daley of Chicago. The point of his primary campaign was to bring indirect pressure on the rest of the leaders through the media and the polls, which he relied on to give his anticipated success in the primaries an importance well beyond the literal arithmetic of the convention votes he gained.

Still, this was a precarious strategy, because a single defeat in the primaries probably would doom his candidacy. But Kennedy calculated, correctly as it turned out, that the contenders for the nomination he took most seriously would be unwilling to endanger their own prospects by running against him.

To bolster the significance of the primaries, Kennedy stressed the civics-books merits of these contests and taunted those candidates who failed to enter them, confident they would not accept the challenge. "Any Democratic aspirant should be willing to submit to the voters his views, record and competence in a series of primary contests," he declared. "Primaries are the ordinary voter's chance to speak his own mind, to cast his own vote—regardless of what he may be told to do by some other self-appointed spokesman for his party, city, church, union or other organization." Kennedy's rhetoric was shrewdly chosen to appeal to the electorate's growing sense of independence from traditional political leaders whom he dismissed as "self-appointed." The opportunity he stressed for the voter "to speak his own mind" helped to enlarge the public importance of the 1960 primaries and contributed greatly to the subsequent resurgence of that institution.

But the question often overlooked in the enthusiasm for primaries was how much of consequence were the voters actually called upon to decide. The answer in 1960 was very little.

Of the seventeen primaries conducted that year, Kennedy entered eight, and in only two of these, Wisconsin and West Virginia, was he seriously opposed. The competition came from Hubert Humphrey, who from Kennedy's standpoint was probably the ideal opponent. Humphrey had enough of a national reputation so that he could not be dismissed. But he could not come close to matching Kennedy's financial resources or his organizational base, which Kennedy had spent so many months preparing. More fundamentally, he was unwilling to challenge Kennedy directly on substantive issues, which Kennedy himself preferred to gloss over.

A self-styled New Deal—Fair Deal Democrat, Humphrey shared the discomfort of many other traditional liberals in the post-FDR period. Because of changing economic conditions, and also because of the red-baiting of the McCarthy era, the liberals had surrendered the initiative. Instead of pushing for new economic and social reforms, many seemed preoccupied with demonstrating their patriotism by talking tough about the Soviet Union. Though sit-in demonstrations in the South were already signaling black impatience with segregation, and Humphrey had first earned national recognition as a civil rights advocate at the 1948 convention, he did not press that cause in his competition with Kennedy. When a civil rights leader publicly hailed him as the John the Baptist of the movement, Humphrey retorted: "You may recall what happened to John the Baptist."

His response to press commentary that there seemed to be few differences on issues between himself and Kennedy was to say: "Then I ought to win because I'm older and have had more experience." He did try to make a point out of Kennedy's wealth, appealing to voter sympathies by likening himself "to a corner grocer running against a chain store."

Against this barren backdrop, the emotion-laden question of Kennedy's religion took on great significance. Some voters rejected him while others supported him, mainly because of his Catholicism. But probably far more important was the impact on a broader segment of voters who were neither bigots nor ardent Catholics. In their minds Kennedy's religion gave his candidacy a special identity, setting it apart from the others, and endowing it with a moral fervor it otherwise lacked. No large policy questions informed Kennedy's candidacy; the religious issue was the only reason it had for existence beyond its own success.

Kennedy's Catholicism had loomed in the background of the campaign from the start. And after an indecisive victory over Humphrey in their first primary in Wisconsin in April, Kennedy brought it to the forefront in West Virginia in May. He challenged the mostly Protestant voters of West Virginia to prove they were not bigots by voting for him. Recalling his war record, Kennedy appealed to patriotism, to fairness, and to religious principles shared by Protestants and Catholics alike. In a dramatic television address, he pointed out that every president swears to support the constitutional separation of church and state. "And if he breaks that oath," Kennedy went on, "he is not only committing a crime against the Constitution for which Congress can impeach him—and should impeach him—he is committing a sin against God."

Humphrey had no way to counter this impassioned appeal. On May 12 West Virginia's Democrats rejected both bigotry and Humphrey and gave Kennedy victory by a huge margin. A few skirmishes remained. But the press, the public and the party leaders were fully as impressed with the West Virginia results as Kennedy intended them to be. And a few weeks later the delegates to the Democratic National Convention ratified the result of the primary by nominating Kennedy on the first ballot.

Kennedy's nomination was by no means inevitable. Had his opponents been more aggressive and more imaginative they might have defeated him. His family fortune was an important asset, particularly against Humphrey's impoverished organization. But some of Kennedy's other rivals, notably Johnson, had access to substantial sources of funding they might have tapped had they been prepared to confront Kennedy in the primaries. Instead they chose to stand back from the active competition and await the verdict of the party's supposed power brokers.

But their judgment was preempted by Kennedy's success in the primaries, particularly in West Virginia. That state had only about 1 percent of the nation's population and sent only 1 percent of the delegates to the Democratic National Convention. Yet Kennedy contrived to transform the contest there into a national referendum on his candidacy. His skill at manipulating political symbols, with the help of television, overshadowed the ebbing power of the party hierarchy and proved the potential of two related forces in presidential politics —media and personality.

The success of Kennedy's candidacy would have substantial impact on future presidential campaigns in both parties as more politicians awoke to the changing political environment, particularly the vulnerability of traditional party leadership. Kennedy's early start would come to be a model for presidential hopefuls, thus helping to lengthen the campaign calendar by many months. And because he owed his victory to the primaries, that somewhat dormant reform would take on new life and added significance.

But as effective as these tactics had been in gaining Kennedy the nomination, they would not suffice for the struggle for the White House against the Republican nominee, Richard Nixon. Kennedy had won the nomination despite most of his party leaders. Now he needed their full support, and also the backing of broader segments of the electorate than he had appealed to in the primaries.

Since he had developed no national program during his race for the nomination, Kennedy fell back on the old strategies and rhetoric of Franklin Roosevelt. To solidify the no longer so solid South, he chose Lyndon Johnson of Texas as his running mate, over the objection of party liberals who considered Johnson too conservative and who resented his willingness to make common cause with the Eisenhower administration.

After years of operating as an outsider, Kennedy now tried to identify himself as a full-blooded Democrat. "This contest is not between the vice-president and myself," he told a California crowd early in the campaign. "This contest is between the Democratic Party and the Republican Party, and in that regard there is no contest." Most voters knew, or thought they knew, what the

Democratic Party had stood for in the past. Kennedy's problem, which he never really solved, was to redefine the party under his leadership for the 1960s.

As he barnstormed the country, the candidate offered a laundry list of promises—civil rights legislation, health insurance for the aged, a raise in the minimum wage—most of them updates of New Deal and Fair Deal pledges. But Kennedy had never been famous as a champion of these causes in Congress, and he lacked sufficient credibility among the interest groups most directly concerned to be their advocate now. After Americans for Democratic Action had grudgingly endorsed Kennedy's candidacy, Arthur Schlesinger, Jr., wrote the senator: "I was prepared for apathy on the part of grass-roots liberals. I was not prepared for the depth of hostility which evidently exists."

Ultimately the liberals' hatred of Nixon helped to overcome their suspicion of Kennedy. But other, more fundamental problems marred Kennedy's efforts to lay out a convincing program, and these were to have a telltale effect on his presidency. For one thing he failed to explain how he would persuade his fellow Democrats in Congress to approve his proposals after they had failed to act on similar measures in the past six years during which they controlled the House and Senate. Moreover, the program Kennedy offered lacked an overview, an ideological and political standard for coordinating his promises and deciding which among them deserved the most immediate and urgent effort.

Instead of a structure of beliefs and priorities, Kennedy coined a slogan; with a bow to the New Deal he promised to lead the nation to a New Frontier. This would be rigorous territory, the candidate warned, but he did not explain who would bear the most hardship. He spoke of sacrifice, but when asked at a press conference what sacrifices he had in mind, Kennedy's response ran to more than two hundred words in the transcript without answering the question. "When I talk about a future which is going to be a very testing one," he concluded lamely, "I am talking about the national mood and atmosphere which takes a broader view of the capacity of the United States to affect events."

Kennedy was more explicit and more strident in warning of the menace of communism abroad. Mindful that the Republicans had long used this issue successfully against the Democrats, he attacked the Eisenhower administration for not rolling back the Iron Curtain in Europe, for allowing Fidel Castro to seize power in Cuba, and for permitting the United States to fall behind the Russians in nuclear armament. This latter charge gave birth to the phrase "missile gap," which his administration would later have to acknowledge did not exist.

If Kennedy's aim was sometimes off the mark, his onslaught nevertheless kept Nixon on the defensive. Getting his party's nomination had been relatively easy for Nixon. Because of Eisenhower's disinterest in partisan politics, his vice-president had shouldered many of the party leadership chores normally assumed by a president during Eisenhower's eight years in the White House. Republican Party leaders came to regard Nixon as a quasi-incumbent, an attitude which persuaded Nixon's strongest potential opponent, New York governor Nelson Rockefeller, to drop the idea of seeking the nomination himself.

But as Eisenhower's legatee, Nixon was obliged to answer for the Eisenhower record, a task made more difficult because he lacked Eisenhower's prestige and broad appeal. His responses to Kennedy's broadsides often sounded weak, almost plaintive. When Kennedy decried economic conditions at home and complained that U. S. influence was declining abroad, Nixon declared: "I'm tired of hearing our opponents run down the United States of America." Painfully aware that his was the minority party, Nixon tried to undercut Kennedy's partisan appeal to Democrats. "We believe that in this year what should come first is not the party, nothing else but America," he told a cheering throng in Hartford.

In an election whose outcome both candidates frequently asserted would be critical for the nation's future, the dialogue often dwelled on the past. Kennedy sought to evoke gratitude for the achievements of the New Deal while Nixon pointed with pride to the peace and relative prosperity brought by Eisenhower. "The campaign raised no clear-cut, decisive issue, and except for the Peace Corps, no new proposals," Sorensen wrote later in *Kennedy*, his firsthand account of the Kennedy presidency.

In the haze of rhetoric, voters had trouble marking the difference between the two candidates. Shortly after the conventions, in a newspaper column which attracted wide attention, the prominent commentator Eric Sevareid complained that both candidates lacked commitment and conviction and described them as "completely packaged products" of "the managerial revolution." The critique reflected Sevareid's nostalgia for the tense and turbulent thirties when, he wrote, young men "sickened at the Republic Steel massacre of strikers . . . dreamt beautiful and foolish dreams about the perfectibility of man, cheered Roosevelt and adored the poor."

Kennedy was stung by this appraisal and worried that Sevareid's feelings were widely held by liberal Democrats. At the candidate's urging, Arthur Schlesinger, Jr., who functioned as a sort of intellectual-in-residence to the Kennedy campaign, dashed off a slim book called *Kennedy or Nixon: Does It Make Any Difference?* designed to answer such carping.

What was most revealing about the book was that for two-thirds of it Schlesinger dwelled on the differences in style and personality between the candidates. Schlesinger berated Nixon for mentioning his wife in his speeches and concluded: "The hard fact is that Nixon lacks taste."

By contrast Schlesinger described Kennedy as "a bookish man," "an exceptionally cerebral figure," and added: "Kennedy is non-corny," whatever that meant.

Schlesinger's efforts tended more to substantiate Sevareid's indictment than to rebut it. But the passions Sevareid mourned were fostered by an unusual era when party lines were barricades between classes with clear and conflicting interests which their leaders represented. Or so many people believed at the time. By 1960 the tides of change had blurred the lines of battle and left political leaders to sink or swim on public perceptions of their own merits and shortcomings.

So it was that as the Kennedy-Nixon campaign wore on, the personal differences between the two candidates increasingly dominated public attention. This was the clearest area of distinction which emerged from the much heralded television debates. Kennedy gained stature, particularly from the first one, mainly because he appeared self-assured while Nixon looked sallow and seemed ill at ease.

As it had in the West Virginia primary, the controversy over Kennedy's religion heightened interest in him personally and added to his appeal. The argument over whether Kennedy gained or lost more votes simply because he was a Catholic can never be definitely settled. But there was no question that the so-called religious issue caught the imagination of the voters and struck a sympathetic chord among many of them for Kennedy. Only the most hardened bigot would have been unmoved when Kennedy, confronting the Protestant ministers in Houston, reaffirmed his belief in separation of church and state and added: "This is the kind of America I believe in—and this is the kind I fought for in the South Pacific, and the kind my brother died for. No one suggested then that we might have a divided loyalty."

The emotions generated by religion, the hullabaloo from the TV debates and the fact that the preelection

polls showed the contest to be neck and neck, helped
account for a record turnout of sixty-nine million on
election day, 62.8 percent of the voting-age population.
Kennedy won with 112,000 more popular votes than
Nixon, less than two-tenths of 1 percent. It was the nar-
rowest margin of the century. His electoral vote advantage was more substantial. But some big states were so
closely divided that a switch of only a few thousand
votes here and there could have given Nixon victory.

The results proved that thirty-two years after Al
Smith's crushing defeat, a Catholic could be elected president, thus substantially broadening the ranks from
which future candidates could be chosen. But the nature
of the campaign, and the narrowness of the victory, left a
host of other questions and problems to face the new
chief executive.

2. Great Expectations

During his campaign for the White House John Kennedy
had cast himself as a president in Roosevelt's activist
mold. Over and over he had vowed to "get America
moving again." On election eve in Boston he had declared:
"I run for the Presidency of the United States because
it is the center of action, and in a free society, the
chief responsibility of the President is to set before
the American people the unfinished public business of
our country."

But the election returns had cast a shadow over these
energetic promises, and over the prospects for Kennedy's
legislative program. Publicly, Kennedy discounted the
limitations imposed by his razor-edge triumph. "The
margin is narrow but the responsibility is clear," he said.
"There may be difficulties with Congress, but a margin
of only one vote would still be a mandate." But in private

he recalled Thomas Jefferson's counsel: "Great innovations should not be forced on slender majorities."

Kennedy's margin was not only slender but extremely shaky. He owed his election to the return to the Democratic Party of most of the constituencies which Franklin Roosevelt had forged into a coalition, particularly the Catholics and blacks. But this alliance was nowhere near as broad or as firm as it had once been. And Kennedy's candidacy, with its emphasis on style and recycled slogans, had presented no new framework of issues and goals to reinvigorate or expand the old political base.

Only in the Northeast did Kennedy have sturdy support. The farm belt and the West had voted almost solidly for Nixon. And though Lyndon Johnson had helped him in the South, the old Democratic ties of that region were plainly wearing thin. Nixon had run ahead of Eisenhower in half a dozen states of the Old Confederacy and had carried two of the biggest, Florida and Virginia.

The weaknesses pointed up by the presidential balloting were mirrored and magnified in the Congress. For the first time in a century, a newly elected president had not increased his party's strength in Congress. Democrats had lost twenty-two seats in the House and one more in the Senate. Their tenuous control of both houses now rested more than ever on the South, whose representatives could be expected to resist liberal legislative initiatives.

Moreover, the Democratic lawmakers from the South, and from most other parts of the country, had no reason to feel obligated to Kennedy. In most congressional districts he had run behind his party's ticket. More than most new presidents, Kennedy would be shackled by the constitutional restraints on the exercise of political power. And Kennedy, who in his days in the House and Senate had not allowed himself to be unduly hindered by party allegiance, now had to reckon with the impact of that lack of discipline on his presidency. He could speak from experience when he told his staff: "Party loyalty or responsibility means damn little" to members of Congress. "They've got to take care of themselves first."

But Kennedy was not prepared to allow himself to become an obscure transitional figure in the White House. Confronted with the pressures growing out of the gap between politics and government—the campaign promises he had made to the voters and the intransigence of the Democratic baronies on Capitol Hill—he responded with the same energy and intensity that infused his candidacy. As a consequence he established patterns and created problems for the presidency that still endure after two decades.

Seeking action, or at least the appearance of action, he turned his attention, and the public's, from domestic policy, where his range of action was limited, to the broader horizons overseas, where he was less restricted. Determined to fire the public's imagination, he set goals for himself and the nation that reached literally to the moon. And to hold the voter's attention during the long periods of stalemate and tedium, he orchestrated his presidency, like his candidacy, around his own personality.

Kennedy and those around him in the White House thrived on crises. Sorensen, often referred to as the President's alter ego, devoted one chapter of *Kennedy* to "The Early Crises—The Bay of Pigs," another to "The Berlin Crisis," and yet another to "The Continuing Crises"—the Congo, Laos, Vietnam, Red China and India. In the atmosphere of crisis the mundane routines of governing could be overlooked and the nation's attention more readily focused on the personality of the president.

The most likely arena for crisis was foreign affairs, where nuclear danger lurked and where the president, as commander in chief, automatically enjoyed patriotic loyalty and respect. Significantly, though Kennedy had spent much of the time between his election and his swearing-in reviewing domestic policy proposals, he decided to focus his inaugural address on foreign policy. "Let's drop the domestic stuff altogether," he told Sorensen as they worked on the final draft of the speech. "It's too long anyway."

Sorensen's contrapuntal cadences and biblical syntax and Kennedy's fervid delivery gave the inaugural address stunning impact. He pledged his countrymen "to pay any price, bear any burden, meet any hardship, support any friend, oppose any foe to assure the survival and success of liberty." For the future he forecast "a long twilight struggle," a continuing crisis, and he exulted in this prospect. "Only a few generations have been granted the role of defending freedom in its hour of maximum danger," he said. "I do not shrink from this responsibility. I welcome it."

His rhetoric pointed the way to adventurism and confrontation abroad. Within weeks of the inauguration, Kennedy allowed the U. S.-sponsored invasion of Cuba's Bay of Pigs to go forward. After its failure he was most disturbed not because the United States had flouted international law and violated its own standards of conduct toward other countries, but because he had miscalculated the expedition's chances for success. "All my life I've known better than to depend on the experts," he said. "How could I have been so stupid as to let them go ahead?"

This misadventure did not deter him from taking further risks abroad. To deal with armed insurgencies flaring in the Third World, he ordered creation of the Green Berets, giving the United States a guerrilla army of its own, or at least an army that used guerrilla tactics. And he found the first use for this elite unit in Vietnam, in the process of expanding U. S. involvement there, a course of action whose painful consequences were only beginning to be felt when the Kennedy presidency ended.

He continued to indulge himself in rhetorical excesses.

With the future of Berlin a sensitive point of dispute between the United States and the Soviet Union, Kennedy visited the divided city and told a cheering throng: *"Ich bin ein Berliner."* The reaction of the crowd was so frenzied that Kennedy himself was taken aback.

Meanwhile Cuba and the Bay of Pigs fiasco gnawed at him, rankling his pride. When the luckless prisoners of the invasion brigade were finally ransomed back to the United States, Kennedy greeted them in the Orange Bowl in Miami with the provocative pledge that their battle flag would be returned to them some day "in a free Havana."

Kennedy was never able to keep that promise. But it was the continuing tension over the Castro regime that led to the ultimate confrontation of his presidency, the October 1962 missile crisis. Later Sorensen acknowledged that the presence of the Soviet missiles in Cuba "made no difference *in fact*" in the balance of nuclear weaponry. "But the balance would have been substantially altered *in appearance*" (his emphasis). On these grounds Kennedy, whose presidency relied so much on appearances, led the nation and the world to the brink of nuclear destruction, outbluffed Khrushchev, and scored a great personal triumph that overshadowed the humiliation of the Bay of Pigs.

The search for challenges and the creation of expectations extended beyond the struggle with communism in the international arena. As his inaugural address indicated, Kennedy's horizons were almost without limit. In the first moments of his presidency Kennedy summoned Americans to "explore the stars, conquer the desert, eradicate disease, tap the ocean depths," as well as to create "a new world of law where the strong are just and the weak secure and the peace preserved." He called for "a grand and global alliance" to vanquish "the common enemies of man: tyranny, poverty, disease and war itself."

Kennedy had hoped to persuade the Soviet Union to

agree to make the effort to "explore the stars" a joint venture with the United States. But the Soviets, who then enjoyed a considerable advantage in space technology, had no interest in such a partnership. Kennedy, who had criticized the Eisenhower administration's space efforts—"to him it symbolized the nation's lack of initiative, ingenuity and vitality under Republican rule," Sorensen wrote—decided to push ahead on his own.

A few months after he entered the White House, Kennedy committed the nation to send a man to the moon by the end of the decade. Whatever the scientific value of this enterprise, it was symbolism on a galactic scale. If Americans could reach for the moon, then, under Kennedy's leadership, nothing on earth should be considered beyond their grasp. But the moon was a long distance away and it would take a long time to get there. The Soviets could be scolded more easily than they could be made to yield. The New Frontier's domestic agenda was bogged down in a balky Congress. Meanwhile Kennedy needed to sustain the public's approval of his presidency and its faith in the expectations he had created. And for this he relied on the attraction of his style and the force of his personality.

Within weeks of his inauguration, Kennedy had made his voice and his face, his manner and his habits, his staff and his family, seem one and indivisible with the office he held. None of his predecessors exploited the prestige of the White House with more telling effect, not even Franklin Roosevelt.

FDR had used radio to reassure, inspire and beguile the nation. Kennedy used the more potent instrument of television for the same purposes, and the impact was geometrically greater. Kennedy's quick wit, virile good looks and crisp manner were ideally suited to the camera. The first president to risk having his press conferences televised live, he converted the reporters into a cast of supporting players who complemented his starring performance. "We couldn't survive without television," he once remarked.

As powerful as it was itself, television was also the key to the other media. Kennedy's televised news conferences became news events in themselves. One survey showed that his press conferences received more coverage in the printed press than those of any of his predecessors, including Franklin Roosevelt. This despite the fact that Roosevelt conducted his press conferences three or four times more often than Kennedy and against the backdrop of the Great Depression and World War II.

During his campaign Kennedy had learned the value of making himself accessible to the press and of cultivating the most influential journalists, and he continued this practice in the presidency. His use of the perquisites of the White House to charm the press prompted the venerable Washington columnist Arthur Krock of the *New York Times* to complain of "news management" in the form of "social flattery of Washington reporters and commentators on an unprecedented scale."

But it was not just Kennedy's invitations to luncheons or dinners or the occasional confidences that captivated the press corps. More broadly, the air of urgency created by Kennedy and his associates as they involved themselves and the country in one crisis after another gave journalists covering the White House a vicarious sense of importance. And the atmosphere was elevated, too. The president entertained and consulted with luminaries of the arts and academe, linking his administration with the world of culture and ideas. "The glow of the White House was lighting up the whole city," said Arthur Schlesinger, Jr., of the New Frontier's early days. "It was a golden interlude." The press corps basked in the glow.

Kennedy heightened this sense of drama by injecting himself personally into controversies. When the big steel companies announced a rise in prices, contravening what

Kennedy had taken to be a pledge of restraint made personally to him, retribution rained down upon them. The president publicly questioned the patriotism of the company managers and encouraged investigations into their economic power by the Justice Department and Congress. But when the price rise was rescinded, the White House swiftly lost interest in the probes; in retrospect, the episode seemed like a personal vendetta. "U.S. Steel picked the wrong President to double cross," one aide later proudly remarked. "Oh, didn't he do a good one," cheered Robert Frost, unofficial poet laureate of the New Frontier. "Didn't he show the Irish all right?"

The incident provided more material for the personal legend being woven about the president, a character pattern dominated by the conceit of toughness. The president's closest associates seemed to relish being called the Irish Mafia, with its suggestion of ruthlessness. For Kennedy himself, "tough" connoted self-discipline and self-control and intellectual and emotional detachment as contrasted with the flabbiness of those who indulged their minds and feelings in sentimentality and commitment to causes of one sort or another.

Kennedy nourished this perception, consciously and unconsciously. In a tribute to Robert Frost after his death, he said he was impressed by many of the poet's qualities, but "also by his toughness." As Henry Fairlie observed in his penetrating critique, *The Kennedy Promise*, "Even the poets on the New Frontier had to be tough." Kennedy once pressed Theodore White to rewrite a campaign pamphlet for use at the 1960 convention, then rejected the renowned journalist's effort. "It would be good copy for Adlai," Kennedy said. "But it's not my style. My style is harder."

The infatuation of the press with the Kennedy mystique extended to his family. His wife, Jacqueline, set new styles in women's coiffures and dress and, having redecorated the White House amid much fanfare, showed off her handiwork in a televised tour. Caroline Kennedy, three years old when her father was inaugurated, was the subject of innumerable feature articles and even of a cover story in *Newsweek*.

Mawkish as this might seem, the public's overall reaction was immensely favorable, as the polls, which Kennedy followed carefully, showed. A few months after he had barely defeated Nixon on election day, a poll showed Kennedy winning a hypothetical rematch by a margin of 62 to 38 percent. After the Bay of Pigs his approval rating soared to 82 percent. "The worse I do, the more popular I get," Kennedy said wryly.

That was really not quite the case. But the poll ratings reflected Kennedy's personal popularity, not his policy goals and accomplishments. Congress understood that, too, and therefore Kennedy's standing in the polls was not directly transferable into political leverage on Capitol Hill. Kennedy might have tried to use his popularity to build public support for his programs. But he was as reluctant to commit himself on issues as president as he had been as a candidate. Instead he relied on the traditional patterns of "inside politics," trying to persuade and bargain with the lawmakers.

In the early days of his presidency Kennedy sought to expand the membership of the House Rules Committee, which sat astride the pathway of legislation, to give it a more liberal majority. Kennedy and his aides begged and bartered for votes supporting expansion, making it a test of personal support for the president. "Let's win this one for Jack, Jackie and little Caroline," his legislative liaison, Lawrence O'Brien, told wavering Democratic congressmen. The maximum effort yielded victory, but by a margin so slight it underlined the obstacles Kennedy faced. "Our honeymoon was over before it began," O'Brien concluded.

The problems did not get easier. Aside from the Peace

Corps, which was quickly adopted, Kennedy proposed few innovations. He sought mainly to strengthen programs put into effect under Roosevelt and Truman. Even so, approval required intensive courting of individual congressmen by the liaison staff, and frequent concessions. The experience taught O'Brien "just how difficult it is to achieve social progress in America."

His diligence helped push through a series of bread-and-butter measures that still held appeal for the old New Deal constituencies; a raise in the minimum wage, and expansion of unemployment insurance and social security, along with a new aid program for depressed areas. But Medicare, federal aid to education and other efforts to break significant new ground foundered.

Moreover the adoption of legislation often required painful compromise. To get an increase in the minimum wage Kennedy had to abandon the idea of extending coverage to laundry workers, whose exploitation he had often cited during the campaign as a symbol of the "icy indifference" of the Republicans.

To avoid antagonizing the Southern support he needed, Kennedy delayed for two years introducing the major civil rights legislation promised in the Democratic platform and in his own campaign statements. He also postponed banning discrimination in federally financed housing, though he had often derided Eisenhower for failing to take this action. All that was required, as Kennedy liked to point out during the campaign, was "the stroke of a pen." In frustration, civil rights advocates mailed bottles of ink to the White House to remind the president of his pledge. Meanwhile, sit-ins and other civil rights protests swelled in the South, and Martin Luther King accused Kennedy of trying to limit black advances to "tokenism."

As the 1962 congressional elections approached, Kennedy sought not to gain ground but mainly to protect what support he had in the Congress, an accomplishment which history had demonstrated was difficult for the party in power. He set out on an ambitious schedule of campaigning for Democratic candidates, but his efforts were interrupted and overshadowed by the Cuban missile crisis.

The Castro regime had been linked to the congressional campaign from the beginning. Republicans had proclaimed that they intended to make the supposed threat from Castro a major issue, and during that summer of 1962 leading Republicans publicly warned of a Soviet military buildup on the island. The administration dismissed the Republican cries of alarm until three weeks before the election, when the president dramatically announced that U-2 flights had discovered hard evidence of the presence of Soviet offensive missiles and warned that the country was in maximum danger.

His success in forcing withdrawal of the missiles not only boosted Kennedy's personal prestige, as the country rallied behind him, but also helped his party. Though preelection polls had shown them to be in serious trouble, the Democrats lost only two seats in the House and gained four seats in the Senate, a remarkable performance for the party in power in an off-year election. And to add to Kennedy's feeling of satisfaction, and to the strength of the Kennedy dynasty, the crop of newly elected Democrats included his youngest brother, Edward Moore Kennedy, who won the president's former Senate seat in Massachusetts.

Kennedy emerged from the election, and from the missile crisis, seemingly more confident of himself and more willing to fulfill his campaign commitments. He finally issued the executive order banning housing discrimination, though he watered it down and timed its announcement, on the eve of the Thanksgiving Day holiday, to create minimum attention.

But it was not until June 1963, when the brutal treatment of civil rights demonstrators by police in Birmingham had shocked the nation, that the president finally submitted to the Congress the far-reaching civil rights program the Democratic Party had promised. That same month he also announced in a memorable speech at American University the resumption of nuclear test ban negotiations with the Soviet Union and called upon the Russian leadership to join the United States in forging "a strategy of peace."

By the fall of 1963 Kennedy was making plans for the 1964 election. He felt certain of renomination and reasonably confident of winning reelection, although he anticipated "a hard close fight," particularly in the South, if, as he expected, Barry Goldwater was the Republican nominee. On the legislative front he was heartened by Senate approval of the test ban treaty, and his aides were confident that other major elements of his program, notably Medicare and civil rights, would win approval in 1964.

Kennedy's assassination came at a time when he believed his presidency was finally gathering momentum. His death cheated him of the chance to test that belief and clouded assessments of his record. Still, it is possible to draft a rough balance sheet.

His most evident achievement was in bringing a sense of vitality and excitement to public affairs which, for a time, increased voter participation and encouraged many young Americans to enter politics and public service. Unfortunately, this atmosphere did not survive long after his death.

On the other side, he committed serious sins of omission. He failed to deal with problems which were not created by him but which worsened during his three years in the White House. One way to illustrate the reasons for his failings is to make a series of assumptions based on a series of ifs.

If the political party system had been healthier and

better equipped to deal with issues, then Kennedy as a congressman would have been less dependent on personality and more concerned with ideology.

If Kennedy had had a close working relationship with a party coalition, then he would have offered clearer choices to the voters as a candidate for the nomination and the presidency.

If Kennedy had been elected with such a mandate, and with such a coalition to support him, he would have been in a stronger position to overcome the constitutional barrier between the presidency and the Congress.

If party discipline had been tighter and the party platform had carried more weight, Democrats in Congress would have been obliged to be more cooperative with the president.

And finally, *if* Kennedy could have made genuine progress with his domestic programs, then he would not have felt the political need to prove his mettle in confrontations with Castro, Khrushchev, and U.S. Steel.

The list of suppositions could go on and on. But these ifs, of course, were not the conditions that prevailed and that molded Kennedy's behavior as a politician and a president. "They've got to take care of themselves," Kennedy had said of the Democrats in Congress. As a Democratic president, Kennedy operated on the same principle, to the detriment of his party and his country.

His emphasis on symbolism and personality distracted attention from the difficult choices that faced the nation. He made compromises because of what he deemed to be political necessity which in the long run proved to be costly, particularly in race relations. Though black voters had made an important contribution to his election, Kennedy delayed keeping his promises of civil rights legislation on pragmatic grounds, fearing to alienate the South. But the result of this temporizing was that by the time he was finally forced to act, the black leadership had become frustrated and mistrustful and Southern defenders of segregation were infuriated anyway. He faced 1964 knowing that the Southern drift away from the national Democratic party was accelerating, and that he had been unable to shape a new alliance.

The successful outcome of the Cuban missile crisis probably saved some Democrats from defeat in the 1962 elections, and this may have been Kennedy's most tangible contribution to his party. But Kennedy's handling of that episode was not the sort of performance that could be repeated. And the contrast between his willingness to gamble for nuclear stakes and his reluctance to risk his prestige in vigorous support of his domestic programs serves to define the values and priorities of his presidency.

Unable to make the government respond to many of the complex problems of the electorate—civil rights, the decay of the cities, the plight of the elderly—Kennedy overdramatized other challenges facing the country, abroad and in space, and overstated his ability as president to deal with them. Kennedy governed by exaggeration. After he was struck down, these exaggerations became part of his compelling and troublesome legacy.

CHAPTER FOUR

1964

1. "A Choice Not an Echo"

Millions of Americans spent the afternoon of Sunday, October 8, 1961, in front of their television sets watching the New York Yankees shut out the Cincinnati Reds in the fourth game of the World Series. But the twenty-two Republicans who gathered in a Chicago motel room that day had no time for baseball. Their minds were on the 1964 election. All were conservatives who had come together from various parts of the country because they shared the conviction that the Republican Party had long been drifting in the wrong direction. By the end of their meeting they had pledged themselves to a common goal. This was nothing less than the takeover of the Grand Old Party and the nomination of Barry Goldwater of Arizona as its next standard bearer.

The organizer of the meeting was F. Clifton White, a jaunty, fifty-two-year-old New York public relations adviser who had been a second-level tactician in the 1960 Nixon campaign. The rest included two obscure young congressmen and an assortment of even lesser-known fund raisers. They were not an imposing group, but their objective was not as unrealistic as it might have seemed. For as Clif White perceived, the established leaders of the Republican Party had an even weaker grip on its controls than their Democratic counterparts had in 1960 when John Kennedy outmaneuvered them.

"The people who had controlled the party for more than twenty years—the party pros to whom the press still paid homage—were in reality on the shelf," White wrote later in *Suite 3505*, his account of the Goldwater campaign. "Most of them were just too old and too tired to answer the bell for another round."

The decline of the established party leadership, which, as White foresaw, paved the way for Goldwater's nomination, was only one aspect of the gap between politics and government which shaped the 1964 quadrennial.

The influence of personality and its disruptive impact were demonstrated by the reaction to two unforeseen and otherwise unrelated events—the remarriage of Nelson Rockefeller, the early favorite for the Republican nomination, and the assassination of President Kennedy. At first glance these two episodes hardly seem comparable. Rockefeller was involved in a melodrama with tawdry undertones. Kennedy's death was an awful tragedy. But they were linked in that both generated intense emotional responses which reflected the personalization of presidential politics and altered the presidential campaign in ways that had little to do with the legitimate concerns of politics and government.

The stress on personality, with its frequent corollary of party divisiveness, also manifested itself in the Republican presidential primaries. Since neither Goldwater nor Rockefeller, the two principal rivals, offered constructive proposals for uniting their party, public and press attention focused on the shortcomings of both candidates. This pervasive negativism permanently scarred both candidates and aggravated the tensions and disagreements within their party.

As Clif White realized, the Republican leadership was ailing even before the campaign. Their influence, like that of their Democratic counterparts, had been undermined by the social and economic flux of the postwar era, and their party's appeal to the public had been declining since Franklin Roosevelt's election. Eisenhower's personal popularity had masked the party's difficulties. But Nixon's failure to capitalize on the Eisenhower legacy in 1960 had sent the GOP once again stumbling to defeat and widened its divisions.

Right through the ideological heart of the party ran a fault line, splitting it left and right. This rift could be traced back to 1912, when Theodore Roosevelt's Progressives deserted the incumbent William Howard Taft and bolted the party. Some of the rebels returned, but the hard feelings still simmered. The conservatives held control during the 1920s, and took the shattering force of the Great Depression. By 1940 the right wing had lost much of its influence over the party's presidential choice, but remained a potent force in Congress, rallying behind the leadership of Ohio's Robert Taft. The conservatives were Franklin Roosevelt's most vociferous opponents. But they clung too long to the lost cause of isolation, and their chief response to the New Deal, and to Truman's Fair Deal which followed it, was a simplistic negativism.

The liberals, or moderates as they preferred to call themselves by the 1960s, had dominated Republican presidential conventions since Wendell Willkie. But they lacked the imagination and intellectual vitality of their Progressive forebears. Their power was based in the big investment houses and law firms of the East and they were not inclined to take chances. While the conservatives fought vainly to turn the clock back, the moderates merely wanted time to stand still. Every four years they had placed their faith not in any substantive alternative to the policies of the Democrats, but in candidates who seemed safely in the middle of the road and who promised to do most of the same things that Democrats had done, but to do them more cheaply. They had nominated Willkie, Dewey, Eisenhower and Nixon, and now, as they looked ahead to 1964, they seemed prepared, though not without misgivings, to give their support to Nelson A. Rockefeller.

This was a choice that White and his cohorts were not prepared to accept. But to stop Rockefeller the conservatives would need to be more aggressive than in the past. White took inspiration from Kennedy's early drive for the 1960 nomination, which White believed had established "a whole new dimension" in American politics. A few weeks after the initial planning meeting in Chicago, White set up shop in a midtown Manhattan office building for an unofficial presidential campaign organization. Ostensibly the group put off commitment to any particular candidate. But it was clear from the beginning that Goldwater was the only realistic possibility and that the group would try to draft him if necessary.

Kennedy had focused on winning primaries to pressure party leaders into supporting his candidacy. But the draft-Goldwater strategy challenged the party leaders more directly, by trying to take their organizations and delegates away from them. This meant an intensive effort at the grass-roots level, where two years or so before the national convention the process began of choosing county and state party officials who would ultimately dominate their convention delegations.

White regarded most current GOP leaders as "sitting ducks" who had "lost touch" with the conservative precinct and district committee members. And with the Democrats in control of the White House, most state governments, and nearly all of the principal city halls, the established Republican leadership had also lost the patronage needed to hold the lower echelons in line. "The situation," White believed, "was ripe for revolt."

In its early stages the drive did not need the support of Goldwater, which was just as well, because the senator was reluctant to commit himself to running. Goldwater had made a name for himself among conservatives during the fifties, when he traveled around the country as head of the GOP Senate Campaign Committee. He had then emerged as a national figure at the 1960 convention, when he became the spokesman for conservatives indignant at liberal changes in the party platform authored by Nelson Rockefeller and accepted by Richard Nixon.

After Nixon's defeat, Goldwater was the logical candidate for conservatives to rally behind. But Goldwater preferred giving speeches to his admirers to scrambling for votes among the uncommitted. And he had no stomach for a long battle against Nelson Rockefeller, who was the clear leader in the public opinion polls for 1964.

Rockefeller himself brimmed with confidence. Seemingly untarnished by his divorce in 1961 from his wife of thirty-one years, he had handily won reelection as governor of New York in 1962. Buoyed by his standing in the polls, he ignored the early stirrings of the draft-Goldwater drive. His aides sought to placate conservative leaders, who were suspicious of Rockefeller's reputation as a big-spending liberal, and hoped to convince them of the inevitability of his nomination. Rockefeller personally courted Goldwater, who told his friends: "Rocky's really not such a bad fellow. He's more conservative than you would imagine."

This was the Republican outlook in the spring of 1963, as it appeared to Rockefeller and Goldwater strategists. But before the year was out, their calculations were overturned twice—first by the remarriage of Rockefeller and then by the assassination of the president.

The fifty-four-year-old Rockefeller married Margaretta Fitler Murphy, who was thirty-six, in May 1963. His new wife had been divorced only weeks before, and she had four children whose custody was awarded to her former husband; gossip was widespread that she and Rockefeller had carried on a prolonged affair before her divorce.

Reaction to the marriage was swift. Ministers denounced Rockefeller from their pulpits. Voters, particularly women, condemned him in letters to their congressmen as a home breaker and a wife stealer. The impact on the Gallup Poll was seismic. Rockefeller, who had been leading Goldwater by more than fifteen points before the wedding, fell behind him by more than ten.

Rockefeller and his supporters insisted that the outcry would subside. But it did not, for reasons that reflected the shallowness of Rockefeller's political support. Rockefeller owed his success in politics mainly to the impression he had created with voters, once described to me by Joseph Persico, one of his speech writers, as "your friendly neighborhood billionaire." His blintz-eating folksiness as a campaigner and the vaguely liberal policies he pursued as governor played off nicely against the austere and autocratic reputation of his family. Rockefeller cast himself as a problem solver in government and politics and avoided involvement with issues and movements that might have helped revitalize progressivism in his party but that he feared might create problems for him.

But his remarriage converted the folksy billionaire into an arrogant philanderer in the minds of many voters. When his poll ratings fell, the conservatives whom he had tried to reconcile to his candidacy scorned him. And the liberals, who had looked to him in vain for leadership, were now too disorganized to help him cope with the Goldwater drive.

Nelson Rockefeller had built his presidential hopes on his personal appeal, not on commitment to issues or to his party. When that appeal turned sour, his hopes were doomed.

As Rockefeller faded, Goldwater's interest in the nomination increased and the Goldwater battle plan came into focus. From the start it had a pronounced Southern tilt, because the state Republican parties in the South, which had been in dry rot for nearly a century, had appeared to be prime targets for the grass-roots insurgency. In the wake of the civil rights ferment of 1963, and the legislative response into which the Kennedy administration was finally pushed, the South became even more important to Goldwater's candidacy—not just as a stepping stone to the nomination, but as a cornerstone for victory in the general election.

Though Goldwater declared himself to be opposed to segregation, he also opposed most federal efforts to desegregate as violations of states rights. By September 1963 the Gallup Poll showed Goldwater leading Kennedy by twenty points among Southern voters in both parties. And his strategists had reason to hope that Goldwater might also benefit from a much discussed "white backlash" against civil rights drives in the North.

Then came Kennedy's death and the succession of Lyndon Johnson. Johnson immediately pledged himself to support and carry out Kennedy's legislative program, most particularly his civil rights proposals. But just as the public's attitude toward Kennedy was dominated by his personality, not his program, the public reaction to the new president was also based mainly on personal factors. The most important of these was that Johnson was the first president from the Old Confederacy in nearly a century.

The strategic considerations for the Republican campaign were dramatically reversed. It was now taken for granted that any Republican would have trouble winning Southern votes against Johnson; on the other hand, Johnson was considered to be vulnerable among liberal voters in the North. Convinced he could not defeat a Southerner, Goldwater told his wife he would not run. He was persuaded to stay in the race, but the change in personalities in the White House helped to sustain the candidacy of Nelson Rockefeller and also to encourage the ambitions of other moderate Republicans whose combined efforts caused Goldwater considerable harm.

The sense of personal loss over Kennedy's death felt

by his countrymen, including many who did not support his policies, produced an emotional reaction which also damaged Goldwater's candidacy. Trying to find meaning for the senseless trauma of the assassination, many Americans fixed the blame on political extremists. Though Lee Harvey Oswald himself had been involved with leftist groups, the odium attached also to extremists of the right, a category that seemed to include some of Goldwater's more vociferous supporters. "By some weird convoluted logic," Clif White complained, "a vast subconscious blame for the assassination rubbed off on Goldwater's supporters." Moreover, this distaste for extremism, and the violence associated with it, also tended to curb manifestations of white resentment against civil rights in the North, taking much of the sting out of the backlash.

With the political forces in ferment, the primaries took on new importance for both Rockefeller and Goldwater. Just as Kennedy had used the primaries to minimize the problem of his religion, Rockefeller sought to demonstrate that he could overcome the reaction to his remarriage, while Goldwater hoped to show that his prospects had not been ruined by Johnson's elevation to the presidency. As it turned out, though, the main impact of the primaries was to demonstrate the faults of both candidates.

The first test came in New Hampshire in February. In officially announcing his candidacy, Goldwater promised to offer "a choice not an echo" and vowed that his campaign would be "an engagement of principles." But his principles were soon drowned out by the reaction to a series of ill-considered off-the-cuff remarks. In short order he proposed to make Social Security voluntary, to launch another exile invasion of Cuba, this time with U.S. air support, and to give NATO field commanders the discretion to use nuclear weapons. Goldwater had been saying such things most of his political life, but no one had paid much heed. Now his remarks made the network news shows and front pages in New Hampshire and around the country. It was not so much the substance of what Goldwater said—this was hard to sort out—which did him harm. More damaging was the general personal impression he created of being reckless and erratic, a stereotype he would struggle vainly to alter for the rest of the year.

The treatment given Goldwater in New Hampshire and subsequent primaries was in part a result of trends in politics and journalism reinforcing each other. With the help of the press, particularly television, John Kennedy had greatly dramatized the primaries in 1960. Accordingly, the press intensified its coverage of the 1964 primaries, and its daily search for the item most likely to catch the eye of the viewer and the reader was most often satisfied by Goldwater's ramblings.

A similar influence on the press was exercised by the immense popularity of Theodore White's narrative of the 1960 campaign, *The Making of the President*. A former *Time* correspondent and also a successful novelist, White contrived to transform the dreary routine of campaigning into a romantic spectacle, endowing hitherto unremarked-upon actions and utterances with profound meaning. The 1964 campaign press corps, having digested White's narrative, seized upon Goldwater's ad libs as portents of his philosophy and his character, to the candidate's growing indignation.

But the harm done to Goldwater did not help Rockefeller. He could not find a substantive point for his candidacy to replace the tarnished appeal of his personality. The level of his New Hampshire campaign was reflected in its climactic event, a sort of vaudeville show at the Manchester Armory, in which entertainment by a folk-singing group and a bagpipe band was interspersed with tributes to Rockefeller from television and movie stars. But neither the friendly billionaire's troupe of imported players nor his own relentless affability could shake the stern judgment of New Hampshire voters on his remarriage. Both he and Goldwater finished well behind Henry Cabot Lodge, Nixon's 1960 running mate, who had become U.S. ambassador to South Vietnam, and whose name was not even on the ballot. From his post in Saigon, ten thousand miles away, Lodge was in a poor position to take advantage of his write-in triumph. But the success of his absentee campaign mocked the assiduous efforts of the two chief candidates and underlined their weaknesses.

Of the two, Goldwater was in far better condition, because he could rely on Clif White's grass-roots effort launched long before. Rockefeller's candidacy was mortally wounded. But he refused to drop out, and his stubbornness, along with their own timidity, kept other moderates from entering the race.

After New Hampshire, Rockefeller and Goldwater met head-on in only one more primary, California's climactic contest in June. In the intervening primaries Goldwater scored a number of unimpressive successes against token opposition. The main thrust of his candidacy was in the large majority of states that had no primaries, or where the primaries did not control the selection of delegates. Here Goldwater benefited from the early efforts made on his behalf and from what came to be called "a national mass movement."

Actually the movement was not massive, except by comparison with its opposition, which was almost nonexistent. It only took a few hundred or in some cases a few dozen voters willing to show up at a critical caucus to assure that the delegates would be for Goldwater. Some were John Birch Society members, paranoid in their fear of the Red menace. Others, particularly in the South, were diehard segregationists. And still others, as Robert Novak pointed out in *The Agony of the GOP*, were simply fed up with the growth of federal power and believed that the "choice not an echo" battle cry of the Goldwater campaign meant that at last the Republicans had offered a genuine alternative to the dominant liberal establishment.

That Goldwater's utterances lacked coherence and substance mattered little. In a campaign bereft of issues, emotions ruled the day.

Impelled by their combination of resentments, aided by the early spadework instigated by the draft movement, the Goldwater supporters swept through the caucus states like locusts. Nearly every day that spring Goldwater's delegate tally climbed steadily, until by the time of the June California primary, despite his unimpressive showing in the polls, Goldwater had a commanding lead in delegates.

The California primary presented the last possibility for the moderates to stop Goldwater. Rockefeller sought to depict Goldwater as a threat to peace. One of his campaign pamphlets asked voters: "Whom do you want in the room with the H-bomb button?" and warned: "The very life of your Republican Party—and, perhaps, our nation's—is up to you." In his desperation to salvage his candidacy, Rockefeller did not stop to consider what impact his own hyperbole might have on the future health of his party; such ad hominem attacks were bound to cause bitterness and division no matter who won the GOP nomination.

At any rate, Rockefeller's assault was not enough to overcome his own drawbacks. The decisive blow to Rockefeller's prospects came three days before the vote when his wife gave birth to a son, reminding any voters who might have forgotten about his remarriage. Goldwater won by sixty thousand votes out of more than two million cast, enough to give him all of the state's delegates and assure him of the nomination.

Still the moderates refused to surrender. Rockefeller, finally conceding defeat, threw his resources behind

Pennsylvania governor William Scranton, who after hemming and hawing for months at last announced his own candidacy. All this accomplished was to turn the convention into a fratricidal brawl. The moderates were bitter in defeat, accusing Goldwater of extremism, and the conservatives were vindictive in victory. In his acceptance speech Goldwater threw the moderates' charges back in their faces, proclaiming "extremism in the defense of liberty is no vice" and "moderation in the pursuit of justice is no virtue."

White, who had been isolated from Goldwater in the closing months of the campaign, heard the speech in his trailer command post outside the convention hall. He listened in stunned dismay to the rhetoric and to the wildly cheering crowd and wondered "if they knew they were hailing disaster and defeat."

However dim Goldwater's prospects seemed, his conservative supporters could rejoice in their triumph over their liberal adversaries. The liberals had nothing to cheer about. The campaign had exposed their bankruptcy of ideas. While the liberals complained bitterly about the negativism of the Goldwater campaign, they themselves were united only by their opposition to Goldwater, and the main reason they gave for their continued resistance was that they doubted his electability. This kind of argument had carried weight with professional party leaders at past conventions, but most of them had lost their power in the Goldwater onslaught.

The intellectual vacuousness of the liberals was matched by their lack of resolve. The New Hampshire primary showed that Rockefeller's candidacy was doomed and displayed Goldwater's vulnerability. Yet none of the moderate leaders was willing to commit himself to a candidacy at that point. Instead they hovered in the wings, relying on the hope that Rockefeller might just manage to prevent Goldwater's nomination, allowing one of them to pick up the prize.

The Goldwater campaign demonstrated that an entrepreneurial candidacy which got off to an early start and demonstrated determination and resourcefulness could overcome a somnolent regular party organization in the GOP as well as in the Democratic Party. Goldwater's victory in the California primary clinched the nomination and gave his candidacy legitimacy in the minds of the delegates and the voters. The enhanced prestige of primaries would influence strategies in both parties in 1968.

But the primary contests cost Goldwater and his party dearly. The bitter fights in New Hampshire and California led to the unseemly discord of the convention, battered Goldwater's reputation and gave the Democrats potent ammunition to use against him in the fall.

2. The Politics of Consensus

The framers of the Constitution would have approved the basic idea underlying Lyndon Johnson's approach to the presidency. This was the concept of consensus. The framers found the idea of consensus attractive because it fit in with their aversion to politics and parties and their faith that Americans were destined to live together in relative harmony. Consensus appealed to Johnson because it helped him to manipulate politics and government.

Consensus politics contrasts with coalition politics. In coalition politics alliances of groups with similar interests compete against each other through the party system for the rewards they seek from government. The potency of coalition politics was best demonstrated in modern times by the forces Franklin Roosevelt assembled and led in the Democratic Party during the early years of his presidency. Consensus politics, on the other hand, assumes that all significant competing interests, and the political parties themselves, will set aside their differences for the sake of achieving common goals. In reality, though, meaningful common goals are hard to agree on and harder to achieve. Practitioners of consensus tend either to offer something for nearly everybody, as Johnson did, or very little to anybody. In either case, some groups are bound to be disappointed and frustrated, leading to hostility and tensions which are often more severe than if the competition between interests had not been avoided in the first place.

Lyndon Johnson's brand of consensus politics was designed as a substitute for political parties in getting the government to respond to what he perceived to be the concerns of politics. Accustomed to bypassing his own party, unwilling to depend upon it for support in the presidency, he extolled the virtues of nonpartisanship and relied on the force of his personality instead of the collective responsibility of the political system. "To me," Johnson explained, "consensus meant, first, deciding what needed to be done regardless of the political implications and, second, convincing a majority of the Congress and the American people of the necessity for doing those things." Johnson himself did most of the deciding and most of the convincing. As he said: "I pleaded, I reasoned, I argued. I urged. I warned." For a time he was extremely persuasive and extremely successful. But eventually the strain his machinations imposed on himself, on the Congress, on his party and on the public wrecked his presidency and intensified cynicism about politics and government.

Johnson had learned to practice consensus politics in his home state of Texas. Like other Southern states, Texas had a tradition of Democratic Party supremacy dating back to the Civil War. With the social and economic changes that followed World War II, Republicans began to stir in the state. But Johnson and other party leaders managed to forestall the emergence of Texas

Republicanism for years by catering to the business interests, who normally would have supported the GOP, and by overlooking the economic grievances of less-advantaged constituencies in the Democratic ranks. This was a cozy arrangement for Johnson and his associates because it preserved their privileged personal status in the state. But it deprived the Democratic Party of ideological identity or purpose. And like most such consensuses, this arrangement contained the seeds of its own destruction. Wealthy conservative interests became dissatisfied with their treatment by the Democratic Party and began backing Republicans. After Johnson was elected vice-president in 1960 he was replaced in the Senate by John Tower, the first Republican to go to the Senate from Texas since Reconstruction. Meanwhile, friction between conservatives and liberals in the state Democratic Party was getting harder to control. It was, in fact, an attempt to placate these consensus antagonists that sent John Kennedy to Dallas in November 1963.

Although the Republicans in the U.S. Senate were a more formidable force than they had been in Texas, Johnson found that his consensus approach could still operate among the lawmakers. By taking care of the personal concerns of individual senators, and by devising convenient compromises, he could generally avoid open clashes with the opposition party and also with his fellow Democrats. His skill at dealing and maneuvering helped him become majority leader and brought him unprecedented power in that position.

The tragic circumstances that elevated Johnson to the presidency were ideally suited to the building of consensus. The mourning nation rallied behind the successor to its fallen leader and partisanship was subdued. Johnson was quick to take advantage of the situation. A few days after the assassination he called the Republican leader in the Senate, Everett Dirksen of Illinois, and asked him to persuade his fellow Republicans "that it was essential to forget partisan politics, so that we could weather the national crisis in which we were involved and unite our people."

Dirksen, an old Johnson crony from the president's Senate days, was not hard to convince. "Well, Mr. President," he replied, "you know I will."

Johnson, by his own account, had many such conversations during his first weeks in the White House with Democrats and Republicans, businessmen and labor leaders, journalists and public officials. As he later wrote: "I brought people together who under ordinary circumstances would have fled at the sight of each other."

The new president adroitly sustained the public mood of unity. When he declared "Let us continue" in his first major address after taking office, he sounded exactly the right note. By making Kennedy's legislative program his own, Johnson offered the badly shaken country what it most wanted, stability and consistency. And in all his utterances, public and private, Johnson stressed his basic consensus theme: "People must put aside their selfish aims in the larger cause of the nation's interest."

But this homily ignored the reality that the resolution of these so-called selfish aims was fundamentally what people expected from politics and government. And it begged the question of for how long and on what basis Lyndon Johnson should be allowed to define the nation's interest.

Nevertheless, the early favorable response of Congress to Johnson's efforts to push through Kennedy's program enhanced his prestige. In the summer of 1964, as the Democratic National Convention approached, Johnson's consensus was holding firm and he seemed on top of the political world.

While the Republicans had battled each other across the country that spring, the only action on the Democratic front had been provided by Alabama governor George Wallace. Having made himself a hero to diehards in the South as a result of his resistance to racial integration, Wallace ventured outside of Dixie to enter primaries in Wisconsin, Maryland and Indiana. Running against favorite-son stand-ins for Johnson, Wallace got enough votes to shock Northern liberals and to demonstrate the political potency of the white backlash. But this was an exercise aimed at building Wallace's prestige in the future, rather than an effort to deny Johnson nomination in 1964. By any reckoning, Johnson's hold on his party seemed beyond challenge. The only political speculation about the Democratic convention in August centered on whom Johnson would choose as his running mate.

Yet Johnson, by his own account, was "beset with many doubts and reservations" about whether he should accept the prize that was clearly his to claim. He needed no one to remind him that he had come to power "in the cruelest way possible, as the result of a murderer's bullet." He was well aware that many people doubted that he could ever have gained the presidency in his own right, because of his Southern origins. And he questioned whether the country would stay united for long behind a Southern president. "The metropolitan press of the Eastern seaboard would never permit it," he felt.

During the spring and summer of 1964 Johnson spent a good many precious hours consulting his friends and advisers about his political future and drawing up a list of the pros and cons of seeking four more years in the White House. Just one day before his nomination was expected to take place at the Democratic convention in Atlantic City, as Johnson tells the story in his memoirs, he drafted a statement ruling out his candidacy. Not until late that afternoon did he allow Lady Bird Johnson to persuade him that "it would be wrong for the country" for him to withdraw.

Obviously Johnson wanted to be persuaded. But it is also clear that at a time when the tides of fortune all seemed to be running in his favor he was deeply concerned about potential pitfalls for his presidency. And this sense of anxiety served to intensify his determination to avoid any discord that might threaten his consensus. Even before the convention opened Johnson had dealt with one potential problem, represented by Robert Kennedy. Johnson had benefited greatly from the emotional reaction to John Kennedy's assassination when he first entered the White House. But as the months passed, and the Kennedy legend grew, Johnson resented the comparisons made with increasing frequency between his own presidency and Kennedy's romanticized tenure in the White House. And he was concerned about the ambitions of Robert Kennedy, who continued in the post of attorney general to which his brother had appointed him and who had become heir to the family political legacy.

The support for Kennedy, which ultimately contributed to a disastrous cleavage in the Democratic Party, was a further manifestation of the politics of personality which had distorted the Republican campaign. At this point in his life Robert Kennedy had never held elective office, or even sought it. On many public issues his views were unknown to the public and, in fact, still largely unformed. Yet the simple fact of his identification with the myths woven about his brother made him a major actor on the political stage with whom Lyndon Johnson believed he had to contend.

Kennedy partisans began lobbying for the attorney general to become Johnson's running mate on the 1964 Democratic ticket, and Kennedy himself, though he said nothing publicly, clearly would have welcomed the opportunity. But Johnson, fearing to give Kennedy a position which he could use as a national forum, wanted no part of that proposition. To squelch the idea he publicly announced, in the month before the convention, that he would not consider any official of cabinet rank for his running mate, thus effectively eliminating Kennedy. The slain president's brother would go on to win election to the Senate from New York and remain a potential rallying point for opposition to Johnson. But for the time being at least, Johnson felt that he had protected his consensus by sidetracking a potential rival.

Meanwhile, he bent every effort to make the Atlantic City convention, marking his official debut as the party's political leader, into a showcase of harmony. After heavy-handed efforts to contrive suspense over his choice of a running mate, he finally settled on Hubert Humphrey, who would help to reassure those liberals who still nursed suspicions of Johnson himself. And to avoid the slightest chance of resistance to his wishes, Johnson insisted on shifting a film memorializing John Kennedy—which he feared might stir emotional support for Robert Kennedy for vice-president—from the convention's opening night to a time after the balloting for vice-president had been concluded.

But not all discord could be so easily muffled. A contingent of civil rights partisans from Mississippi, sixty-four blacks and four whites, calling themselves the Freedom Democratic Party, showed up at the convention, demanding that they be given credentials in preference to the all-white delegation of the state's regular Democratic Party which had been chosen under its traditionally segregated practices.

On strictly procedural grounds the Freedom Democrats had a weak case. But their protest against the racism long practiced in the South and tolerated by the North had a powerful moral and emotional appeal, and quickly became the focus of public attention at Atlantic City. Feverish negotiations ensued behind the scenes until a compromise of sorts was dictated by Johnson himself from the White House and accepted by the convention. The Freedom Democrats were given two votes at the convention. But far more important, the assembled delegates decreed an end to segregation in the Democratic Party, North and South, for the future. In an official resolution the convention empowered future conventions, starting in 1968, to refuse to seat delegations from states whose Democratic parties practiced racial discrimination.

Only two Southern delegations walked out in protest, and the harmony the president had sought was restored. But the episode had important and discordant implications for the future. It served to demonstrate the militance of black leaders determined to eradicate all the vestiges of segregation, an attitude that would in time help to undermine the traditional New Deal coalition. More broadly, by making the first significant change in its rules since 1936, when the requirement of a two-thirds majority for nomination was eliminated, the convention opened the door to a wave of revisionism which would ultimately plunge the party into turmoil.

For the time being, though, Democrats were as united behind the Johnson-Humphrey ticket as even Johnson could wish. This was in sharp contrast to the condition of the Republicans after their San Francisco convention. Goldwater's nomination and his unyielding acceptance speech had left many moderate Republicans, from office holders down to rank-and-file voters, disaffected with their own party's candidate.

This created a splendid opening for consensus politics, and Johnson moved swiftly to take advantage of it. Within his campaign, Johnson created a so-called Frontlash program destined to overshadow the threatened white backlash. The Frontlash operation, as Johnson explained it, was intended "to make it as easy as possible for lifelong Republicans to switch their votes in November to the Democratic column." Frontlash played on Republican fears of Goldwater's extremism and at the same time sought to reassure them about Johnson. Announcing formation of a committee of prominent Republican business leaders pledged to support his candidacy, Johnson declared: "I shall never seek to be a labor President, or a business President, a President for liberals or a President for conservatives, a President for the North or a President for the South—but only President for all the people." In *The Party's Over*, David Broder tells of Johnson showing White House visitors a poll indicating that liberals, conservatives and middle-of-the-roaders all considered him to be one of them. "They all think I'm on their side," he bragged.

This consensus politics turned into a grand and insidious delusion. But given the context of the campaign, there was no one to point out that the emperor of consensus had no clothes.

Goldwater had led people to anticipate that his challenge to Johnson would become a clash of issues and ideas. It was nothing of the sort, and in large part this was Goldwater's own fault. Early in the campaign, Goldwater later revealed, he visited Johnson in the White House to promise he would not challenge the president's handling of Vietnam or civil rights. Goldwater explained that he was acting in the interest of national unity, but he was also probably gun-shy about discussing war and race as a result of his primary scars. Johnson eagerly accepted the offer and pledged to exercise similar restraint. "The President seemed relieved," Goldwater wrote. And no wonder. Goldwater had spared him from having to defend his positions on the most sensitive questions of the day, which were also the questions most demanding of reasoned debate.

Whatever Goldwater's understanding was of his agreement with Johnson, their conversation did not prevent the president from trying to set aside, in the most emphatic terms, voter concerns about the fighting in Indochina. "We are not about to send American boys nine or ten thousand miles away from home to do what Asian boys ought to be doing to protect themselves," he declared.

Nor did the private pact between the two candidates

hinder Johnson's Frontlash operation from exhuming a broad range of Goldwater's utterances from the primary campaign and from his earlier writings and speeches and recycling them through the press. Time and again, with less and less patience, Goldwater was obliged to explain what he really meant when he suggested selling the Tennessee Valley Authority, or when he talked about a nuclear defoliation of the jungles of Laos.

And so Goldwater was kept most of the time on the defensive, particularly trying to dispel the fear that he would be too eager to push the nuclear button. Goldwater never actually advocated starting a nuclear war. As Charles Mohr of the *New York Times* pointed out, "He just talked about it all the time." During one thirty-minute address in which he sought to set the nuclear issue to rest, Mohr calculated, Goldwater had used words such as "nuclear weapons" and "devastation" a total of twenty-six times.

And Goldwater's efforts to take the initiative bogged down in negativism and inconsistency. He was against communism. But so was everyone else. He was against big government. But he had no alternative to government programs. He was for an income-tax cut. But he had voted against the tax cut proposed by Kennedy and enacted under Johnson.

The polls showed Goldwater trailing Johnson by thirty to forty points, a hopeless margin. Johnson could have coasted to victory. But he drove himself on, determined not just to win but to win by a margin so huge that it would set to rest all doubts about the legitimacy of his presidency, reinforce his consensus and provide a mandate for the hazy vision of the Great Society which he had made the cognomen of his administration. Johnson had set for himself the goal of being president of all the people. And as he campaigned that fall, cheered on by huge throngs, it seemed he would not be satisfied unless literally all the people voted for him.

"I just want to tell you this," he cried to a crowd that swarmed around his motorcade in Providence, Rhode Island, "we're for a lot of things and we're against mighty few." Johnson held out the promise of the Great Society as a boon for everyone. But he never got around to explaining how it would work. "In fact," David Broder reported after a week-long campaign tour with the president, "Johnson has been able to get by this campaign by doing little more than defending the policies that have been at the root of American policy since the establishment of the United Nations, the passage of the first foreign aid bill and the enactment of the Full Employment Act of the 1940s."

As election day arrived, no one doubted the result, including Goldwater. Richard Kleindienst and Robert Mardian, two of his Arizona advisers, found the senator that morning outside his hilltop home in Phoenix, peering through a telescope, one of the technical devices he surrounded himself with. The candidate sighted in on the polling place in town, where he spotted his Hispanic housemaid waiting her turn in line. "Look at that damn woman," he muttered. "She's going to vote against me, too."

Despite his maid, Goldwater carried his own Arizona and five Southern states. That was all. Lyndon Johnson's margin was huge enough to satisfy even him. He defeated Goldwater with 61 percent of the vote—the largest popular vote margin up to that time. The Democrats gained two seats in the Senate, thirty-seven in the House and five hundred in state legislatures around the country. Voter turnout fell to 61.9 percent from 62.8 in 1960.

Some analysts contended afterward that Goldwater's debacle proved that an ideological candidate cannot succeed. But Goldwater was no ideologue. Ideologues have programs, however doctrinaire. Goldwater had only a set of complaints. He was an amateurish candidate. He did not try to control the right-wing groups which supported him, and he refused to disavow those, like the John Birch Society, which could not be controlled, thus doing a disservice to the more rational conservatives who backed his candidacy. He seemed more like a missionary than a candidate, but he was most comfortable addressing the already converted.

Goldwater's candidacy made casualties out of numerous Republican office holders, but in the long run the nation suffered more than the GOP. Because of Goldwater's inadequacies, and the nature of the nominating process which allowed him to prevail despite his failings, there was no real challenge to Lyndon Johnson, no one to raise the questions about Vietnam and the Great Society which needed to be asked, and for which Johnson, as the country ultimately learned, had no good answers.

Johnson reveled in his triumph and in the whopping majorities the Democrats had won in the new 89th Congress. But he knew that such advantages could be worn down against the Madisonian wall separating the president and the Congress. Indeed, in the flush of victory he felt that the political clock was already running against him. "I was just elected President by the biggest popular margin in the history of the country, fifteen million votes," he told his congressional liaison staff a few weeks after the election. "But just by the nature of the way people think and because Barry Goldwater scared the hell out of them, I have already lost about two of those fifteen." Furthermore, he predicted, as Rowland Evans and Robert Novak recounted in *Lyndon B. Johnson: The Exercise of Power*, that if more troops were shipped to Vietnam, "I may be down to eight million by the end of summer." Then he gave the marching orders for his agents on the Hill: full speed ahead.

Even before the 1964 election, Johnson had done quite well with Congress, getting approval for the civil rights legislation initiated by John Kennedy and for the launching of his own war on poverty. But this had just whetted his appetite for the smorgasbord of programs he now demanded. The breadth of his agenda reflected Johnson's zeal to preserve his consensus, offering something for nearly every national interest of consequence. Besides the major goals of Medicare and federal aid to education, he presented a long list of programs in areas ranging from arts and humanities and Appalachia to water pollution and weather forecasting.

And then there was the voting rights bill, pushed to the forefront by black demonstrations in the South, and urged upon the Congress by Lyndon Johnson in a televised address to a joint session, climaxed by the exhortation, "We shall overcome." "On this issue," the president declared, "there must be no delay, no hesitation, no compromise with our purpose."

But in fact this same unrelenting urgency pervaded Johnson's attitude on every measure, including many that lacked the moral and constitutional imperative of voting rights. Time and consensus did not permit the setting of priorities. Johnson drove himself, his aides and the lawmakers to the utmost, and occasionally to distraction. Furious because on one occasion he could not reach his domestic affairs adviser, Joseph Califano, Johnson ordered that a telephone be installed in Califano's office lavatory. And one October night he kept the House in session until past midnight so it could pass a highway beautification bill before Johnson entered the hospital for removal of his gall bladder.

In its first year the 89th Congress passed eighty-four of the eighty-seven major bills Johnson submitted to it, establishing a record that matched, and in some ways exceeded, what was accomplished in the heyday of the New Deal. But still Johnson was not satisfied. When Congress resumed in January 1966, Johnson refused to lower his sights for domestic policy.

Under Johnson's prodding, the lawmakers sent the White House some more parchment for presidential signature. But they were now visibly dragging their feet, amidst a rising chorus of criticism from both parties and the public. And by the time the Great Society Congress adjourned, only two weeks before the 1966 elections, the president and his party were awash in troubled waters.

Their difficulties were a measure of the failure of consensus as a strategy for using government to meet the needs of the electorate. That failure can be traced back to the 1964 campaign. Johnson might have tried to build a coalition in his own party around a framework of limited but explicit goals. But a lifetime of experience in Texas and in Washington counseled against that approach. Instead, Johnson sought to reach voters across the political spectrum with sweeping but hazy promises —"We're for a lot of things and we're against mighty few." Goldwater, with little credibility and without a coherent viewpoint, was unable to pin him down.

The magnitude of his triumph enhanced his personal standing, but Johnson, as he told his legislative lobbyists, knew the impact of this success was transitory. Sooner or later the Congress, impelled by its institutional prerogatives and individual political concerns, would balk. And sooner or later certain elements in the consensus would become jealous and impatient. Like some political monster, the consensus could only be kept alive by fast-feeding it with the rewards of government.

Accordingly, Johnson set a breakneck pace for the Congress, which was bound ultimately to irritate the legislators. Moreover, Johnson's timetable allowed little opportunity for explanation of his programs and for public debate of their merits. Anyway, this was not Johnson's style. He made such a fetish of secrecy that his subordinates feared, with good reason, that if they divulged information about his intentions, the president would certainly scrap these plans and probably punish the offending official to boot.

Johnson put his personal stamp on the presidency as much as, or arguably more than, did his two immediate predecessors, Eisenhower and Kennedy. But he used his personality differently and got different results. Eisenhower and Kennedy had great personal advantages. Johnson could not match Ike's fatherly dignity or Kennedy's youthful vigor and flair, qualities which gained them a popular following.

Lacking such traits, Johnson sought to focus his powerful personality internally. With rare exceptions, such as his appeal for voting rights in a crisis atmosphere, he tried to engineer support through private persuasion rather than public pressures. Johnson was more comfortable dealing with the leaders of groups than appealing directly for the support of the members of these groups. The leaders, Johnson believed, could handle their followers for him.

He liked to tell the story of the prominent Baptist who called the White House to complain to the president that the aid to education bill, then before the Congress, unfairly benefited Catholics. The aide who took the call mentioned that the president at the moment was relaxing in the White House pool with none other than Billy Graham.

After a pause, the caller asked: "Is that *our* Billy?"

Yes, it was, he was told. Did he want the president to come to the phone?

"Oh no," the mollified Baptist replied. "Just give the President my very warm regards."

In this case, and in a number of others, Johnson's cultivation of interest-group leaders paid off. But there were limits to the loyalties these leaders could command on a personal basis. And there were also limits to what Johnson could accomplish as president on a personal basis.

In Medicare and civil rights Johnson could point to enduring achievements which met widely felt concerns of the citizenry. But in other areas his programs suffered from hasty preparation and lack of public debate and understanding. To a large extent they were expressions of Johnsons's own will rather than responses to voter wants and needs. Because some of it was ill-conceived, or underfunded, or both, his war on poverty bogged down before it could come close to achieving the expectations raised for it. In the cities black unrest turned to violence, undercutting the national enthusiasm for civil rights and for elevating the poor. Resentment against the president mounted, in the Congress and in the country.

But above all else, as a source of divisiveness, there was Johnson's other war, the one he preferred not to talk about, in Vietnam. With openness and candor during the campaign, Johnson might have won public support for a consistent policy for dealing with Vietnam. But he did not want to risk diminishing his anticipated landslide by a full-dress debate on such a controversial issue. In the months following the election, despite his campaign pledge not to send American boys "to do what Asian boys ought to be doing," Johnson sent tens of thousands of young Americans to Vietnam. This he was able to do on his own, as commander in chief. But he was reluctant to ask for the economic sacrifices needed to finance the war and to keep inflation under control. This would have required a public debate which Johnson feared might damage the consensus he counted on to enact the Great Society programs.

Instead, his war policy was founded on secrecy and dissembling, as it had been from the beginning. In August 1964 Johnson used the confused reports of a purported North Vietnamese attack on U.S. destroyers to railroad through a panicky Congress the Tonkin Gulf resolution, which gave him a blank check to take military action in Indochina. The constitutional validity of this resolution was as hazy as its language. But Johnson was content to rest on it, rather than to answer the questions that would have been raised by a request for a more explicit authorization.

He ran "the dirty little war" behind the country's back, all the while creating the impression that peace was just around the corner. Instead of choosing between guns and butter, Johnson promised both in his 1966 State of the Union address. And he chose to ignore the growing strain on the federal budget by refusing to ask for an income-tax increase.

But Johnson could not sustain this mirage indefinitely. As casualties increased in Vietnam and inflation climbed at home, the president began to lose his prestige, his credibility and his consensus. He was caught in crossfires between domestic critics who complained he had gone too far with the Great Society and those who grumbled he had not gone far enough, between hawks who wanted to escalate the war and doves who wanted to call it off.

In his isolation, Johnson became more resentful of his critics, many in his own party. As the 1966 congressional campaign got under way, the president kept his distance while Democratic office seekers battled for their political lives. In a final blow to his party and his own credibility, he planned a last-minute campaign tour, then called it off and denied that he had ever considered such a venture.

The GOP had been expected to regain some of the ground lost to the artificially large Democratic majorities of 1964. But the results exceeded every Republican expectation. They gained forty-seven seats in the House and three in the Senate, thus recovering all the ground lost in 1964 and more.

Striving to put the best face on the debacle, Johnson said: "I think we're all glad to see a healthy two-party system." This was a dubious diagnosis coming from a leader whose quest for consensus had aggravated the chronic ailments of his own party.

CHAPTER FIVE

1968

1. The Rules of the Game

Because he deceived the country—and himself, too—about Vietnam, Lyndon Johnson has borne most of the blame for the great damage done by the war to American society and politics. Certainly, by conducting the war without congressional sanction or public understanding of the costs and aims of his policies, Johnson demonstrated the dangers of the personalization of the presidency.

But Vietnam also brought home another distortion created by the gap between politics and government—the absence of a responsible and effective opposition to the president. Johnson did not lack for detractors. What was missing during the fateful years when he escalated the war was an organized force with the prestige to oblige him to explain and define his policies and with the resources to present constructive alternatives of its own.

In a classic study of the American political parties published in 1950, a committee of the American Political Science Association laid down this maxim: "The fundamental requirement of accountability is a two-party system in which the opposition party acts as the critic of the party in power, developing, defining and presenting the policy alternatives which are necessary for a true choice in reaching public decisions. The opposition most condu-

cive to responsible government is an organized party opposition."

Our parties have always had difficulty in living up to
this standard in opposition for some of the same reasons
they have had a hard time providing a responsible government. In opposition as in control, the parties have
been hampered by the tendency of their leaders to ignore
collective policy goals, by laxness of discipline, and by
the absence of an effective national party structure. In
opposition, a party faces additional handicaps. It has limited access to the councils of state and usually has no
single leader to rally around and help it gain attention.
The result of these hindrances was typified in the 1930s
when the Republicans were unable to unite on a clear
alternative to Roosevelt's handling of the economy or to
his response to the threat of aggression abroad.

As the U.S. involvement in Vietnam deepened, Republicans once again found themselves in the opposition role.
But for the GOP presidential candidate in 1964, the normal problems of the system were exacerbated by the
divisions in his own party caused by the struggle for the
presidential nomination and by his own reputation for
recklessness. So he foreclosed the option of debate. As
we shall see in the next section of the book, in 1968 the
Republican candidate made essentially the same decision
for different strategic reasons.

This default by the Republicans was particularly damaging to the political system because the war in Vietnam
was prolonged, frustrating, and increasingly resented.
Opposition to the war spread and intensified. But, unable
to find an outlet in the Republican Party, the opponents
turned first to the campuses and streets and then to the
president's own party. They succeeded in preventing the
president from seeking renomination. Yet the nature of
the political system limited the positive potential of the
opposition to the war. The antiwar movement itself became enmeshed in the politics of personality, which ob-

scured its purposes. Within the Democratic Party, the movement was blocked by the party hierarchy and the party's rules. The net result of the opposition to the war was to leave the Democrats deeply divided and embarked on the precarious road to reform.

As he started the last year of his presidential term, which had begun so promisingly in 1965, Lyndon Johnson was beset on many fronts. The Republicans in Congress, reinforced by the 1966 election, combined with increasingly recalcitrant Democrats to block his legislative proposals. The economy was out of joint, pushing him toward the necessity of seeking a belated tax increase. The violence in the ghettos of Detroit and other cities in 1967 had sharpened racial tensions and given impetus to George Wallace's independent candidacy for the White House.

And aggravating all these difficulties was Johnson's fundamental problem—the war in Vietnam. Limited wars have always been unpopular with Americans, as evidenced by the political price Harry Truman paid for the Korean War. But Johnson suffered more damage than Truman for his limited war, because of the nature of the struggle in Vietnam and the changing nature of American society, particularly the political environment.

Vietnam was a trackless morass. No one was sure exactly when it began and no one could tell when or how it would end. All that was clear was the cost in blood and treasure, which mounted steadily every week. It was the first war fought on television, and it penetrated the national consciousness as had no other conflict Americans had fought. "The living room war," critic Michael Arlen called it.

Confused by the welter of television images, body counts, and victory claims, accustomed to supporting the president against foreign foes, most Americans were disturbed but slow to pass judgment. The strongest and earliest negative reaction came from students and faculty on college campuses, and as their protest swelled, through the press, it spread to a sizable segment of middle-class professionals.

It was true that the students had a certain amount of self-interest at stake, since their lives could be disrupted by the draft. But most also could get deferments. At any rate, the students and their allies in the protest movement had broader concerns and motives. Taken together they were a phenomenon of the times and an illustration of how the changes of the postwar era had blurred the classic divisions which had been the basis of past political coalitions.

Opposition to the war was considered to be the liberal position. Yet a good many of the war's opponents had reached a level of income (or in the case of the students, their parents had) which in the thirties would have inclined them to conservatism on the economic issues then dominating politics. The shifting of the New Deal class alignments in the Vietnam controversy was also reflected in the overall support for the war by blue-collar workers. They had been among the most consistent backers of New Deal liberalism. But they took the so-called conservative position on the war because their ethnic backgrounds made them militantly anticommunist, they resented the social values and life-style often flamboyantly exhibited by the younger war protesters, and they believed they had a stake in the jobs the military buildup for the war provided.

The upper-middle-class citizens who actively opposed the war were secure enough economically to afford the luxury of a moral protest. And their educational level and access to information tended to make them skeptical of the government's claims about the progress and the purpose of the fighting.

Their counterparts in the fifties would have been inhibited by the lingering chill of McCarthyism. But the mood of the country in the sixties was more favorable to citizen activism and there were more citizens eager to act. With a minimum of formality and discipline, and with a maximum of zeal and energy, they made themselves into a formidable force for political protest.

The opposition to the war took inspiration and example from the civil rights drive earlier in the decade. The overall strategy was similar—to force political change through demonstrations and protests. Many of the same leaders were involved, and support was drawn from some of the same sources.

But there were some conspicuous exceptions. Despite the efforts of Martin Luther King, blacks were not attracted to the protest against the war in significant numbers. Also absent from the antiwar movement were many of the leaders of organized labor who had given important backing to the civil rights drive but who supported the war for economic and ideological reasons.

And in general the protest against Vietnam had a much harder time than the civil rights movement in gaining broad support among the general public. The civil rights drive in its early years had aimed mainly at practices and laws in the South, which few people outside that region were willing to defend. Moreover, the rulings of the federal courts provided opponents of racial segregation with a legal foundation to bolster their appeal to standards of fairness and morality. The Southern response—stubborn resistance to the court decrees and suppression of demonstrations—helped build sympathy for the civil rights cause and added to the political pressure which ultimately forced action by the president and the Congress.

The war was a much more ambiguous issue. It offered no villains like Bull Connor, no martyrs like Medgar Evers—only victims. The protest against the war could find no recourse in the courts, and only a few supporters in the Congress. As for the president, who had made the civil rights cause his own, it was his own policies which were the target of the protest, and he was unyielding in his refusal to significantly alter them.

The protest movement was left with no choice but to challenge the president directly in the political arena. Clearly the Republican Party would be inhospitable ground for such a venture. Most of its leaders publicly supported the president on the war; if they criticized Johnson at all, it was for not being hawkish enough. Besides, the liberals in the antiwar movement felt more at home in the Democratic Party, and it was there they decided to concentrate their efforts.

In the summer of 1967 a group of dissidents against the war set up an organization called the National Council of Concerned Democrats and informally deputized Allard Lowenstein, an inexhaustible thirty-eight-year-old veteran of the civil rights movement, to find a candidate to challenge Johnson. Lowenstein firmly believed that national policy could be changed by working through the political system. "When a President is both wrong and unpopular, to refuse to oppose him is both a moral abdication and a political stupidity," he declared.

American presidential politics had never seen an enterprise quite like this before. The war-protest movement provided both an issue and a constituency in search of a candidate, a reverse of the usual situation in which the candidate seeks support so he can get elected. The movement demanded a leader whose ambition for office would take second place to his convictions, and someone like this was hard to find.

The most obvious prospect was Robert Kennedy, who had somewhat latterly come around to disagreeing with Johnson on the war and who was considered the president's strongest potential rival within the Democratic Party. But the very factors that accounted for Kennedy's strength also made him in some ways an inappropriate figure to lead the protest against the war.

Robert Kennedy's appeal was in large part a function

of the politics of personality that flourished in John Kennedy's White House. It derived from a sentimental yearning for a restoration of Camelot and from the dynastic view of Lyndon Johnson as a usurper to the throne and Robert Kennedy as the rightful heir. The danger was that if Kennedy had yielded to Allard Lowenstein's urgings to lead the peace movement into battle against Johnson, his personal rivalry with Johnson would have overshadowed and diminished the case against the war.

Of course there was more to it. Conventional wisdom held that Johnson could not be beaten. "The Democratic National Convention is as good as over," Democratic National Chairman John Bailey declared in January 1968. "It will be Lyndon Johnson and that's that." Few people outside the inner circle of the peace movement were prepared to quarrel with that assessment, and Kennedy was not among them. "I can't run if there's no chance," Kennedy told his friend Jack Newfield, the New Left journalist.

Even when Lowenstein finally found a willing challenger, Senator Eugene McCarthy of Minnesota—an articulate critic of the war, though a strangely remote personality—it did not alter the prevailing political judgment. But Lowenstein pressed on with his organizing efforts on McCarthy's behalf, prodding the candidate into entering the New Hampshire primary. When critics derided McCarthy's efforts, Lowenstein told them: "Wait until he wins a few primaries, and we'll see what happens."

His hopes for McCarthy rested on political symbolism, tied to success in the presidential primaries, much the same formula John Kennedy had used in 1960. If McCarthy could make a respectable showing in New Hampshire and then improve on that performance in future primaries, perhaps Johnson could be pressured into de-escalating the war. If the president refused, then maybe the party would rebel and turn to McCarthy or, in a deadlock, to Kennedy. This was a long-range strategy and its essential ingredient was tying the protest against the war to the public's antipathy toward Johnson.

The strategy was, however, overtaken by events. At the end of January, the communists launched their Tet offensive in South Vietnam, a display of strength made more shocking to Americans by its variance from the reassuring picture the administration had presented. Suddenly public opposition to the war—or at least the way Johnson was conducting it—mounted sharply, and McCarthy's campaign in New Hampshire absorbed the benefit. He received 42 percent of the vote in the March 12 balloting against Johnson's write-in candidacy, which had been managed by state party leaders—a result translated by the press into a McCarthy victory.

The implications of Tet and of McCarthy's strong New Hampshire showing hit hard in Wisconsin, where Johnson's name was on the ballot for the next primary. Dispatched to the scene, Lawrence O'Brien reported back to the president that he was likely to be "badly defeated," perhaps by as much as two to one. Meanwhile, Robert Kennedy, having reassessed his position, had announced his own candidacy four days after the New Hampshire vote, not "merely to oppose any man" but rather "to propose new policies."

Johnson, who had allowed plans for his own campaign to go forward while he pondered whether or not to run, now had little choice. As an incumbent president he probably could count on loyal party leaders delivering a majority of the delegates at the convention. But given the mounting opposition to the war, and to himself, such a victory would strain the party to the breaking point and probably assure a Republican victory in November. By dropping out of the race, he could hope to defuse resentment against him, preserve his dignity and operate as president with greater freedom. On March 31 Johnson stunned the nation by announcing his withdrawal, and at the same time a limited bombing halt, intended to draw the North Vietnamese to the negotiating table.

Like everyone else, Hubert Humphrey was thrown off balance by the President's abrupt decision. But he soon rediscovered his old ambition for the White House. Having served as Johnson's understudy, he now became his stand-in as a candidate, inheriting Johnson's backing among the party hierarchy. He continued to support Johnson on the war, and became the new target for the hard-core opposition, which had not been lessened significantly by the pause in the bombing.

Nevertheless, Johnson's withdrawal cleared the way for Humphrey's nomination because of the underlying weakness of the peace movement as a political force. For it, too, depended too much on the politics of personality. The antiwar leaders had relied on the widespread antagonism to Johnson himself to focus and popularize their protest. With Johnson out of the race, and out of the line of fire, the antiwar leaders had to fall back on their relatively narrow base on the campuses and among middle-class liberals.

Building a broader base in the country, and in the Democratic Party, among working-class voters and blacks would have required an extensive education and organizing campaign. The antiwar leaders had neglected to undertake such a grass-roots drive earlier, and after the president's withdrawal they had little time left before the convention. Moreover, as they came to realize, the restrictive party procedures controlling the nominating process severely limited their ability to use the campaign itself to reach out to rank-and-file Democrats.

Whatever else he had lost, Lyndon Johnson could still count on one of the prime assets of incumbency, the backing of the Democratic Party hierarchy, which he could turn to Humphrey's advantage. This loyalty had little to do with Johnson's or Humphrey's stands on issues. Rather it reflected the resentment, almost universally shared among office holders, of any insurgency as threatening to themselves. This attitude was supplemented by the reality of the President's continuing control over much of the Federal largesse that helped sustain party leaders with their own constituents. This was an appeal that could not be matched by the leaders of the antiwar insurgency.

Also the politics of personality seemed to turn against the insurgents. On the new political scene, the personal antagonism toward Johnson was partly replaced by resentment against Robert Kennedy, whose candidacy divided the ranks of the antiwar forces and bolstered the determination of their opponents. Many of the McCarthy supporters, who months before had hoped in vain for Kennedy to run, now regarded him as an opportunistic interloper.

On the other side of the political fence, some party regulars still resented the way Kennedy had ridden roughshod over the party establishment in managing his brother's presidential campaign. Others were disturbed and threatened by the ideological intensity of his left-wing advisers and by the emotional frenzy and overheated rhetoric of his campaign. Just as "dump Johnson" had been the battle cry of the antiwar movement, "stop Kennedy" now became a major theme of the Humphrey campaign. As Humphrey later acknowledged: "A large share of the money pledged to me came from New York business leaders who feared and distrusted Bob."

For his part, Kennedy seemed to have no more admiration or affection for the party establishment than his brother had. Midway through his campaign, after he had addressed an assemblage of party regulars at a Jefferson-Jackson Day dinner in Omaha, I asked him how he thought his speech had been received. "I don't know," he said with a shrug. "They're not my kind of crowd."

They were not Eugene McCarthy's crowd either. In 1968 the party leaders belonged to Johnson, and to his surrogate candidate, Hubert Humphrey. Their support was based not so much on ideological grounds as it was on concern for their own positions and authority, which the insurgent candidacies placed in jeopardy. The realization that their influence had been declining increased their anxiety. However, they still clung to control of the nominating apparatus, a ramshackle collection of procedures and customs which had accumulated since the days of Andrew Jackson. Far better than the insurgents, they understood the rules of the game, some of which they made up as they went along, and as a result they were able to determine the outcome of the campaign.

This advantage more than offset the continuing decline in the vitality of their organizations and their inability to muster broad support in the primaries for either Johnson or Humphrey. McCarthy's strong showing in New Hampshire had been followed by his impressive victory over the president in Wisconsin and by Kennedy's success in the Indiana primary against the state's governor, Roger Branigan, who entered the race at Humphrey's behest and with his blessing.

Humphrey wanted no more such embarrassments. The timing of the official announcement of his candidacy exempted him from having to compete directly in any of the remaining primaries. Instead, he concentrated on the nonprimary states, which sent most of the delegates to the national convention.

This was no great sacrifice on Humphrey's part. In 1960, when party leaders were uncertain and divided on their choice of a candidate, John Kennedy had used his success in the primaries to pressure and persuade them into backing his candidacy. But in 1968 most party leaders closed ranks at once behind Humphrey, who had the

influence of the White House behind him, and were prepared to stand firm regardless of the outcome of the
primaries.

The symbolic impact of the primaries was thus diminished; as to their tangible importance, it was less than met
the eye. By official count, the sixteen states and the District of Columbia which held some form of primary
chose about 40 percent of the 3,084 convention delegates.
But that figure was misleading; the sentiment of the voters
in primaries was not necessarily reflected by the delegate support a presidential candidate received at the convention. In six states delegates could run without letting
voters know which presidential candidate they preferred;
and in one of these states, New York, delegates were
prohibited from stating their preference. In three of the
biggest primary states—New York, Pennsylvania, and
Illinois—party leaders, not primary voters, selected a
substantial proportion of the delegates.

In some states, although presidential candidates' names
appeared on the ballot, this competition, known as a
beauty contest, did not necessarily control the support of
the convention delegates. In Pennsylvania, for example,
McCarthy received nearly 80 percent of the vote in the
beauty contest but emerged with less than 20 percent of
the state's delegation.

In the nonprimary states procedures often were even
more arcane and the results more frustrating for the antiwar forces. Time was a major handicap. The key to the
success of Goldwater's campaign in the GOP was the
early effort to penetrate the lower echelons of the party
machinery. Because of their late start, the Kennedy and
McCarthy candidacies were at a hopeless disadvantage in
a number of states.

The process of picking convention delegates in many
states was handled as a routine part of other party business and began (and sometimes finished) a year or more

before the convention. By the time Eugene McCarthy announced his candidacy on December 2, 1967, nearly a third of the delegates to the Democratic National Convention had already been selected, the vast majority firmly committed to whomever the local party organization favored. In fact, a good many of them had not been elected but simply appointed by party officials who themselves had been chosen by rank-and-file voters in 1966.

The most common method of selecting delegates was through state conventions whose proceedings were usually dominated by party officials. Delegates to these gatherings were generally chosen through a process that began with precinct caucuses which in theory were open to all Democrats. The actual practice was quite different. In some states the rules gave party officials broad discretion in deciding when and where caucuses would be held. In ten states there were no written rules at all governing this or any other aspect of the delegate selection process; in ten other states the rules which were supposed to exist were inaccessible to outsiders. Under these conditions organization leaders were free to hold caucuses at their own convenience, and at the inconvenience of the insurgents, often with little or no advance public notice.

And even when the insurgents managed to find out about a caucus session and showed up in respectable numbers, they were sometimes stymied by the high-handed tactics of the regulars. At three congressional-district caucuses in Indiana, for example, the chairman simply adjourned the meeting after the regular party slate had been nominated without even recognizing the McCarthy supporters present. One such session, tape-recorded by a McCarthy partisan, lasted all of twenty-two seconds.

Under the unit rule, in use in at least fifteen states, the majority could compel unanimous support from a delegation for its position or candidate, regardless of the minority. Proxy voting, which permitted the votes of absentees to be cast by some authorized person at the caucus, offered another opportunity for abuse. In Hawaii, regular organization leaders cast proxy votes from precincts that had not even been organized, one of which was an urban renewal area made up mostly of vacant lots. At a township caucus in Missouri, where McCarthy supporters appeared to be in the majority among those present, the local party leader announced that he held 492 proxy votes, about triple the total attendance at the caucus, which he cast for his own slate of delegates.

The unit rule had been common practice in the Democratic Party for over a century, as had many of the other appurtenances of the nominating procedure on which the organization relied. One reason criticism of these practices mounted in 1968 was the war and the passion and anger it brought to politics. For the insurgents, their protest against the Vietnam War made ordinarily dull procedural questions literally a matter of life and death. They believed, not without reason, that the rules had robbed them of a fair chance to broaden political opposition to the war.

More generally, the assault on the rules reflected the growing unwillingness of many voters to accept the traditional role of the party as the definer of political choices. The party's loss of influence had earlier manifested itself in the increasing tendency of voters to make decisions based on the personality of political leaders, rather than on party allegiance. Now, for an important segment of the citizenry, the protest against the war provided another channel and another motive for challenging the party.

The two groups, the party regulars and the insurgents, looked at the nominating process and the party machinery from entirely different perspectives. After the New York primary in June, where they had won a majority of the delegates on the ballot, McCarthy supporters protested bitterly because they were allotted only fifteen of the sixty-five at-large delegate seats doled out by the organization.

The answer to their complaint came from Monroe Goldwater, legal adviser to the state party: "By and large the controlling factor in the selection of at-large delegates has not changed," he said. "The telling factor is 'what have you done for me lately?' " By way of further explanation, the party's state chairman, John Burns, said: "If I ignored the people who have helped me with the organizational work and appointed strangers, just because they're for McCarthy, I'd have a revolution on my hands."

Goldwater and Burns, like other regulars, considered the party to be something like a private club which had been entrusted to their stewardship. Public participation was desirable on occasion, but not at the expense or inconvenience of the regular members.

To the "strangers" who supported McCarthy, the party was a means to an end, which they were determined to use to their best advantage. The revolution that Chairman Burns worried about was already building, and it erupted at the convention in Chicago.

The bizarre and tragic circumstances of the 1968 campaign helped to rally support against the nomination procedures. Robert Kennedy's assassination after his victory in the California primary eliminated all but the slimmest chance of Hubert Humphrey's nomination being prevented. The leaders of the McCarthy campaign, who had battled against the rules, usually in vain, all through the campaign, decided as a last desperate tactic to mount a series of credential challenges to pro-Humphrey delegates, contending that they had been selected in violation of state laws and the guarantees of the U.S. Constitution.

To promote their cause, the antiwar forces established

an ad hoc commission of sympathetic party leaders, headed by then governor Harold Hughes* of Iowa to gather evidence about the delegate selection procedures and make recommendations for reform. The Hughes Commission report, titled "The Democratic Choice," a compendium of reform proposals, was completed just before the convention opened. With the convention machinery controlled by Humphrey supporters, the insurgents had only a faint hope of prevailing in 1968, but they were already looking ahead to the future.

As expected, the credentials committee of the convention rejected all the procedural challenges brought by the McCarthy campaign. The committee did, however, vote to unseat the regular Mississippi delegation, on the grounds that it had been selected in violation of the 1964 convention edict against discrimination, and replaced it with a biracial delegation from the state. More important for the long run, the committee recommended creation of a special party commission to study problems of delegate selection and to aid the state organizations in carrying out reforms.

To give added weight to the commission idea, the McCarthy delegates introduced a resolution embodying major recommendations of the Hughes Commission and laying down strict new dicta for the 1972 presidential campaign. Their resolution abolished the unit rule, called for delegates to be chosen in the same year as the convention and required state parties to give all Democrats a "full and timely opportunity to participate" in the process. Some Humphrey delegates agreed to back the proposal to placate the insurgents. Other regulars were too distracted by the chaos at the convention to realize the potential import of the measure. Chicago police and anti-

* Not to be confused with Governor Richard Hughes of New Jersey, who, as it happened, chaired the party's Special Equal Rights Committee, created by the 1964 convention to establish standards to enforce the convention's antidiscrimination resolution.

war demonstrators were battling in the streets outside the convention hall while insurgent and regular leaders inside clashed over the party platform. In the confusion, the insurgent proposal for delegate selection reform passed by a narrow margin.

The convention ended two days later, having nominated Hubert Humphrey and Edmund Muskie and beaten back the challenge of the antiwar forces to adopt a Vietnam peace plank in the party platform. The party regulars had won the battle of Chicago. But, as they would learn in 1972, they had lost control of the party.

2. The Politics of Negativism

For John Kennedy, his narrow margin of victory and an obstinate Congress widened the gap between politics and government that confronted him in the presidency. He relied mainly on his personal appeal, abetted by a crisis atmosphere, to overcome his difficulties. Lyndon Johnson, mindful of Kennedy's frustrations and blessed with a landslide victory and a duly responsive Congress, depended on the strategies of consensus to work his will on the government. But both presidents, struggling against the fundamental defects of the political and governing structure, created expectations they could not fulfill and problems they could not solve.

The controversy over Vietnam had produced massive protest demonstrations, splintered the Democratic Party, prevented the renomination of its president and raised doubts about the nation's role in the world. At the same time, racial violence triggered by Martin Luther King's assassination seared the cities, turned black against white and underlined the tragic truth that a century after Emancipation race relations remained an unresolved dilemma. The combined impact of these traumas was comparable to the shock waves from the Great Depression and the Second World War.

Enter Richard Nixon and the politics of negativism.

Nixon liked to attribute his reemergence as a presidential candidate in 1968, after his earlier reverses, to the pull of destiny, rather than his own efforts. "No man, not if he combined the wisdom of Lincoln with the connivance of Machiavelli could have maneuvered or manipulated his way back into the arena," he claimed.

But Nixon was too modest. His engineering of his comeback showed Lincoln and Machiavelli a trick or two. With the latest innovations of political technology to aid him, he was able to build support without making commitments. Avoiding direct confrontation with his foes, he allowed them to defeat themselves. Most important, by catering with varying degrees of subtlety to the mixture of discontents that gripped the electorate, he made himself the chief beneficiary of ill-will. His negative strategy, as standard-bearer for the opposition party —in the face of the problems dividing the country—was in large measure responsible for making the 1968 presidential campaign an exceptionally dismal example of the irrelevance of the political process.

One way or another Nixon had figured prominently in every national election since 1952. As well as anyone he understood the failings of the system—the lack of accountability, the focus on distractions, the inherent sense of public frustration. These defects, shrewdly exploited, led to his triumph in politics but also, when he sought to govern, ultimately contributed to his downfall.

Neither Vietnam nor race was an issue that offered the possibility of swift and simple solution. Still, the presidential campaign theoretically presented the opportunity for constructive debate on the choices open to the country for dealing with both problems. But any voter who looked to the candidates for such illumination would have been turned away in disappointment.

George Wallace's third-party candidacy, born out of racial hostility, broadened as it became an outlet for the more general discontent with the war, demonstrations and street crime. But this enterprise never became more than a protest movement. Wallace had a genius for sensing and voicing the grievances of millions of working-class and middle-class voters against the bureaucracy, the courts, the leaders of the two major parties and the established order in general. But after he had promised that "When I get to be President I'm gonna call in a bunch of bureaucrats and take their brief cases and throw them in the Potomac River," Wallace had no persuasive remedy to offer the crowds that cheered his outbursts.

As for Hubert Humphrey, his candidacy was imprisoned by the incumbent president who had been its chief sponsor, and by Humphrey's own past. Humphrey learned the limits of Johnson's toleration of deviation from the administration's Vietnam policy at the Chicago convention. The nominee-to-be had reached agreement with the antiwar forces on a compromise platform plank that called for a further reduction in the bombing of North Vietnam. But the president was furious. "This plank just undercuts our whole policy," he complained to Humphrey over the phone from the White House. "And by God the Democratic Party ought not to be doing that to me and you ought not to be doing it; you've been part of the policy." Fearful of the president's opposition Humphrey backed down, and did not dare to differ with Johnson again on this issue until the closing stages of his campaign.

The vice-president had scarcely more room to maneuver on the issue of race. To many, the rioting in the ghettos seemed clear evidence of the miscalculations of Lyndon Johnson's Great Society. If Humphrey raised questions about these programs, he would again risk offending the president. But Humphrey's own record, in any case, would have kept him on the defensive against the white backlash which both Nixon and Wallace sought to exploit. No one in politics had fought harder than he for the advances made by blacks which now provoked white resentment.

On the face of things, Nixon seemed the candidate freest and best qualified to take a fresh look at the war and at racial tensions. But he would have none of that. From the inception of his candidacy Nixon had decided that he would avoid positions that might embroil him in controversy and cost him votes. His present reading of the national mood dictated against taking such risks and so did his past experience. Looking back on his defeat by John Kennedy in 1960, he put part of the blame on his spending "too much time . . . on substance and too little time on appearances." His conduct in 1968 showed that he had taken that supposed lesson to heart and mind.

The course Nixon charted for himself in 1968 was tortuous; he was obliged to dodge and duck while most of the time standing still, and to play not to his own strengths but to other men's weaknesses. As he examined his prospects after the 1964 Republican debacle, Nixon realized that the supremacy of the party's Eastern establishment leadership had been ended by the Goldwater candidacy. Influence was shifting to more conservative forces in the West and South. Nixon lacked the popular appeal to those regions that had carried Goldwater to the nomination. And his defeats for the presidency in 1960 and for the California governorship in 1962 stamped him as a loser and made him a questionable commodity everywhere.

The party chieftains were not powerful enough to prevent some candidate with strong personal support from taking the nomination by storm, as Goldwater had. But if no such dynamic contender emerged, then the party regulars would wield considerable influence in the competition, and they might be persuaded to give their support to Nixon as the safest of the available options.

Accordingly, his first move was to ingratiate himself with party leaders by demonstrating his loyalty, a quality on which in their declining condition they placed a higher premium than ever. He campaigned dutifully for Goldwater in 1964, making 150 appearances in thirty-six states in what he knew to be a losing cause. And right after the election he called a press conference to praise Goldwater's efforts and, more to the point, to read Nelson Rockefeller out of the party for failing to back Goldwater.

For the next two years, while Johnson began running into trouble, Nixon spent much of his time touring the country raising funds for the party and then speaking for its congressional candidates in the 1966 election. He took a bow for his contribution to the big GOP victory and then abruptly announced that he would take "a holiday from politics" for six months.

For the time being, Nixon realized he had nothing to gain from the glare of public attention and, given the rising controversy about the war, might actually have a good deal to lose. He preferred to let the spotlight turn on George Romney, who after his reelection as governor of Michigan had forged ahead in the polls among prospective 1968 Republican presidential candidates.

Knowing the intense public scrutiny to which a presidential front-runner is subjected, and also knowing Romney, Nixon believed the bumptious governor would not stand up well to that sort of examination. His appraisal of Romney proved justified. The governor's clumsiness in dealing with the national press, capped by his admission that he had been "brainwashed" by Johnson administration officials after a 1965 visit to Vietnam, sent his candidacy into a steep and irreversible decline.

Romney stubbornly tried to compete against Nixon in the New Hampshire primary and challenged him to debate the issues. But Nixon promptly turned him down, claiming such an encounter would only help the Democrats. And when Romney's own polls showed him trailing by a vast margin, he dropped out of the race.

Fortunately for Nixon, the much maligned Rockefeller then announced his candidacy. He prudently chose not to enter any primaries. But the mere fact that Rockefeller was seeking the nomination and getting attention in the press helped enhance the significance of Nixon's victories in the four subsequent primaries he entered. Though he was unopposed, his staff nevertheless claimed that his triumphs were proof that he had overcome his past tendency to defeat.*

The lack of real competition contributed to the smooth functioning of Nixon's tightly organized campaign, which was arranged to protect him against stumbling into the sort of controversy that had brought Romney down. To Richard Whalen, one of "the bright young men" the candidate had recruited as a speech writer and issues adviser, it seemed "as though Nixon were being assisted by a team hired in a package deal with IBM."

By introducing the massive use of direct mailing, computers, and other techniques of modern merchandising, Nixon's managers sought to transform presidential campaigning from an uncertain art into a manageable science. His formal announcement of candidacy was made in a letter received on the same day by 150,000 New Hampshire households. Ultimately Nixon's computers would store the candidate's positions on sixty-seven different issues and spew out that information under Nixon's signature to voters around the country.

---

* Rockefeller did win the Massachusetts primary in April, which Nixon did not enter, with a write-in vote. Write-in campaigns were also conducted for Rockefeller, and for Ronald Reagan, in Nebraska and Oregon, but Nixon won these primaries as well as the contests in Indiana and Wisconsin.

No foreseeable pitfall was overlooked. Even the elephants trotted out as party symbols at Nixon rallies were first given enemas by the candidate's advance men to insure against the embarrassment of an act of nature.

But the centerpiece of the Nixon campaign's technology was its use of television commercials. In June 1967, H. R. Haldeman, Nixon's ranking advance man and later his White House chief of staff, sent him a memo proclaiming that "the time has come for political campaigning—its techniques and strategies—to move out of the dark ages and into the brave new world of the omnipotent eye." The gist of Haldeman's message was that a candidate could reach a much larger audience, with greater ease, through television commercials than through the traditional frantic schedule of personal appearances. Just as important, he could have better control over the message. The same notion had occurred to other politicians, but it was the Nixon campaign that had the resources and foresight to take maximum advantage of the concept.

Nixon went through the customary routine of speeches and interviews, structured and paced in his case to limit the possibility of impromptu complications. More significant, though, because they were seen by vastly more voters, were the television commercials in which Nixon answered questions from local voters. His advisers had concluded, Nixon said, "that the more spontaneous the situation the better I come across."

But the spontaneity, like the appearance of competition in the primaries, was illusory. The participants were carefully selected by Nixon's aides, and the exchanges carefully edited before they were screened. The important point, as William Gavin, one of Nixon's media advisers, explained, was not what Nixon said but how he was seen. "Reason requires a high degree of discipline of concentration; impression is easier," Gavin wrote in a memo. In a TV film "the candidate can be shown better

than he can be shown in person because it can be edited
so only the best moments are shown."

Against the hazy backdrop created by his film editors,
Nixon deftly practiced his negative strategy on Vietnam
and race. In dealing with Vietnam his negativism was
relatively passive. His standard campaign speech included
the promise: "New leadership will end the war and win
the peace in the Pacific." He calculated that was enough
to appeal to dissatisfaction with the war. He did not risk
an explanation of how peace would be achieved.

When Lyndon Johnson announced his withdrawal
from the presidential campaign and the cutback in the
bombing of Vietnam, Nixon declared a moratorium on
discussion of the war while he studied the North Vietnamese response to Johnson's overture. As peace talks
dragged on in Paris, Nixon prolonged his moratorium,
explaining that he wanted to avoid any statement that
might intrude on the negotiations. While the war ripped
the Democratic Party apart and divided the country,
Nixon declared: "The pursuit of peace is too important
for politics as usual."

On the race issue Nixon's negativism was more active
and discernible. After the ghetto riots in the spring,
Richard Whalen submitted an impassioned proposal for
Nixon to respond by calling for an "open society" in
which government and business would work in partnership to create opportunities for blacks in housing and
employment. Nixon read the memo and filed it. With an
eye on the white backlash he began to talk more often
and more ominously about the menace of riots and street
crime and the need for law and order. "The first civil
right of every American," he told the voters, "is the
right to be free from domestic violence."

Nixon's only declared opponent, Rockefeller, had
turned out, as Nixon expected, not to be much of a

threat. Rockefeller's candidacy was the kind only a billionaire could indulge himself in. He spent vast sums of money flying around the country in hopes that he could convince party leaders that Nixon was a loser, while only Rockefeller could win the White House for the GOP, an argument that relied heavily on public opinion polls.

Nearly everywhere Rockefeller went outside the Northeast, party leaders gave him a cold reception. At one point I asked Leslie Slote, the governor's press secretary, how long Rockefeller could continue this futile enterprise. "Don't worry," Slote said loyally, "there are things going on that you and I don't know about—I hope."

Slote's guess was wrong. The decisive blow came just before the convention when the Gallup Poll, which Rockefeller had counted on to prove that the party needed him to win, instead showed Nixon beating Humphrey while Rockefeller was only tied with him.*

Only one serious problem loomed on Nixon's horizon as the convention opened. This was Ronald Reagan, who had made himself a hero to conservatives in the 1964 campaign with a stirring speech in which he argued Goldwater's case far better than Goldwater ever had himself. With his election as governor of California in 1966, Reagan had become a national political figure and a potential presidential candidate.

Unsure of himself in national politics, and pledged to serve out his full four-year term in California, Reagan moved slowly at first. But under the tutelage of Clifton White, the engineer of the draft-Goldwater drive, he proved to be an apt pupil. Though Reagan did not officially declare his candidacy until the day the convention

* A subsequent Harris poll showed Humphrey beating Nixon and losing to Rockefeller. The net result was to demonstrate the questionable reliability of polls and make their results worthless to Rockefeller.

opened in Miami Beach, his appeal was clearly growing, particularly among the erstwhile Goldwater supporters in the South and West who now dominated the party.

But Nixon's partisans invoked the specter of Rockefeller to block the Reagan drive. They warned conservative delegates tempted to back Reagan that as Goldwater's political heir his candidacy would produce a repeat of the 1964 debacle. And they told the moderate delegates inclined to vote for Rockefeller that unless they helped put Nixon over the top on the first ballot, Reagan might stampede the convention his way.

This possibility was not entirely out of the question. To head off the Reagan threat Nixon promised Southern delegations to the convention that he would not select a running mate who would divide the party, language they correctly took to mean he would not pick a liberal. He also confided that he took a dim view of court-ordered school busing. It was not the role of the federal courts, he said, "to be a local school district and make the decision as your local school board."

This was what the Southerners wanted to hear, and it was enough to hold the line against Reagan. The next night Nixon won the nomination with 692 votes, just fifteen more than the majority he needed. And he promptly kept the first part of his bargain with the South by picking as his running mate Spiro T. Agnew, the governor of Maryland, an erstwhile Rockefeller partisan, whose only previous claim to national attention had come when he condemned a group of moderate civil rights leaders for racial violence in Baltimore.

Though the Southern delegates were satisfied on the vice-presidency, their constituents back home needed continued reassurance from Nixon on the race issue as the general election unfolded. George Wallace made this necessary. With his candidacy booming in the wake of the spring riots, Wallace was getting increasing attention not only from Democrats but also from Republican voters. He was a threat in the suburbs of the North as well as in the South. But it was in the South, and in the border states, that Wallace's initial base was substantial enough so that he was in a position to carry states that Nixon needed for an electoral majority.

To protect his Southern flank against Wallace, and to bid for the backlash in the North, Nixon quickly wrote off the black vote. In *An American Melodrama*, a superb chronicle of the 1968 campaign, Nixon is quoted as telling Republican leaders in Pennsylvania, who contended he needed black support to carry that state, that he would not campaign for black voters, adding: "If I am President, I am not going to owe anything to the black community."

As for Wallace, Nixon tried to dismiss him as a spoiler who could not possibly win the White House, all the while competing hard for Wallace's support. As he barnstormed the South, Nixon chipped away at the federal courts. And he reiterated demands for a restoration of "law and order," a code phrase that was generally assumed to be aimed mainly at the specter of black lawlessness and black disorder.

On Vietnam, Nixon's early resolve to stand pat was hardened after the Democratic convention. The disarray in Chicago, transmitted into the nation's living rooms by television, was soon reflected in the polls, giving him a substantial lead over Humphrey. Under these circumstances, having promised at the convention "to bring an honorable end to the war," Nixon decided to leave Vietnam at that.

Apart from his general aversion to controversy, Nixon was worried about offending Lyndon Johnson, who, as Nixon always kept in mind, still had the power to control events. When Richard Whalen tried to persuade Nixon to challenge Johnson directly on the war, he was struck by the impassive expression on the candidate's face. He thought, as he wrote in *Catch the Falling Flag*, "I might as well be talking to Humphrey. Nixon looks just the way Humphrey must look when his people tell him to break with Johnson."

Fearful of pushing Johnson into breaking the deadlock in negotiations, Nixon warned his speech writers against attacking the president. "If there's peace they'll vote their pocketbooks, Democratic prosperity."

It was an additional demonstration of the inflated power of the incumbency. Not only could Lyndon Johnson dominate the Democratic campaign to choose his replacement, but also he could influence the tactics of the Republican standard bearer.

Nixon's refusal to disturb the status quo in Indochina ultimately cost him votes, and almost cost him the election. At the end of September Humphrey finally moved an inch or two away from Johnson's position on the war, indicating his willingness to halt the bombing. The departure was more semantic than real, but the symbolism gave Humphrey a badly needed boost. And he gained more impetus in the final days of the campaign, when Johnson announced a bombing halt and an apparent breakthrough in peace negotiations. But at the last minute the South Vietnamese government balked at Johnson's arrangement, and this may have been all that saved Nixon from being a loser again.

The landslide victory that seemed possible in September turned into a cliff-hanger; Nixon won by about 500,000 votes, not much more than his margin of defeat in 1960. He took 43.4 percent of the vote and 302 electoral votes to Humphrey's 42.7 percent and 191 electoral votes. Wallace received 13.5 percent and 45 electoral votes, all in the Deep South. The turnout of eligible voters dropped to 60.6 percent from 61.9 percent in 1964 and 62.8 percent in 1960.

Just as the closeness of the election made it hard to define the reasons for Nixon's victory, the blur of his campaign made it even more difficult to foretell his presidency. A few weeks before election day I had talked about this with John Sears, a young lawyer who was among the most thoughtful and forthcoming of Nixon's aides. "These things run in cycles," Sears said as he sipped a Scotch and water. The country had been pushed too hard and too fast under Kennedy and Johnson. "That's why people are at each other's throats. It's time to change the pace and mood."

Nixon believed, or so Sears thought, that the next president's first priority must be to help the country calm down and slow down and heal its wounds. "Then it will be time to move forward again," Sears said.

On the morning after election day, when he finally claimed victory, Nixon made a point of recalling a sign displayed at one of his rallies which said, "Bring Us Together," and added: "And that will be the great objective of this Administration, to bring the American people together."

That made it sound as if John Sears was right. But the next day I phoned Henry Kissinger, whom I had met when he had been a campaign adviser to Nelson Rockefeller. Kissinger, I knew, viewed Nixon with contempt. When I asked him if Nixon could bring the country together, Kissinger snorted: "If he did, it would be the first positive thing he's ever done."

Neither John Sears nor Henry Kissinger was naive. But as it turned out, Sears, who respected Nixon and had worked closely with him, was wrong about the new president. And Kissinger, who disliked him and barely knew him, was dead right.

Nixon's campaign had not been designed to help him unite the country, or indeed to govern it at all with any degree of consistency. The Republican gains in Congress had not been substantial enough to overturn Democratic control of both houses. So the perennial conflict between the legislature and the executive seemed certain to continue, just as Madison had foreseen even before two competing parties emerged to heighten the potential for institutional rivalry.

More important, the two issues that had hung over the campaign without ever really being addressed, Vietnam and race, still dominated the scene. And in both cases Nixon's choices were limited and difficult. As he had come to realize during the campaign, though he would not acknowledge it publicly, the national interest demanded that he wind down the war. On the racial front, despite his attempts to placate the South, the Supreme Court's reading of the Constitution would ultimately compel him to preside over the elimination of legal school desegregation in the South "root and branch."

Given these imperatives, Nixon might have tried to reconcile the diehard segregationists and the diehard hawks among his supporters to their inevitable disappointment, and at the same time reach out to the young and the blacks to broaden his base of support. In this way he might have kept the unifying promise of his victory statement. But this would have been a formidable challenge, particularly since Nixon had done nothing to prepare for it during the campaign.

Instead, Nixon tried to offset the contradictions between the rhetoric of his campaign and the obligations of his office by falling back on the negativism which had infused his candidacy. In this he relied heavily on the views of his former campaign manager, now his attorney general, John Mitchell. Adding the Nixon and Wallace vote together, Mitchell came up with the makings of a new conservative majority. The problem was to forge this coalition while bringing both the war and school desegregation to an end. The ill-conceived answer was to use the opposition to the war and the support for civil rights as rallying points.

Nixon dragged out the military withdrawal from Vietnam through his first term and beyond, interspersing it with "incursions" into Laos and Cambodia and escalations of the bombing. When demonstrations inevitably erupted, Nixon called upon the "silent majority" to support him in defying "the minority who . . . try to impose [their will] on the nation by mass demonstrations in the streets."

On school desegregation Nixon first tried to defy the Supreme Court, then sought to change its membership. When his second successive Southern Supreme Court nominee, Harrold Carswell, was rejected by the Senate after Carswell's past indulgences in bigotry had been exposed, Nixon publicly denounced the Senate for "malicious character assassination." He asked "the millions of Americans living in the South" to bear witness to this "act of regional discrimination," and vowed not to nominate another Southerner for the High Court until the makeup of the Senate had changed.

In the White House Nixon was a prisoner of his own strategy as a candidate. Having failed to foster public backing for constructive approaches to dealing with the war and racial tensions as a candidate, he sought to divert attention to the strident protests against the fighting in Indo-China and racist practices at home. But this gambit would turn out to be less effective in the Oval Office than on the stump during the artificial atmosphere of the campaign.

The acid test of Nixon's attempt to win support through the enemies he had made came in the 1970 Congressional campaign. Nixon unleashed Vice-President Agnew, and then himself, in an unprecedented effort by a national administration to influence a midterm campaign. Agnew ranted against "radical-liberal" lawmakers and warned Americans against being "intimidated and blackmailed . . . by a disruptive radical and militant minority."

Nixon climaxed his own campaign efforts by climbing

on top of the presidential limousine to stretch out his arms in a V-for-victory salute to an unruly crowd of antiwar demonstrators. When the crowd predictably hurled stones at the presidential motorcade, Nixon's advisers considered that reaction to be a tactical triumph for their side.

Such antics had only limited appeal to the electorate, particularly since the country was plunging into a recession and unemployment was rising. On election day the Republicans lost nine House seats and eleven governorships, while winning two seats in the Senate. This was a meager harvest for the extensive effort made by Nixon and Agnew. Moreover, whatever ground Nixon had gained in the Senate, he had paid a price for it in the hardening of Democratic opposition and in the unease among Republican moderates.

Instead of healing the country's divisions, Nixon had aggravated them. The word "polarize" came into frequent use to describe the impact of the president's actions and rhetoric. He had made himself something of a hero in the South and to many "middle Americans" elsewhere. But he had turned a good part of the rest of the country against him. What was more ominous, Nixon had become persuaded by his own harsh pronouncements that the White House was actually a fortress under siege by foes who had to be crushed, no matter what the cost.

CHAPTER SIX

1972

1. "The Greatest Goddam Change"

In February 1969, three months after Hubert Humphrey's defeat by Richard Nixon, and three years before the official start of the 1972 presidential campaign, the Democratic National Committee announced the creation of a twenty-eight-member Commission on Party Structure and Delegation Selection to carry out the Chicago convention's promise of reform. Under the chairmanship of George McGovern, then a little-known senator from South Dakota, the commission conducted hearings in seventeen cities, heard testimony from five hundred party leaders, sifted through three thousand pages of staff analysis and in November issued its report, called "Mandate for Reform." At the heart of the report were eighteen "Guidelines" laying down a new set of laws and standards to govern Democratic parties in every state and terrritory in selecting delegates to the 1972 national convention. Some guidelines were only recommendations, but most were mandatory. Together they were intended to correct what the commission called "the profound flaws in the Presidential nominating process" exposed by the 1968 campaign. After his first look at the new rules, Lawrence O'Brien, newly installed as the Democratic National Chairman, hailed them as "the greatest goddam change since the two party system."

Some state parties resisted the changes at first. But under the threat of having their delegations barred from the national convention, the vast majority accepted the overall thrust of the new political order. The impact on the 1972 campaign was dramatic. Never had the competition been so open or so intense. More than twenty-one million Americans participated in the caucuses and primaries, nearly double the number of those who had taken part in 1968, and by far the greatest mass involvement in American political history in the choice of a presidential candidate.

But the campaign culminated in a convention which in bitterness and confusion rivaled the 1968 confrontation in Chicago. And that convention sent forth as its standard-bearer the chairman of the reform commission, George McGovern, who in an election which saw the lowest voter turnout since 1948, carried only one state, Massachusetts, and the District of Columbia—the worst electoral college defeat inflicted upon a Democratic nominee in this century.

When the returns were in, angry party officials, labor leaders and other regulars, most of whom had strongly opposed McGovern's candidacy, denounced the reforms. They blamed the guidelines for the nomination of McGovern, the divisions in the party and its overwhelming defeat. But the assault on the reforms, which continues to the present, missed the point. Despite Larry O'Brien's exuberant appraisal, the controversial reform and guidelines boiled down merely to modifying part of the machinery of the political system. They were an attempt to adjust to the changes wrought in the Democratic Party, and in the overall electorate, during the past decade.

But these revisions in procedures did not address the fundamental causes of change, which were rooted in the widening gap between politics and government—the social and economic ferment which fragmented political constituencies, the consequent undermining of the parties' capacity for organizing coalitions for candidates and delivering results from government, and the mounting burden of expectations and demands on the government, particularly the presidency. The hallmarks of the gap—the irrelevance of politics and the unaccountability of government—had during the sixties contributed to conditions which troubled the lives of nearly every citizen.

The war in Vietnam, which had been started and widened by presidential fiat, its conduct marked by miscalculation and deceit, still dragged on, adding to the national sense of waste and frustration. Bland promises of prosperity, unsupported by explicit programs establishing priorities among the goals and beneficiaries of government policies, were mocked by cycles of recession and inflation which seemed to surge along on their own capricious and destructive course. In the great cities, the nerve centers of American society, the populace was constantly confronted with blight, crime and racial hatred.

The electorate did not necessarily expect swift and easy solutions. But the failure of political leaders to address these varied crises openly and candidly, and the misleading assurances of progress that were offered instead, intensified the cynicism of the voters, which in turn, of course, further weakened the institutions of politics and government. It was this combination of turbulent and divisive forces, far more than the McGovern Commission guidelines, which shaped the destinies of George McGovern and the party he tried to lead.

McGovern did not dictate the reforms, any more than the reforms dictated his nomination, though he did take better advantage of them than his competitors. The work of the McGovern Commission was part of a widespread, often grudging response by political leaders to a surge of public interest in making the electoral process more open and more equitable. Like the reform drives in the late nineteenth and early twentieth centuries, this latest effort had a variety of causes. Its origins could be traced back to John Kennedy's candidacy in 1960, which demonstrated the weakness of the party hierarchy and the potential significance of presidential primaries. Reform got another lift from the controversy over Mississippi's segregated delegation to the 1964 convention, and more broadly from the drive for black voting rights which called attention to a variety of restrictions on the franchise. Then came the war and the bitter struggle for the 1968 Democratic nomination, which brought the party's delegate selection procedures under attack. The old system had survived for so long mainly because hardly anyone outside a small circle of party functionaries paid attention to it. When that circle was greatly expanded by the candidacies and conventions of the 1960s, change was inevitable.

The drive for reform extended beyond the national Democratic Party to the Republican Party, to the states and to the Congress. Reflecting its narrower base and tighter organization, the GOP's rules for delegate selection were more codified than the Democratic procedures. Nevertheless, the Republicans saw the 1968 Democratic experience as reason to put their own house in order. With little fanfare the 1968 Republican convention had created a Delegates and Organization Committee to review nominating procedures and to report to the 1972 national convention.

By the fall of 1969, as the McGovern Commission was in the midst of its deliberations of proposed rule changes, a good many states were already in the process of renovating their voting statutes. Some were moving to adopt primaries, others to discard residence barriers to registration and voting. And in 1971 Congress approved, and the states swiftly ratified, the Twenty-sixth Amendment,

giving eighteen-year-olds the franchise in state and federal elections.

But the McGovern Commission was probably the most
significant and ultimately the most controversial bridge-
head for reform. Initial support for the commission had
by no means been unanimous. The leadership of the AFL-
CIO, though not all its member unions, regarded the
commission as part of a reformist scheme to take over the
party. Its chief representative on the commission, I. W.
Abel, president of the United Steel Workers of America,
did not attend any of the commission's meetings and
hearings. Some state party leaders, particularly in the
South, resented the commission from the start as a threat
to their authority.

But these were exceptions. The makeup of the commission reflected the acceptance by most national party
leaders after the 1968 convention of the fact that some
sort of rules revisions had to be made. Far from being a
group of radical "goo-goos," as its critics later contended,
the commission membership was dominated numerically
by Democratic regulars, most of whom had supported
Humphrey's candidacy in 1968. Humphrey himself, as
the party's titular leader, personally approved McGovern's selection as chairman. Humphrey considered Mc-
Govern to be "a regular Democrat" who could get along
with both reformers and the establishment. McGovern's
style as commission chairman was restrained; when controversies flared he usually tried to find a middle ground.

The staff was young, aggressive and committed to reform. As in the case with most such commissions, the
staff did most of the spadework and prepared the first
drafts of the guidelines. But all the guidelines were debated and most were substantially revised by the commission. The most controversial of the new rules sought
to put teeth into the party's nominal commitment against
discrimination and led many states to establish firm numerical quotas for women, young people, blacks and

other minorities on their delegations. These guidelines were the handiwork of the commissioners themselves, who failed to anticipate the storm they would create.

But the burden of finding a certain number of women, young people and blacks to fill out their slates of delegates fell equally on all presidential candidates. For all the furor over the quotas, and the questions of equity they raised, the quotas had no bearing on which candidate won how many delegates in each state.

The group of guidelines which struck directly at the confusion and arbitrariness of the delegate selection process had far greater influence on the choice of a standard-bearer. These reforms reinforced the 1968 convention's prohibition against the unit rule, banned proxy voting, required the selection of delegates within the year of the convention and public notice of delegate selection caucuses, all but eliminated the power of party officials to appoint delegates and encouraged delegate candidates in primaries to declare themselves as supporters of a presidential contender.

The publication of the eighteen guidelines in November 1969 provoked no great public protest. The guidelines were technical and their practical effect uncertain. Besides, the first presidential primary contest was still more than two years off. Not until the 1972 campaign was well under way did most of the state party leaders realize that the special advantages they had enjoyed in the past had been stripped away and their influence on the nominating process greatly diminished.

In January 1971 McGovern resigned the chairmanship of the commission and became the first declared candidate for the Democratic presidential nomination. Leadership of the commission, which still faced the task of prodding the state parties into compliance with the guidelines, was turned over to Donald Fraser, a reform-minded Minnesota congressman. But the foundation for the changes had been laid while McGovern was in charge, and for this the party establishment would never forgive him.

McGovern's candidacy, though, caused little alarm among the regulars; they simply did not take him seriously. McGovern had gotten only a flicker of national attention in 1968 when he announced his presidential candidacy a fortnight before the convention and sought to rally supporters to the slain Robert Kennedy behind him. Afterward, he returned to the obscurity to which most senators from small states are consigned.

At any rate, many party leaders, along with most of the press, took it for granted that the next Democratic presidential nominee would be Edmund Muskie of Maine. Only three years before, Muskie had been, like McGovern, just another senator from a small state. But as Hubert Humphrey's running mate in 1968, Muskie, by contrast with the other national candidates, had comported himself with dignity and strength. Edward Kennedy had been the early favorite for the nomination. But unanswered questions about the auto accident at Chappaquiddick Island in 1969, in which a young woman passenger in Kennedy's car had drowned, appeared to eliminate him and open the way to Muskie's candidacy. Then, on election eve in 1970, a powerful televised address in which Muskie, speaking on behalf of Democratic congressional candidates, shamed Nixon and Agnew for their campaign rhetoric, made the Maine senator the acknowledged front-runner.

But Muskie and his advisers made the mistake of believing their own press clippings, overlooking the fact that the circumstances which had elevated him had not really tested his capacities or his beliefs as a national candidate. Also overlooked, though Muskie's campaign manager, George Mitchell, had been a member of the McGovern Commission, was the impact of the changes wrought by the new guidelines. Muskie set about running for the nomination as if the traditional procedures were still in place and he were the incumbent president. In effect, he sought to revive Lyndon Johnson's consensus.

But the politics of consensus that had worked to re-elect a sitting president in 1964 were ill-suited to the circumstances of the country as the 1972 campaign approached. Under Richard Nixon's negative stewardship, the discontents of the 1960s had deepened and the divisions multiplied. In *State of the Nation*, a survey of the American mood in 1971 and 1972, William Watts and Lloyd Free found that while most Americans pronounced themselves satisfied with the material circumstances of their personal lives, "an air of uneasiness is abroad in the land." Only 37 percent of the public approved of the way the nation was being governed, 53 percent agreed with the proposition that "what you think doesn't count very much," and 50 percent felt that "the people running the country don't really care what happens to people like yourself."

Though citizens shared a general sense of alienation from their government, they had little else in common. No unifying purpose or leadership pulled them together. Instead, all across the demographic map a range of pressures drove various groups at cross-purposes to each other. Hostility between blacks and whites intensified, and new conflicts developed, pitting city against suburb, the affluent against the poor and sometimes the older generation against its offspring.

The social ferment of the 1960s had created a broad new cleavage in the land that came to be called "the social issue." Two best-selling books published in 1970 defined the forces in opposition. In *The Greening of America*, Charles A. Reich, a Yale Law School teacher, heralded "the coming American revolution" which, he confidently predicted, would ultimately transform the political structure. "This is the revolution of the new generation," Reich wrote. "Their protest and rebellion, their culture, clothes, music, drugs, ways of thought and liberated life style are not a passing fad. . . ."

The rebuttal came from two political analysts, Richard M. Scammon and Ben J. Wattenberg in *The Real Majority*. They depicted most Americans—"the unyoung, the unblack and the unpoor"—as personally terrified of street crime, protests and permissiveness, all elements of "disruptive social change," and warned: "When voters are afraid, they will vote their fears."

Every public issue of consequence contributed to disharmony. Weariness with the Vietnam War was widespread, but Americans were sharply split about the conditions under which the war should be ended. Many young people supported amnesty for draft violators, but most other Americans opposed it.

A majority of blacks and whites resisted the idea of forced busing as a remedy for segregated schools. But twice as many blacks as whites believed that some form of busing, mandatory or voluntary, was needed to give their children a chance at a better education.

Although the law of the land was now on the side of integration, social and economic forces pushed blacks and whites apart. White flight to the suburbs segregated schools in the North faster than the federal courts could desegregate them in the South. And as the suburbs resisted low-income housing, big-city ghettos steadily expanded to enclose more blacks.

In their frustration, the black leaders became more militant in their demands, adding to the strains on the old Democratic coalition. A strategy conference of about three thousand black leaders, in early 1972, denounced "forced integration," demanding instead community-controlled schools financed by an equal share of tax revenues. The threat which that proposal posed to white taxpayers was matched by the resentment of Jewish voters at another conference resolution accusing the state of

Israel of "forceful occupation" of Arab territory and condemning that country's "expansionist policy."

The blacks were only one of a number of groups flexing their political muscles. Feminists banded together to help push the Equal Rights Amendment through Congress to the consternation of a good portion of Middle America, and in an even more controversial area, pressed hard for liberalization of abortion laws. The feminists, like the black leaders, and the advocates for the claims of Hispanics, welfare recipients, draft violators, and homosexuals, all looked to the political process and particularly to the Democratic presidential campaign for a chance to air their grievances and gain promise of redress. No cause was without merit and each cause had its own dedicated constituency. But each also had its own built-in opposition.

This splintering of old allies and proliferation of new interest groups ran directly counter to the basic premise of Muskie's candidacy and assured its failure. Muskie was determined to find the middle ground and hold it. This is a strategy better designed for general election campaigns when the attention of the entire electorate is focused on two major party candidates. But the competition for the presidential nomination within the Democratic Party in 1972 had no center, only a cluster of fragmented constituencies, many of them at war with each other.

By trying to position himself in the middle, Muskie failed to appeal strongly to any of the various groups fastened on their own particular interest. And by his occasional shifts from left to right and back again on such issues as Vietnam, Muskie succeeded mainly in creating an impression of vacillation and opportunism—a perception that encouraged other candidates to enter the race.

At one time or another a total of fifteen prominent and not-so-prominent Democrats launched or tried to launch presidential candidacies. Some dropped out early and some who stayed until the end were mainly indulging their own egos. But their numbers showed how factionalized the Democratic coalition had become and how difficult it would be for anyone to reassemble it.

The roll call of contenders covered the full range of the party's ideological spectrum from Shirley Chisholm, the black congresswoman from Brooklyn, and New York City mayor John Lindsay on the left to Los Angeles mayor Sam Yorty and George Wallace on the right. In the middle, more or less, was Hubert Humphrey, making his third try for the presidency, who counted on support from such traditional party bulwarks as organized labor, blacks and Jews.

And finally there was George McGovern. Less known than any of his major rivals, his obscurity at first helped him with an electorate mistrustful of the more familiar political crowd. But McGovern had other more positive initial assets: his early declaration of candidacy, his total personal commitment to the contest, and, most important, his passionate opposition to the war.

McGovern had been among the first senators to challenge the point of American involvement in Indochina, as far back as August 1963. In declaring his candidacy for the presidency, he pledged that if elected he would announce "a definite early date for the withdrawal of every American soldier." Though U. S. troop levels in Vietnam were declining, there remained a significant segment of Americans intensely opposed to the fighting and eager to use the presidential campaign as an outlet for their protest. They helped to provide McGovern with desperately needed financial support and with a cadre of political operatives seasoned by the 1968 campaign.

While Muskie counted on the efforts of prominent political leaders—"We built from the top down," a Muskie adviser said—McGovern dispatched political guerrilla leaders to the hustings to find and build support at the local level. The potential payoff for such gritty labor was vastly increased by the reform guidelines. In the states that selected their delegates through caucuses and conventions, where the antiwar forces had been frustrated in 1968, elimination of the unit rule and proxy voting, public postings of meetings, and the creation of a written body of rules opened the way to the McGovern insurgency. Ultimately he won nearly four hundred delegates, more than a third of the total number of delegates picked in caucuses and conventions.

But the main battlegrounds of the campaign were the primaries. Because of the reform guidelines, and also because of the heightened public interest in primaries, their number increased from seventeen in 1968 to twenty-three. The primary states now included nine of the nation's ten largest—all but Texas—and together chose two-thirds of the delegates to the convention.

The impact of the increased number of primary states was reinforced by the guidelines which curbed the power of party officials in these states to appoint delegates and prodded them into listing the presidential preference of delegates on the ballot. The overall result tied the makeup of primary-state delegations to the popular vote for president more closely than before and converted the primaries from mainly a symbolic test of personal appeal into decisive competitions for actual delegate strength. It was the primary states which gave McGovern about 1,200 of the 1,500 delegates he needed for a convention majority and assured him of victory.

Certainly the guidelines benefited McGovern's candidacy. But other factors also contributed to his ultimate success: the efficiency of his organizing effort, the mistakes of his opposition and the reaction of the press and the public to the events of the campaign. The three primary contests that were most important to his campaign —New Hampshire, which established him as a formidable contender, Wisconsin, which made him the leader in the race, and California, which gave him the margin he needed for victory—were conducted under rules that were little changed from preguideline campaigns.

McGovern's strong second-place finish in New Hampshire, which Muskie had been expected to win overwhelmingly, was interpreted by the press as a victory for McGovern and a setback for Muskie. Muskie's prestige was damaged and his confidence shaken. After his poor fourth-place finish in the Florida primary, where Wallace rode a tide of antibusing sentiment to victory, Muskie lost his front-runner status and his temper, too. He lashed out bitterly not just at Wallace but at Wallace's supporters, who he implied were racists.

McGovern, who had made only a minimal effort in Florida, where he finished sixth, was more restrained and shrewder. He labeled Wallace an "extremist" but added that many who voted for him "did so because they are deeply frustrated and disgusted with the way their government is ignoring their concerns and interests." Presenting himself as the only candidate prepared to respond "to the angry cry from the guts of ordinary Americans against a system which is really bothering people in this country," McGovern had some success in appealing to the same pool of alienated voters who were attracted to Wallace. In the Wisconsin primary in April, he scored well among Catholics and blue-collar workers in such Archie Bunker enclaves as Kenosha, Racine, and South Milwaukee.

Still, there was no sign that McGovern, any more than the other candidates, had found a way to reconcile the racial resentments and harsh feelings which infused the hard core of Wallace voters in 1972, as in 1968. When Wallace was shot and seriously wounded in May, on the eve of the Maryland and Michigan primaries, which he won handsomely, his wounds eliminated him as a force in the campaign. But he remained in the background as a disturbing reminder of the divisions within the party, of the disillusionment of many Americans with the political

and governing system, and of the failure of Democratic
leaders to offer positive programs that could match the
appeal of Wallace's demagoguery.

Meanwhile, as McGovern gained ground on his other
rivals, his own views on the problems underlying the
national discontent came under closer scrutiny and
mounting criticism. The debate, such as it was, typified
the folly and frustration of presidential politics. With
little expectation that campaign proposals will be transformed into reality and with no tradition or mechanism
for rational discourse, issues in presidential campaigns are
generally reduced to slogans and epithets, hurled back
and forth by each side to stir emotions for or against a
candidate.

McGovern was accused by his opponents of radicalism
and recklessness. Some of the criticism unfairly distorted
the record. But McGovern, acting sometimes out of
what he deemed political necessity and at other times out
of simple carelessness, gave his critics good grounds for
complaint.

McGovern's opposition to the war, the centerpiece of
his candidacy, had considerable potential appeal. But Mc-
Govern hurt his own case by likening Nixon to Hitler
and by proclaiming that the Senate chamber "reeks of
blood"—outbursts which to millions of patriotic Americans made him seem wild-eyed and dangerous.

McGovern's own convictions and his need for support
on the campuses compelled him to advocate an uncondi-
tional amnesty for draft violators, though polls showed
that only about 20 percent of the voters accepted the
idea. His advisers hoped that some of the voters who
disagreed with him on this point might at least give him
credit for having the courage of his beliefs.

But McGovern ruined that possibility by muddling his
positions on other matters. He said he was opposed to
criminal penalties for marijuana but not in favor of
legalizing it; he personally believed in a woman's right to

abortion but he did not support abortion on demand as federal policy. As he seemed to say one thing, then another, his foes accused him of extremism or shiftiness or both.

The proposal most damaging to his candidacy was his scheme for welfare reform, which relied on giving a government grant to every American, regardless of economic status. The upper and middle classes would return all or part of their "demogrants" to the government in taxes; poor people would keep the entire amount to supplement their earnings. Because the economic ramifications of the plan were difficult to calculate, McGovern's advisers warned him to stick to its broad principles in explaining it. Nevertheless, McGovern began using the figure $1,000 for the size of the demogrants.

By going into details he had trapped himself. During the California primary campaign, in a televised debate with Humphrey, who had become his chief opponent, McGovern was inevitably challenged to say how much his plan would cost. The embarrassed candidate was forced to admit that he just could not tell, nor could anyone else. After the debate, when his campaign manager, Gary Hart, mentioned the $1,000 plan, McGovern snapped: "I wish I had never heard of the goddam idea."

Welfare reform was then and is now a problem demanding serious public debate. McGovern's unhappy experience is sometimes cited as evidence of the futility of raising such issues with voters who are depicted as apathetic and ignorant about substantive matters. But the real blame for the flop of the $1,000 plan goes back to the haphazard nature of presidential campaigns, which resulted in the complex reform being presented before the candidate or his staff fully understood it.

Despite the controversy over demogrants, and Humphrey's general onslaught against him, McGovern won the California primary in June with 44 percent of the vote to 39 percent for Humphrey. Under the winner-takes-all rules governing the contest, he was entitled to all of the state's 271 delegates, enough to clinch the nomination.

But McGovern's foes would not give up. Banding together on the convention credentials committee, two weeks before the convention itself opened in Miami Beach, they pushed through a ruling which divided the California delegation proportionately among all the candidates who had competed in the primary. The pretext for this change was one of the McGovern commission's own guidelines which called for proportional representation. But this guideline was merely a recommendation, not mandatory, and a number of states besides California had rejected the idea. The maneuver temporarily cut McGovern's delegate total in California from 271 to 120 and placed his nomination in jeopardy. The outraged McGovern forces on the credentials committee retaliated by unseating fifty-nine delegates from Cook County, controlled by Mayor Daley, claiming they had been handpicked by the mayor in violation of one guideline and did not fairly represent minority voters, in violation of still another guideline.

When the convention got under way, McGovern won back his rights to the full California delegation after a bitter floor fight. He was aided by a hotly disputed procedural ruling from the convention chairman, Lawrence O'Brien, who by this time had good reason to wonder about his initial enthusiasm for the guidelines.

McGovern's foes based their diehard opposition to his candidacy on the grounds that he could not unify the party. This argument became a self-fulfilling prophecy. At any rate, the old coalition was so badly battered that any candidate would have had trouble patching it together. Humphrey, who was McGovern's closest competitor, would have been estranged from the reformers and liberals who backed McGovern, particularly if McGovern's defeat had been achieved by the switch of the

California delegation. Moreover, the weakness Humphrey displayed in competing for blue-collar votes against Wallace in the primaries would certainly have been exploited by Nixon.

With the nomination safely in McGovern's grasp, his emissaries urged Mayor Daley, in the interest of party unity, to accept a compromise, under which about half of his fifty-nine delegates would be seated. Daley refused, and stayed out of the convention.

Daley did not really want to make peace with the McGovern forces, nor did most of the other regulars. For years they had been losing power and now McGovern and his reformers had taken away most of what remained of their influence over the choice of the presidential nominee. For the time being this authority mattered more to them than regaining the White House, a cause which most privately conceded to be already lost.

2. Split Screen

Far more than most modern presidential candidates, George McGovern seemed determined to offer explicit answers to the major questions before the public. He pledged to end the war and bring home all American troops within ninety days of his inauguration. He vowed to cut the defense budget by $30 billion over three years and save another $222 billion by closing a variety of tax loopholes. He promised to spend $10 billion of the savings to help create new jobs, another $3 billion to expand Social Security benefits, and $15 billion more to provide local tax relief for financially burdened homeowners. He called for new ethical standards to guard against the corruption and abuse of federal authority.

The candidate's hope was that these and other proposals would help reconcile his Democratic campaign adversaries, keep faith with his early supporters and unite his party behind him. But the voters he needed to reach did not heed him. His message, whatever its merits, was drowned out by some of the distortions of the political process. McGovern became entangled in the inherent irrationalities of vice-presidential selection. The press, absorbed with character analyses, took him to task for his folly. With his integrity and competence called into question, he could not offset the power of the incumbent president to dominate events and their perception. The result was not just that McGovern suffered a humiliating defeat. More important, because the country tuned McGovern out, the 1972 campaign became another contest for the presidency which offered no meaningful debate on the urgent issues of the day—the management of the war, the supervision of the economy, the response to racial tensions and the uses of presidential power.

In each of the previous quadrennials examined here, the reasons for the lack of relevance had been somewhat different, of course, according to the circumstances and the candidates.

In 1960 the erosion of traditional party allegiance and ideological distinctions during the postwar era led to the emphasis on style and personality in the contest between Kennedy and Nixon.

In 1964 the fratricidal conflict within the Republican Party crippled Goldwater's candidacy and left Johnson free to avoid specifics and to pursue his all-encompassing consensus.

In 1968 Humphrey was inhibited by fear of his chief sponsor, the incumbent president, from offering fresh approaches, while Nixon was able to exploit the resentments and disillusion created by the old regime.

But common to all these competitions and underlying the tactical differences were the inherent imbalances and limitations of the political and governing system which narrowed the options of the candidates and governed their fortunes. So it was with McGovern in 1972. It is not necessary to overlook his tactical blunders to recognize the damage done to his candidacy by conditions he did not create and could do little to control.

For all practical purposes, George McGovern's campaign against Richard Nixon ended when and where it began, at the national convention in Miami, with his choice of a running mate. To fully understand that episode, it helps to recall the origins and development of the vice-presidency, an office that the early critics of the Constitution condemned as "dangerous and useless."

In keeping with their nonpartisan philosophy, the framers of the Constitution intended the vice-presidency as a consolation prize for whichever presidential candidate finished second in the electoral college tally. They failed to anticipate political parties which would nominate both a vice-president and a president and deliver unified support to both. This is what happened in 1800 when Jefferson, the Democratic candidate for president, and Aaron Burr, his running mate, finished in a deadlock, ahead of John Adams, the Federalist incumbent president.

The election went to the House of Representatives, where on the thirty-sixth ballot the tie was broken largely through the efforts of Hamilton, who persuaded his Federalist friends that Jefferson would be the lesser of two evils. That episode cost Hamilton his life in a duel with Burr and led to the Twelfth Amendment, which established separate ballots for president and vice-president.

But by ending the chance of a deadlock, and the possibility that a vice-presidential candidate could be selected by the House as president, the amendment eliminated what was left of the incentive the authors of the Constitution had relied on to attract able men to the vice-presidency. For more than a century the nation's second highest office was mainly a repository for Throttlebottoms who passed their time keeping an eye on the president's health and presiding over the Senate.

In the modern era, as the president's power and prestige enlarged, some of the magic rubbed off on the vice-presidency. The opportunity to share, however modestly, in the attention showered on the president made the vice-presidency a convenient launching pad for the White House, as Hubert Humphrey and Richard Nixon had demonstrated.

But the anomalous nature of the office remained, as McGovern pondered his choice in Miami. Measured in real power, the vice-presidency in itself was next to nothing, but in potential it could be everything. All this depended on the president, his physical well-being, his political strength and his attitude toward his vice-president. A prospective vice-president had to be willing to gamble his ambitions on long-range circumstances over which he had no control. On the other hand, a presidential candidate considering a running mate was simply looking for someone to help him win a ninety-day campaign.

This contradiction of purposes had made vice-presidential selection a disjointed exercise, blurred by conflicting egos, aspirations and judgments. Adding substantially to the confusion for presidential candidates who, like McGovern, had to struggle to the bitter end to secure their own nominations, the vice-presidency became an afterthought, a choice made in haste and exhaustion. No wonder that all concerned with such deliberations often had difficulty explaining their actions afterward.

Not until the morning after his nomination did McGovern instruct his staff to produce a list of possibilities for the vice-presidency. With the party in disarray, his need to find someone who could exert a healing influence was critical. But as Gary Hart recalled in *Right from the Start*, McGovern's advisers, still euphoric from their victory of the night before, were in a lighthearted mood. When the name of New Orleans mayor Moon Landrieu was proposed, Ted Van Dyk, McGovern's chief issues adviser, objected. "Can't you see the headlines?" he said: "Moon over Miami?"

"I can't get over this," another aide remarked. "Here we sit, unshaven, worn out, knocking down U. S. Senators."

One U. S. senator who was almost knocked down was Thomas Eagleton of Missouri. Someone had heard a rumor that Eagleton had drinking problems and a family history of mental illness. But a quick check turned up no supporting evidence, and Eagleton's name made the final list, though not at the top.

McGovern's first choice was Edward Kennedy, who quickly turned him down; Kennedys did not run for vicepresident. Next was Walter Mondale of Minnesota. But he was more interested in getting reelected to the Senate. For a while Mayor Kevin White of Boston seemed the likely choice. But that idea did not go over well with Kennedy or with other members of the Massachusetts delegation, who nursed local grievances against him.

With time running out, Eagleton began to look better and better. McGovern scarcely knew him, having met him briefly on two occasions. But he was a Catholic, he was from a border state, and he had good connections to the labor movement, all areas where McGovern himself was weak.

"I think I'll go with Tom," McGovern told his advisers.

Eagleton quickly accepted, "before you change your mind," he told McGovern. Then Frank Mankiewicz, a McGovern adviser, took the phone to ask if there was anything in Eagleton's background that could cause trouble for the campaign. The answer was a flat no.

That settled it. After a seemingly interminable roll call, prolonged by the insistence of nearly every group in the party on putting forward its own token candidate to grasp a moment of precious prime time, the delegates endorsed McGovern's choice. The band played "Happy Days Are Here Again," FDR's old anthem, and for the moment it was possible for Democrats to dream of victory.

Almost immediately afterward, McGovern's staff heard the first hard information on Eagleton's troubled background. Within a few days the essential elements of the story were clear. The forty-three-year-old senator had been hospitalized three times for nervous exhaustion following previous campaigns and on two of those occasions had received electric shock therapy. He had concealed these facts from the voters in Missouri, just as he had from McGovern. But after Eagleton's nomination, the Knight newspapers had received an anonymous tip about his medical history, and their reporters were now digging into the senator's past.

McGovern and Eagleton hurriedly called a joint press conference to beat the Knight papers to their scoop, and then both tried to ride out the storm. McGovern insisted, somewhat implausibly, that he would have chosen Eagleton even if he had known of his past, and later, in a phrase that would echo through the rest of the campaign, declared he was "a thousand percent" behind Eagleton.

McGovern soon found himself caught between two emotionally powerful waves of opinion. The country, dependent on a strong leader in the White House, had little tolerance for weakness, particularly a weakness as ill-defined and unpredictable as mental illness, in the background of the man who would stand first in succession. Said Matthew Troy, the blunt-spoken leader of New York's Queens County, one of the few party officials who had supported McGovern, "I have nine kids. I don't want to see them destroyed because some unstable person might become President." A storm broke in the press. The *New York Post*, the *Washington Post*, the *New York Times*—all influential liberal papers sympathetic to McGovern's candidacy—urged that Eagleton be dropped from the ticket. Not only did Eagleton have health problems, his critics pointed out, but he had not been forthright about them.

McGovern wavered. He let it be known that he was reconsidering his initial decision to stick with Eagleton. Meanwhile, though, feelings were running high on the other side. As Eagleton barnstormed the country, defending his fitness, he gained support from those who sympathized with underdogs in general and those who felt special compassion for victims of mental illness.

Alarmed that Eagleton's illness would become the main issue of the campaign, McGovern's staff and supporters urged him to act. In another joint press conference, on July 31, eighteen days after Eagleton's nomination and a week after the disclosure of his health problems, Eagleton announced his withdrawal. "The public debate over Senator Eagleton's medical history continues to divert attention from the general national issues . . . ," McGovern explained.

But dismissing Eagleton shifted the focus of the debate from Eagleton's health to McGovern's character. One line of attack asserted that by waiting for public reaction before forcing Eagleton from the ticket, McGovern had demonstrated that he was not any more high-minded than traditional politicians. "In the 'old politics' this sort of maneuvering was an accepted technique for approaching tough decisions, euphemistically known as 'keeping your options open,' " William Greider wrote scornfully in the *Washington Post*. "The 'new politics' of the McGovern campaign . . . will have to think of something different to call it." The Eagleton affair, said the *New York Times*, had damaged McGovern's "image" as "an unusually candid Presidential candidate."

But what was the so-called "new politics" supposed to mean? McGovern himself, as Greider wrote, "has always insisted that he is above all a pragmatic politician." His claim to being different, so far as it went, was based mainly on his professed willingness to deal frankly with issues that other politicians ducked and on the positions he took on those issues. The Eagleton affair had nothing to do with substantive issues. The case turned on public attitudes toward Eagleton's medical history and toward his deception of McGovern. For his own sake, and Eagleton's, McGovern tried to sway opinion in Eagleton's favor and overdid it. But when that effort failed, McGovern had no choice, under the "new politics" or the old, but to find another running mate.

While some critics in the press were exposing McGovern as duplicitous, others were depicting him as an incompetent. Acknowledging that McGovern had "bad luck," James Reston nevertheless argued that "he has also misjudged the problem of picking a Vice President" and "overrated the efficiency of his new young staff." The columnist Joseph Kraft contended that "the Senator from South Dakota has not shown the one thing a Presidential candidate must show—the capacity to govern."

The Eagleton affair was certainly a dismal episode, reflecting no credit on any one concerned. But the judgment that McGovern's choice of his running mate was evidence of his unfitness to manage the country's affairs does not stand the test of comparison with other instances of vice-presidential selection. The discussions leading up to McGovern's selection of Eagleton were terribly confused, but no more so than the conversations preceding John Kennedy's offer of the vice-presidency to Lyndon Johnson in 1960, in the hope and belief that he would not accept it. After that imbroglio, which created resentments that endured for years, Robert Kennedy confided to a friend: "My God, this wouldn't have happened except that we were all too tired last night."

It is true that McGovern's aides were not as diligent as they might have been in examining Eagleton's background. But how carefully had Richard Nixon's staff in 1968 looked into the background of Spiro Agnew in a state whose politics was famous for the laxity of its ethical standards? No one thought to raise that question until the summer of 1973, when Agnew was in the process of plea bargaining to avoid imprisonment for bribery and tax evasion.

"We were no longer McGovern, presidential nominee," Richard Dougherty the candidate's press secretary wrote of the post-Eagleton atmosphere. "We were McGovern in trouble." Dougherty, himself a veteran of the *New York Herald Tribune* and the *Los Angeles Times*, imagined journalists around the country saying to their colleagues: "What went wrong today? What's he done now?"

The Nixon forces, who had long complained of being unfairly abused by the press, found it hard to conceal their delight and surprise at what seemed to them to be a reversal of form. Victor Gold, veteran of countless battles with the press as press secretary to Spiro Agnew in 1972 and before that to Barry Goldwater in 1964, told me: "I used to think that you guys were out for *our* blood. But I can see now that you're just out for anybody's blood."

But the press did not set out to wreck McGovern's candidacy, any more than it had tried to destroy Agnew, Nixon or Goldwater. The press was guilty not of malice but of trying to cater to the standards and values of the public it must serve to survive. Like the public, the press is drawn to dramatic events and personalities, which can be more readily described than can the complex of forces and issues that set the stage for history.

Because of the personalization of the presidency, voters' decisions about presidential candidates are heavily based on perceptions of such ephemeral traits as toughness, trustworthiness, and competence. The press, as a result, relentlessly examines the events of the campaign for revelations of character strengths and flaws. The Eagleton affair was perceived as profoundly revealing of

McGovern's character, and this perception was transformed into a reality that overshadowed all else.

McGovern's efforts to find a replacement for Eagleton added to his embarrassment. His first five choices turned him down. Finally he settled on R. Sargent Shriver, whose ties to the New Frontier and to the Kennedy family, McGovern hoped, would generate some badly needed enthusiasm for the ticket. But the situation was too far gone for Shriver or anyone else to salvage. For McGovern, the vice-presidency had turned out to be just as "dangerous and useless" as its original critics predicted.

George McGovern would have had trouble catching up with Richard Nixon in any event. He trailed the president by twelve points in the polls in June, after his victory in the California primary. But after the convention and the Eagleton affair, that margin almost doubled. The blight that Eagleton cast over his candidacy deprived McGovern of the chance to pull together the major elements of his party, cut Nixon's lead, make a contest out of the campaign and force Nixon to confront him and defend his administration.

Nixon had no desire to do that, and as it turned out, no need to. Agnew and other surrogates carried the burden of the battle against McGovern, while Nixon, except for brief excursions in the final two weeks, remained in the White House and in command of the country.

This was the role he had carved out for himself, long before the campaign year got under way. Opinion surveys after the 1970 congressional elections made clear that Nixon's negative strategy could not sustain him politically. His much heralded hopes of constructing a New Republican Majority were being undermined by the war, which dragged on despite his promise to end it, and even more so by the economy, which was afflicted by both inflation and unemployment.

In midsummer of 1971 Nixon moved abruptly and dramatically to help himself on both fronts. Reversing his previous unyielding opposition to increased government intervention in the troubled economy, he installed sweeping controls on wages and prices.

The war was much harder to deal with directly, in large part because of the intransigence of Washington's South Vietnamese ally. Nevertheless Nixon presented himself to the country as a peacemaker by announcing he would travel to the People's Republic of China to seek normal relations with that country.

The controls steadied the wobbly economy for a while. But they did not remedy the basic causes of inflation and unemployment any more than the visit to China brought peace to Asia. In neither case did Nixon seek public support in advance of his actions, nor did he make clear the ultimate purpose of his moves. But both the imposition of controls and the overture to the Chinese provided the short-term political boost he needed by fostering the perception of Nixon as a bold and forceful leader.

The voter view of the two competing parties in 1972 was a split television screen. While the Democrats battered each other in the early primaries, Nixon was shown at the Great Wall and parleying with the Chinese leaders in Peking. Later, as Humphrey and McGovern debated in California, the nation watched Nixon and Brezhnev in Moscow, reaching agreement on a SALT treaty.

A few weeks after Nixon's return from his success in Moscow, the president and his vice-president were renominated by the Republican convention, whose carefully scripted harmony provided a striking contrast with the Democratic disorder of the previous month. Nixon, seeking to underline another contrast, said of Agnew: "I thought he was the best man for the job four years ago. I think he is the best man today. And I'm not going to change my mind tomorrow."

As he watched the campaign develop from the Oval Office, Nixon saw no reason for concern. It was true that investigators had learned that the June burglary and bugging of Democratic Party headquarters in the Watergate complex had been arranged by his own campaign committee, which Nixon had wanted to be "the most efficient and effective . . . organization humanly possible." And McGovern had hammered away at this disclosure from the stump, charging that it was a sign of pervasive corruption within the Nixon administration.

But details were hard to come by. With the exception of the *Washington Post*, the press seemed far more interested in recounting the bickering within McGovern's campaign than probing into Nixon's operation. Certainly McGovern's charges had little impact on the voters. They reelected Nixon by a margin of eighteen million votes, a bigger victory even than Lyndon Johnson had won against Barry Goldwater.

To those around Nixon, Watergate seemed to be little more than another joke on McGovern, and another indication of the futility of his candidacy. "If McGovern had kept after the Watergate," Henry Kissinger quipped after the election returns were in, "he would have made wiretapping popular."

3. The Breaking Point

"A strict observance of the written laws is doubtless *one* of the high duties of a good citizen, but it is not the *highest*," Thomas Jefferson wrote, years after he had sidestepped the Constitution to make the Louisiana Purchase. "The laws of necessity, of self-preservation, of saving our country when in danger, are of higher obligation."

Jefferson's rationale was not very different from the claim made by Richard Nixon that many of the abuses lumped under the heading of Watergate had been perpetrated to protect the national interest. In addition, Nixon argued in exculpation that he was not the first president to flout the law to advance his own political interest. "My reaction to the Watergate break-in was completely pragmatic," he wrote later. "If it was also cynical, it was a cynicism born of experience. . . . I could not muster much moral outrage over a political bugging." And as the scandal unfolded, beginning with the discovery of the break-in and bugging of Democratic headquarters, Nixon and his aides sought to justify themselves by recounting stories of Lyndon Johnson being bugged by John Kennedy during the 1960 campaign and of Barry Goldwater and Nixon himself being bugged by Johnson in 1964 and 1968.

Whether or not those reports were accurate, it was true that since Jefferson's time, presidents had often strained and sometimes exceeded the Constitution's limits on their power, usually in times of national crisis. The difference was that Nixon, responding to political imperatives and what he claimed to be the national interest, reached further beyond the law than any of his predecessors. Finally he passed a breaking point; his presidency cracked and then collapsed in the rubble of Watergate.

The implications of this disaster extended far beyond Nixon's attempt to suppress evidence linking the leadership of his reelection campaign to the burglary of Democratic national headquarters. The offenses lumped together under the rubric of Watergate grew out of the deterioration in the political process which began before Nixon's election but which accelerated under his presidency.

The most dramatic cause of the impairment to the system was the cumulative legacy of bad faith and erosion of presidential accountability centering on the war in Vietnam. John Kennedy had established a significant U.S. military involvement in Vietnam with little public or congressional debate. Lyndon Johnson, after pledging not to expand that commitment, had shipped 500,000 troops to the battleground. Nixon, after promising to end the war, had widened it. Not only did Nixon exceed his legitimate authority in prosecuting the war, he also abused his power in trying to subdue opponents of the war and in punishing others who for one reason or another were deemed to be "enemies" of his regime.

The crisis in accountability which Nixon precipitated was fostered by the decline in strength and influence of both political parties. The deep divisions within the Democratic Party paved the way for Nixon's election in 1968 and permitted him to win reelection in 1972 by an immense margin without his policies being seriously challenged. Nixon's own Republican Party lacked the vitality or cohesion to gain control of Congress and to be anything more than unquestioning accessory to his conduct of his campaigns and of his presidency.

Most of Nixon's predecessors in the White House had also chafed under the restraints imposed by the Constitution and by the political process. But Nixon's frustration was compounded by circumstances and by his own predilections. Selected by a hair's-breadth margin to lead a fractious country, he had adopted policies and rhetoric which provoked intense animosity. He was the first elected Chief Executive in this century to begin his presidency facing an opposition-controlled Congress, and his efforts to loosen the grip of the Democrats on Capitol Hill in 1970 had intensified partisan and institutional antagonisms.

Dwight Eisenhower had managed to live comfortably with Congress when the Democrats took control after the 1954 elections. But Eisenhower, unlike Nixon, could rely on his immense personal popularity to keep the Democrats in check. Just as important, Eisenhower was willing to settle for presiding passively over the nation's affairs; Nixon, more than any Republican president since Theodore Roosevelt, was determined to shape and direct events.

The center of his concerns, and the principal cause of continuing controversy over his use of power, was the war in Indochina. Nixon had promised to end the war, but he was determined to end it on his terms, which he called "peace with honor." That required not only prolonging the fighting in South Vietnam but extending the war to Cambodia and Laos. For legal justification he relied on his so-called inherent powers as commander in chief to send troops into battle without a congressional declaration of war.

This authority had been asserted by presidents throughout history, mainly to deal with temporary and limited emergencies. As a constitutional doctrine it remained ill-defined and controversial. The inherent powers doctrine had served as the main justification for Lyndon Johnson's escalation of the Vietnam War, though Johnson could also cite the Tonkin Gulf resolution, approved by Congress in 1964, which empowered him to take "all necessary measures to repel any armed attack against the forces of the United States and to prevent any future aggression."

But the language of the resolution was so vague and its origins so dubious that soon after he took office Nixon simply discarded it. Instead, he rested his constitutional defense for the invasion of Cambodia solely on what he claimed to be "the right of the president of the United States under the Constitution to protect the lives of American men."

Those on Capitol Hill and in the press who had increasingly challenged the legality of Johnson's war in Vietnam were more outraged by Nixon's thrusts across other borders without even the semblance of Congressional backing. Opposition to the president mounted in the Congress, which in 1971 called for an end to the fighting in Indochina at "the earliest practicable date," and flared in the streets and on the campuses.

Nixon fought back. If the president had inherent powers to defend the national security overseas, it was not too large a leap for Nixon to believe that he was equally free to defend those interests at home, using whatever tactics came to hand, open and covert. His Justice Department wiretapped journalists and his own aides to stop leaks about the supposedly secret bombing of Cambodia, arrested ten thousand antiwar May Day demonstrators, most of them illegally, and went into court to prevent the publication of the Pentagon Papers.

This official chronicle of the U. S. involvement in the war in Vietnam reflected most directly and most unfavorably on previous administrations. But Nixon worried that it would provide ammunition to critics of his own policies in Indochina. More fundamentally, he feared that unless he acted to prevent publication, "it would be a signal to every disgruntled bureaucrat in the government that he could leak anything he pleased while the government stood by."

After the Supreme Court rejected his attempt to stop the presses, the president sought to retaliate against Daniel Ellsberg, the former Pentagon consultant who had helped assemble the papers and later gave them to the press. Ellsberg was indicted. But Nixon complained that the FBI was not aggressive enough in getting evidence against him. "I did not care about any reasons or excuses," the president wrote later. "I wanted someone to light a fire under the FBI . . . and to keep the departments and agencies active in pursuit of leakers."

By this time the attitude in the Nixon White House toward dissent had reached a point of reckless aggressiveness which Nixon speech writer William Safire later defined as "the political philosophy of the pre-emptive strike, which is rooted in an attitude of 'us against them,' a golden rule turned by perverse political alchemists to read: 'Do unto others before they do it unto you.' " In keeping with this credo, a secret White House investigative unit called "the plumbers" burglarized the office of Ellsberg's psychiatrist, seeking information to discredit Ellsberg. Nixon claimed not to have known about the break-in before the fact. But he later acknowledged that "given the temper of those tense and bitter times and the peril I perceived I cannot say that had I been informed of it beforehand, I would have automatically considered it unprecedented, unwarranted, or unthinkable."

Though Nixon's abuses of power stemmed mostly from his conduct of the war, his assertion of almost untrammeled presidential authority extended to other areas. In 1970, when opposition mounted in the Senate to the nomination of G. Harrold Carswell for the Supreme Court, Nixon proclaimed "the Constitutional responsibility of the President to appoint members of the court" and argued that he should "be accorded the same right of choice . . . which has been freely accorded to my predecessors of both parties." By ignoring the Senate's constitutional duty to advise and consent, Nixon reinforced Carswell's opposition in the Senate and contributed to his defeat.

Unable to control the Senate or the House on this and other matters, Nixon embarked on a policy of refusing to spend, or impounding, funds appropriated by Congress for projects he opposed. Other presidents had used the impoundment power from time to time, but none as broadly as Nixon, who tried to convert impoundment into what was in effect an item veto on spending bills to contravene policies and priorities established by Congress.

Just as Nixon governed as if the president was above the law, he campaigned as if the president was above and outside of the political process. After his abortive intervention in the 1970 congressional elections, Nixon turned his back on his own party in 1972. While his lavishly financed campaign committee devoted itself to his reelection, most other Republicans were left to fend for themselves. He ignored the Republican National Committee and kept its chairman, Kansas senator Robert Dole, at a distance, so much so that Dole wisecracked that the only way he could see the president was to watch him on television. Nixon knew that party leaders resented this treatment, but he convinced himself that the success of his own candidacy would "give the Republican Party the new majority momentum that would give it a whole new lease on life."

But that theory did not square with the results in November. Republicans gained a scant twelve seats in the House, leaving them still fifty votes behind the Democratic majority. In the Senate, which Nixon had tried to conquer in 1970, the Democrats gained two seats.

Nixon was convinced nevertheless that his own landslide victory had at last given him a mandate to tame the Congress, and the balky bureaucracy, too. "There are no sacred cows," he told members of his White House staff on the day after the election. "We will tear up the pea patch." Just to drive the point home, he demanded the resignation of all political appointees, an action "meant to be symbolic of a completely new beginning."

Actually, though, Nixon seemed to have little new in mind; he returned to the tactics of his first term, only with greater force and emphasis. Shortly after the election he stepped up the bombing of North Vietnam and then announced broad new impoundments of funds appropriated by the Congress. At the same time, he began selecting his most trusted White House aides for posting in the cabinet agencies to strengthen his control over the executive branch as he girded for confrontation with the Congress.

But the anticipated battle had only begun when Nixon was crippled by Watergate. To prevent disclosures of past abuses of power, he sought to extend that power even further, claiming that executive privilege shielded the evidence and witnesses sought by investigators. But this strategy failed and served to focus public resentment against what came to be called, in Arthur Schlesinger, Jr.'s, phrase, "The Imperial Presidency."

Within a few months of his immense victory at the polls, opinion began to turn against Nixon. Americans had been willing to tolerate his claims to power in the belief he was guarding the national interest. But when they realized that Nixon had used his power to advance his own interests and protect his own skin, they steadily lost patience with the president.

The incumbency, which had been of such great benefit during the campaign, now became an added burden for the beleaguered chief executive. When oil and gas supplies dwindled during the Arab oil embargo in the winter of 1973, the public's resentment of the shortages added to the anger against Nixon and bolstered the drive for impeachment.

During a congressional recess in January 1974, I accompanied Angelo Roncallo, a Republican congressman, on a twenty-mile walk through his Long Island district to test the mood of his constituents. At every service station on the road from Massapequa to Cold Spring Harbor, long lines of cars waited for gas. "How are things going?" Roncallo asked a woman waiting in a Cadillac.

But this constituent had no interest in small talk. "Angelo, I'll follow you for twenty miles and drive you home on one condition," she offered.

"What's that?" Roncallo inquired.

"Impeach the son of a bitch," she said.

By his own reckoning, Roncallo talked to more than 250 voters, only two of whom had a kind word for the president. "How soon people forget the good things a man does," said Mrs. Roncallo, who kept her husband company on the hike.

"If I were Nixon," the congressman said wryly, "I wouldn't run again."

He went back to Washington bearing a message from the grass roots that was being delivered to his colleagues across the country.

As voter attitudes toward Nixon changed, the political parties began to adjust their positions accordingly, but both Republicans and Democrats were slow to respond. With few exceptions, the Republicans, taking their cue from their national chairman, George Bush, defended the president at first, complaining that the Democrats were trying to exploit the scandal to reverse the results of the election. When the Watergate charges became too serious to dismiss, Republican leaders then tried to put the blame on Nixon's campaign organization, the Committee to Re-elect the President, often referred to as CREEP.

In March 1974, in a speech to a Republican meeting in Chicago, Gerald Ford, who had become vice-president after Spiro Agnew resigned in disgrace, called CREEP "an arrogant elite guard of political adolescents." During the 1972 campaign, Ford complained, CREEP "ran roughshod over the seasoned political judgment and the seasoned political experience of the regular Republican Party organizations in all of our fifty states."

All one thousand regular Republicans in the audience stood and cheered. But it would have been hard to find a single one of them who had uttered a word of public protest when they were supposedly being trampled upon during the campaign. Nor, for that matter, had anyone heard Ford himself voice any complaints. And of course the fact remained that it was a convention of "regular Republicans" which had nominated Nixon and given him its blessing and his place on the ballot.

The Democrats seemed almost as awkward in responding to the early revelations of Watergate. Some held back from criticizing Nixon because, they claimed, they wanted to avoid making the scandal a partisan issue, though it was hard to see how anything could be more partisan than a Republican campaign committee organizing a burglary of Democratic Party headquarters.

Others privately worried that too much talk about political scandal might eventually embarrass Democrats as well as Republicans. Republicans were not alone in indulging in some of the unsavory campaign-financing practices that were spotlighted by Watergate. After the Republicans suffered serious losses in state and local elections in November 1973, Democratic National Chairman Robert Strauss, whose own handling of illegal contributions as party treasurer later came under investigation by the Watergate special prosecutor, contended that Watergate had no significant impact on the vote. Strauss's appraisal was contradicted by the admission of some GOP leaders that they had been badly hurt by the scandal. Not until the spring of 1974, when Democrats won a series of special congressional elections in traditionally strong Republican districts, did Strauss and most other members of the party hierarchy acknowledge the importance of the scandal to voters.

After the 1972 campaign, Rick Stearns, McGovern's deputy campaign manager, concluded that McGovern had been unable to arouse public indignation about Watergate because "political parties as institutions are in such disrepute that sabotage directed against a political party fails to arouse the average American." The general performance of both parties during Watergate could only serve to support that cynicism. It was not surprising that when the disclosures of Nixon's conduct provoked widespread demands for restraining the presidency, few people called for the strengthening of political parties as an instrument for curbing presidential excesses.

The one heartening aspect of the prolonged and dismal episode was that its denouement offered some support for the concept of accountability. After solemn deliberation, the House Judiciary Committee approved three articles of impeachment, Nixon was forced to resign, and Gerald Ford was sworn in as his replacement in August 1974. "Our long national nightmare is over," the new president said. "Our Constitution works; our great Republic is a government of laws and not men. Here the people rule."

His message reassured the nation, but the reassurance would have been more enduring if Ford had better understood his own words. John Coyne, a White House speech writer who had suffered through the Agnew and Nixon debacles, had like many Americans taken hope from Ford's first speech as president. On the September Sunday when Ford granted Nixon a full pardon for his Watergate crimes, Coyne heard the news on the radio and thought, as he told me later: "My God, here we go again."

CHAPTER SEVEN

1976

1. Unintended Consequences

Late in January 1976, Jimmy Carter's quest for votes in the New Hampshire primary took him to the Felton Brush factory in Manchester, where the manager, Al Burtt, greeted him wearing a smile and a "Reagan for President" button. While Carter set off on a handshaking tour of the plant, Burtt, a life-long Republican, told me that if Ronald Reagan failed to win the Republican nomination, he intended to vote for Carter in November. "Jimmy Carter is basically a businessman like me," he said.

Primary day in New Hampshire was still four weeks off. But Carter had just finished first in the precinct caucus balloting in Iowa and it was already clear that his candidacy had different meanings for different people. Indeed, Carter offered a range of identities from which voters could choose according to their own predispositions. "I'm a businessman, I'm a farmer, I'm a planner, I'm an engineer, I'm a nuclear physicist, I'm a politician and I'm a Christian," he liked to tell the crowds that gathered in New Hampshire's churches and schools.

But more important in the political climate of 1976 than all the things Carter was, or claimed to be, was what he was not. Very definitely he was not from Washington, a fact he rarely failed to point out. "It's like a wall has been built around Washington," I heard him tell voters shaken by the ordeal of Vietnam and the upheaval of Watergate. "A lot of us are outsiders. We don't see why these strange things happen in Washington."

Washington's failures and betrayals over the preceding decade had paved the way for Jimmy Carter's success. Deepened public suspicion of the national government enabled him to convert his limited experience as a one-term Governor of Georgia into a major asset.

Just as important to Carter's conquest of the party were the reforms which had been sponsored by the antiwar liberals. The rules changes opened the gate to even broader participation in the nominating process in 1976 than in 1972. But in the face of public cynicism, the liberals were unable to develop goals and programs to rally the millions of primary voters. Operating in an ideological vacuum, the reform machinery had unintended consequences. The elaborate apparatus increased the emphasis on timing and tactics, rather than on issues and experience, and was converted by Carter into an instrument for exploiting the weaknesses of his rivals.

The reforms had come under attack immediately after the 1972 election from a coalition of Democratic Party regulars, spearheaded by the AFL-CIO's Committee on Political Education (COPE). They sought to cut back the McGovern Commission's guidelines, which they blamed for the Democratic debacle in November, and to restore their former dominant role in the party and in the nominating process. On the other side were the so-called New Politics forces, a loose alliance of Kennedy, McCarthy, and McGovern partisans and some sympathetic labor leaders, who were determined to preserve the main thrust of the guidelines. The major battleground was a new delegate selection commission chaired by Barbara Mikulski, then a Baltimore city councilwoman and later a member of Congress.

The most significant efforts to change the rules were intended to limit the increased impact of the primaries. One major proposal was to make all incumbent Democratic senators, congressmen and governors automatic delegates to the national convention, free to vote for whomever they chose, regardless of the outcome of the primaries. Another revisionist idea was to increase the number of delegates that could be appointed by state party committees. Both moves would have strengthened the hand of the party regulars, and also of the AFL-CIO, whose substantial campaign contributions have always given the labor federation considerable influence with office holders and party leaders.

Both proposals were drastically watered down. Governors, senators and congressmen would be invited to the convention but denied voting privileges unless, of course, they were chosen in the same way as other delegates. Party committees would be allowed to appoint more delegates, but their choices would have to reflect the presidential preferences of primary voters.

An even more complicated wrangle ensued over proportional representation, the issue that the anti-McGovern forces had seized upon to challenge the results of McGovern's victory in the winner-take-all California primary. Despite the position they had taken then, the regulars shifted their ground. They argued that proportional representation could ruin the party by encouraging so many candidates that no one could gain a majority except by bargaining with a host of splinter groups.

Once again the reformers gave a little ground but won their main point. Presidential candidates would have to reach a threshold of at least 15 percent of the vote in caucuses and primaries to be awarded any delegates. And the reformers agreed to create a loophole which in some states made it possible for a presidential candidate to win all or nearly all, the delegates, even if each of his delegates was elected only by a plurality of the vote.

The most emotional confrontation was over quotas and affirmative action. This issue did not directly affect the choice of a presidential candidate but nevertheless held symbolic importance for both reformers and regulars. The 1972 guidelines required state parties to encourage both participation in their overall activities and representation in their convention delegations by women, young people and members of minorities—"in reasonable relationship to their presence in the population." A footnote to the guidelines specifically disavowed the use of mandatory quotas to meet these goals. But faced with the "reasonable relationship" criterion and the threat of a challenge at the convention, a number of states had resorted to procedures which, whatever they were called, amounted in effect to quotas.

The pressure to achieve demographic balance did not alter the relative delegate strength of the presidential contenders, which was based on the outcome of the primary and caucus voting. But it did greatly change the makeup of the delegations to the 1972 convention—whether they supported Humphrey, McGovern or someone else—in a way that was dramatically evident to the nation watching on television. The proportion of black and women delegates tripled compared with 1968; the number of delegates under thirty increased tenfold.

But the presence of so many new faces meant that a good many familiar ones had been excluded, in some cases for no reason except that they were neither black, young, nor female. The old-line party leadership complained bitterly that affirmative action, and the way it was enforced, was illogical and unfair. By singling out particular groups for affirmative action, the regulars contended, the reforms had alienated other groups who, not incidentally, made up a majority of the electorate.

The reformers agreed to make the footnoted ban on quotas more explicit and stringent. But they insisted that the affirmative action rules be written to refer specifically to "minority groups, native Americans, women and youth." Moreover, the new rules urged that participation in the party by these targeted groups should reflect their presence in the Democratic electorate. And a special party commission was established to review compliance with the rules by the state parties.

The attack on reform had been beaten back. Except for some relatively minor concessions, the main points of the guidelines had been maintained and in some cases even extended for 1976. But for the reformers, their successful defense proved to be a hollow triumph. In fact, the long and bitter argument over procedures which had engaged the Democratic leadership was in large part misleading and self-deceptive on both sides. Despite all their rhetoric about ideals and principles, both the regulars and the reformers had been mainly concerned with shaping the contest for the 1976 nomination to suit their respective preferences. But each side's view of the future was clouded by bitterness over the past and illusions about the present. The regulars still accused the reformers of dividing the party in 1968 and forcing McGovern down their throats in 1972. The reformers still condemned the regulars for crushing the antiwar insurgency in 1968 and for turning their backs on McGovern in 1972.

But in blaming the reformers for their loss of power and the general weakening of their party, the regulars confused cause and effect. The Democratic Party, and their hold on it, had been declining for years as broad transformations in American society changed voter interests and broke down old allegiances. The reforms had only formalized these and carried them out to their inevitable conclusion. Even if they had undercut the guidelines, the regulars lacked the influence with the voters to reestablish and maintain the control over presidential nominations which they had once enjoyed.

The reformers were equally self-deluded. Some saw the establishment of the rule changes as a good in itself, but their reverence for abstractions was not shared by most voters. Others regarded the reforms as an instrument for progress, a means to stir the enthusiasm of the electorate for a great cause.

But what cause? The protest against the Vietnam War, which had been the original rallying point for reform, had ended with the war itself. Having established no agenda beyond halting the fighting, and having never reached beyond members of the upper middle class and their offspring, the protest movement left behind no foundation for the future. To be sure, social and economic inequities abounded. But proposals to remedy them recalled the rhetoric and expectations of the Great Society, which most Americans now considered stale and overblown. Vietnam and Watergate had dramatized and enlarged the gap between politics and government, increasing cynicism and apathy about politicians and their promises. To set new goals and new directions, and arouse public enthusiasm, the reformers would have to overcome stiff resistance, and they lacked the will and imagination for the challenge. Instead they fell back on the vague hope that the procedures which they had just successfully defended would somehow work out for the best. They failed to grasp that in the absence of some fundamental purpose to drive the machinery they had developed, this apparatus itself would dominate the contest for the presidency.

Neither the original McGovern Commission guidelines nor the updated version produced by the Mikulski Commission required the states to adopt primary laws. But faced with the array of rules, some state parties concluded that primaries presented the surest and simplest road to compliance. Moreover, the reforms and the increased attention bestowed by the press on primaries had greatly increased their significance. Consequently, some states adopted primaries as the best means of sharing in the national political limelight and assuring their influence on the nominating process.

At any rate, between 1972 and 1976 seven more states joined the primary roster, bringing the total to thirty, nearly double the figure of seventeen in 1968 when Hubert Humphrey and the Democratic Party regulars beat back the challenge of the antiwar insurgents at the Chicago convention. And the proportion of Democratic convention delegates selected by primaries rose accordingly, from 40 percent in 1968 to nearly 75 percent in 1976.

Further transforming the nomination process was the new federal campaign finance law, passed in the wake of Watergate. The sleazy aspects of political fund raising had long been tolerated under the old Federal Corrupt Practices Act, but the revelations of the financing abuses in Nixon's 1972 reelection campaign had shocked the public and roused the Congress into action.

In 1968 Nixon had raised the healthy sum of $34 million to fund his campaign for nomination and election. But in 1972, when the president faced no serious challenge for renomination, his finance chairman, Maurice Stans, exploited the advantages of the incumbency to collect the unheard-of total of $52 million. About $10 million of this was in secret gifts, some of which turned out to have been illegally contributed by corporations and some of which was used to finance the felonies of Watergate.

In 1974 Congress established a new set of rigorous standards. Individual contributions to a candidate for the presidential nomination were limited to $1,000. (In 1972, Clement Stone, a Chicago insurance broker, had himself given Nixon $3 million, and individual contributions of five figures were not uncommon.) For preconvention campaigns, spending limits were imposed for each state, an overall ceiling of $10 million was set for each candidate and a system of federal subsidies was established providing matching grants for gifts of up to $250. The federal government also undertook to finance the general election campaign, giving each major party candidate in 1976 a total of $22 million.*

The new financing regulations, like the proliferation of primaries, stemmed from the best of intentions. Both changes sought to correct flaws in the political process by making the system more open and more equitable. The spread of primaries gave voters a greater chance to participate, and the Democratic Party reforms tried to give more weight to that participation. The new financial law reduced the advantage of wealthy candidates and the influence of wealthy contributors, created incentives for small givers and a federal largesse to aid the less affluent contenders.

But both sets of reforms were just extra patches on the crazy-quilt design of American politics. They tried to improve the political machinery while leaving untouched its connection with—or more accurately, its disconnection from—government. The reforms eliminated almost all that remained of the privileged influence party leaders had once exerted over the choice of a presidential nominee. That privilege had originally been justified on the grounds that party leaders could win the support of voters and influence the decisions of government. Whatever the merits of that case once had been, they no longer held water. But the reforms failed to provide any process or institution to fill the job party leaders could no longer adequately fill.

The reforms achieved an increase in quantity, but this did not, despite the hopes of the reformers, produce an improvement in quality. More candidates and more voters participated in the reformed selection process, but the

* The figures are periodically adjusted for inflation. In 1980 the overall preconvention spending limit for each candidate was $14 million; the general election subsidy was $29.4 million.

debate was no more substantive, the alternatives no clearer. The shortcomings of this change in procedures argue that, barring the invention of a substitute for political parties, the best hope for significant reform lies in constitutional change which would strengthen the parties as a link between politics and government, oblige candidates to offer voters meaningful choices and give voters reason to believe that a candidate, once elected, could be held accountable for his pledges.

The reforms in operation in the 1976 campaign worked in the opposite direction, and in some ways against each other, aggravating the existing distortions of the system. The expanded primary schedule elevated the importance of tactical and organizing skills unrelated to a candidate's experience in governing or his views on the issues. While the increase in primaries created a greater need to spend, the finance law imposed new limits on both contributions and spending. Even more than before, the campaign took on the aspect of an athletic event, a prolonged elimination tournament, in which candidates were measured against expectations created by themselves and by the press, and the results of each week's competition overshadowed all else.

Of the ten Democrats who sought their party's presidential nomination in 1976, one understood the workings of the system and the potential for manipulating its machinery better than the rest. He was Jimmy Carter, who, in December 1974, a month before the conclusion of his four-year term as governor, officially announced his candidacy. The success of George McGovern's antiwar candidacy in 1972, along with Muskie's failure in that campaign, seemed to prove that a candidate needed strong ideological appeal to win in a system dominated by primaries. But Carter's 1976 strategy was based on an opposite premise. He was able to demonstrate that a candidate without any discernible ideology could win by running harder and calculating more carefully than anyone else.

Planning for his candidacy had begun soon after the 1972 Democratic convention. The mechanistic basis of his strategy was outlined in August 1974 in a memorandum from his campaign manager, Hamilton Jordan, quoted in *Marathon*, Jules Witcover's narrative of the 1976 presidential campaign. Jordan emphasized the importance of the sequence of primaries, pointing out that the results of one primary "can have a profound and irrevocable impact on succeeding primaries and a candidate's abilities to raise funds and recruit workers." Of particular significance, Jordan advised Carter, were the early primaries, because the press took "an exaggerated interest" in these contests. More important than the results, he said, was how the results were interpreted by the press. "Handled properly, a defeat can be interpreted as a holding action and a mediocre showing as a victory."

In early 1975, while most of his rivals were still occupied with their duties in Washington, Carter began translating Jordan's plans into action. He spent 250 days on the road that year, concentrating mostly on the states where the important early contests to which Jordan had called attention would be waged. But he went to almost every state, wherever there was a chance to win a few delegates, and to get the attention of the press.

Carter's planning and his labors helped him to benefit from the continuing disarray in the Democratic Party, particularly among the liberals who had dominated the 1972 campaign. To begin with, most liberals had counted on Edward Kennedy running in 1976. But in September 1974 the senator announced that his obligations to his family would prevent him from running. Another reason, though he chose not to mention it, was the persistent memory of Chappaquiddick and the questions about that tragedy he had never really answered.

With Kennedy out of the race, more than a hundred

liberal leaders gathered in Chicago in March 1975 to plan their strategy for the campaign. But it was a futile exercise, because they had no candidate. Disheartened by McGovern's defeat, his old supporters had little enthusiasm for any of the active or prospective champions of the left. "They are going to have to show me something more before I give another six months of my life to any of these characters," Jerome Grossman of Massachusetts, an erstwhile McGovern partisan, told me.

By the time of the New Hampshire primary in February 1976, a flock of liberals had entered the race—Morris Udall, Fred Harris, R. Sargent Shriver and Birch Bayh—and in addition, a write-in campaign was mounted for Hubert Humphrey. But none of them came close to matching Kennedy's personal appeal, and none had found a viewpoint or an issue to distinguish himself from the rest. They divided the liberal vote among them, while Carter, the least liberal candidate, and most assiduous campaigner, came in first with 28 percent. It was enough, as Jordan's memo had foreseen, for the press to stamp him as the front-runner.

About all the liberals could agree on was the importance of stopping George Wallace, who was making his fourth try for the presidency. Liberals had underestimated him before and they were determined not to make that mistake again, a concern that reflected their awareness of the increased public cynicism toward government to which Wallace appealed. As it turned out, their preoccupation with Wallace worked to Carter's advantage.

In the immediate aftermath of the attempt on his life in 1972, some thought Wallace was finished as a national political leader. He was said to be ravaged by pain and so heavily sedated that he could not function as governor. In the winter of 1973, along with a small contingent of other reporters, I stood at Wallace's bedside while the governor, wrapped in a blanket which covered his catheter, talked defiantly of running again in 1976. "Maybe I can't campaign as much as I used to," he said hoarsely. "But I can still campaign." He still considered himself a bona fide Democrat and claimed a constituency in the party. "There are a lot of folks out there that believe me and will support me."

That was just what the liberals feared. By 1975 Wallace had regained some of his strength, as a result of a rigorous program of physical therapy. He was still paralyzed from the waist down and confined most of the time to a wheelchair. Yet the liberals regarded him as a formidable threat, a tacit acknowledgment of their own inability to cope with the mood of the country.

Many voters remembered Wallace not just as a defender of segregation but as a blunt-spoken enemy of the federal government and all its works, and viewed his candidacy as the best available outlet for their own frustration. After Kennedy's withdrawal, Wallace took the lead in the polling tests of Democratic presidential prospects. In October 1974 two former McGovern aides, Patrick Caddell and Robert Shrum, published an analysis of the forthcoming campaign which predicted that, given the new party rules providing for proportional representation, "Wallace—with an immovable bloc of a quarter to a third of the Democratic electorate—could come to the convention with as many as 40 percent of the delegates." Few believed that Wallace could actually be nominated. But many feared he could disrupt the convention and leave the party once again divided in the general election campaign.

In a state of near panic, the liberals sought a candidate who could defeat Wallace in the 1976 Florida primary, the scene of his greatest triumph in 1972. They soon convinced themselves that only a Southerner stood a chance of success, and just as quickly settled on Carter as their choice. If Carter was not exactly a liberal, he seemed at least no worse than a moderate conservative.

Moreover, Andrew Young, the black civil rights leader who had dealt with Carter in Georgia, assured the liberals that the former governor was "all right on race." Young himself was quite prepared to take his chances with a Southern moderate, having grown weary of Northern liberals, who he felt "know all the answers to black people's problems, but don't know any black people."

Wallace had been an important factor in Carter's calculations from the very start. Jordan had originally hoped that Wallace would decide not to run, in which case he advised Carter "to make every effort to court Wallace and gain his friendship." After reminding Carter that he had used Wallace's name effectively in bidding for segregationist votes in his 1970 campaign for governor, Jordan suggested that Carter might win Wallace's backing for the presidency "if he saw in your candidacy an extension and continuation of his earlier efforts."

Of course that plan had to be scrapped when Wallace became a candidate himself. But Carter readily switched from the role Jordan had envisaged for him as Wallace's friend and political heir to become instead Wallace's principal adversary. Unified liberal support eased the transition for him. Young had argued that the anti-Wallace forces must not divide their backing among other candidates. "Don't bring all the good guys down here and have Wallace chew them up," he counseled.

Morris Udall, like the other liberal candidates, obeyed Young's admonition and allowed Carter to fight it out in Florida with Wallace and with Henry Jackson, who was vying with Wallace to demonstrate his opposition to school busing. As he watched Carter gain momentum, though, Udall became uneasy. "If Jimmy wins down there," he warned Leonard Woodcock, whose United Auto Workers union was part of the anti-Wallace coalition, "he doesn't expect to go back to raising peanuts."

But Woodcock, Young, and their allies had only one goal at the moment—beating Wallace. If they thought about Carter's future at all, it was as a vice-presidential running mate for Hubert Humphrey. Only after Carter had triumphed in Florida did the liberals come to appreciate the extent of Carter's shrewdness and resourcefulness. By then it was too late to stop him if they had wanted to.

Carter had borrowed a good deal of Wallace's thunder. Like Wallace, he proclaimed himself an outsider and an enemy of the bureaucracy and of traditional political leaders. This was a familiar stance for Carter. He had campaigned against the local courthouse clique when he first ran for the state senate in Georgia, and against the "big shots" when he ran for governor. In Pennsylvania, where his primary victory made his nomination inevitable, Carter declared that political bosses generally opposed him "because I don't yield to them and I don't trade with them. My obligations are to the tens and hundreds of thousands of folks just like you all over the country."

Unlike Wallace, though, Carter steered away from bigotry. Indeed, his willingness to challenge Wallace directly won him a substantial body of black support. And he passionately assured them: "I would rather die than disappoint the black leaders who have come forward to say: 'I have confidence in this man.'" Moreover, Carter softened the edge of his protest against the political and governing establishment with a message of hope, buttressed by his Southern Baptist religion. "We can have a government," he promised countless times, "that's as good and honest and decent and truthful and as fair and idealistic and compassionate and as filled with love as the American people are."

Carter's theme of love and trust provided his candidacy with a measure of idealism and served as a substitute for issues and ideology. Though his staff at his Atlanta headquarters produced a flood of position papers on foreign and domestic affairs, Carter shifted his ground when he thought it convenient and made plain that he viewed such statements as of secondary importance. "I don't care how much you talk about issues or how many numbers of Senate and House bills you can name," he told a group of Washington lobbyists, "if the people don't believe that when you're in the White House you're going to do something about the problem and that they can trust what you tell them."

More even than most of his peers, he resisted committing himself to any coherent point of view. "I never characterize myself as a conservative, liberal or moderate," Carter said proudly early in his campaign, "and this is what distinguishes me from my opponents."

It was a measure of the intellectual exhaustion of the party and of the electorate that Carter was not required to make further disclosure of his beliefs or intentions. His skill at maneuvering his way through the morass of the primary schedule, and at manipulating the liberals' dread of George Wallace provided him with the early momentum Jordan had hoped for and made it possible for him to withstand a series of embarrassing defeats in the final primaries.

Like Kennedy and McGovern before him, Carter had won the nomination despite the putative leadership of the party. But these leaders, increasingly uncertain of their own role and weary of past divisions and defeats, submitted peacefully to the hero of the primaries.

Their pragmatism was reflected by the conduct of Chicago's Mayor Daley, one old-line leader who had managed to preserve his prestige and with whom Carter had dealt with accordingly. For all his oft-expressed disdain of bosses, Carter had chosen not to challenge Boss Daley's slate of delegates in the Illinois primary and had treated the venerable mayor with elaborate courtesy throughout the campaign, while Daley maintained a public stance of neutrality.

On June 8, the last primary day of the campaign, Carter came in first in Ohio but lost New Jersey and California to California governor Edmund G. (Jerry) Brown, Jr., a late starter in the contest. Carter had won only five of the final fifteen primaries, he was about three hundred delegates short of a majority, and Brown was still full of fight.

But Daley saw a chance to make up for his humiliation at the 1972 convention by appointing himself final arbiter of the 1976 campaign. In a postprimary appraisal he chose to ignore the evidence of Carter's weakness and to emphasize instead the importance of his victory in Ohio, which Daley proclaimed to be "the ball game." Carter had shown such strength, the mayor said, that "I'll cast my vote for him and there'll be a Carter victory" at the convention in New York.

With Daley's backing, and accompanying endorsements from Wallace and Henry Jackson, unity at the convention was assured and Carter could afford to joke about past bitterness. "Our bicentennial convention has been one of decorum and order without bickering," he told the delegates at Madison Square Garden. "Among Democrats that can happen only once every two hundred years."

In a prudent gesture to the liberals, who had contributed more than they intended to his victory, Carter picked as his running mate Senator Walter Mondale of Minnesota, Hubert Humphrey's protégé and one of the liberals' brightest hopes. "By choosing so devoted and unquestionable a liberal as Senator Mondale," the *New York Times* declared approvingly, "the Democratic nominee has strongly suggested that the kind of Presidency he has in mind is in the more progressive tradition of the party."

About the kind of presidency Carter intended, the *Times*'s guess was just as good as anybody else's. But no one could do more than guess. Overshadowed by the unusual Democratic harmony and optimism about regaining the White House were some unanswered questions about the party's standard-bearer. A Louis Harris poll taken shortly before the convention showed that most voters liked Carter for not being part of "the Washington establishment" and considered him "a man of integrity." Most citizens interviewed also believed that Carter had gained the nomination "without being obligated to anyone except the voters, and that is good." But as Carter prepared to confront Gerald Ford, he had yet to explain what he considered his obligations to be.

2. The Ink Blot Test

Just as Watergate helped launch Jimmy Carter's candidacy, it gave Gerald Ford a flying start in the presidency. The scandal had been for most Americans exactly what Ford called it, a prolonged "nightmare." Once it ended, the chief executive became the chief beneficiary of the overwhelming national sense of relief.

Moreover, Nixon's neurotic presence was an excellent act to follow. Ford's directness and unpretentiousness provided a refreshing contrast. The country was willing to overlook the fact that it was Nixon himself who had made Ford's presidency possible by choosing him as his successor under the Twenty-fifth Amendment, and that Ford, ignoring all the evidence to the contrary, had fiercely defended Nixon's innocence to the last. For the time being, a spirit of amity and reconciliation prevailed. AFL-CIO president George Meany visited the White House for the first time in a year. General Motors, acceding to a personal appeal from Ford to curb inflation, shaved a percentage point off a projected price increase on its new model cars. The Congressional Black Caucus came by for a friendly meeting and so did congresswomen backing the Equal Rights Amendment. As Ford noted, "Even Bella Abzug smiled."

Heartened by the response, eager "to set an activist

pace from the start," Ford moved with unexpected grace, blending modesty and candor with a touch of boldness. Pledging "communication, conciliation, compromise and cooperation" with the Congress, he told a joint session of his former colleagues: "I do not want a honeymoon with you, I want a good marriage." Risking the wrath of his party's conservative wing, and the danger of being upstaged by his own understudy, Ford chose as his vice-president Nelson A. Rockefeller, whose excessive credentials for the position won the president further accolades. "For ten years this nation has suffered from cardiac insufficiency," Hugh Sidey wrote in *Time*. "Now the heart is beginning to beat again under Jerry Ford."

Then Ford pardoned Nixon and the cheering stopped.

Ford, like Nixon, used his power irresponsibly to serve what he considered to be his own interests. With this one abrupt action, he ended his honeymoon with the country, wrecked his marriage with the Congress and ruined whatever chance he might have had to gain approval of a legislative program of his own.

The pardon weakened Ford's ability to deal with the Democrats in Congress and dissidents within his own party. Helped by his incumbency, he survived a challenge for the presidential nomination, but the struggle drained his time and energy. In the general election, since Ford had not much of a record to defend and Carter had few coherent proposals to offer, the outcome turned once again on impressions of the candidates' characters.

From the moment of his succession to the presidency, Ford had brooded privately about the legal problems Nixon had left behind him. The new chief executive worried that the controversy over custody of Nixon's tapes and papers, and the continuing investigation of Nixon's role in the Watergate cover-up, would become a prolonged distraction for him and for the country. His secretary of state, Henry Kissinger, one of the few whose counsel Ford sought, advised Ford that giving Nixon a pardon "was the quickest, really the only way to clear the center stage." Ford had already made up his own mind anyway; he wanted "to get the monkey off my back." On September 8, 1974, one month to the day after his swearing in, without any warning and with scant explanation, he announced his decision to a stunned country.

Ford had been braced for criticism but not for the storm of indignation that broke over his head, or for the resignation in protest of his press secretary, Jerry Ter Horst. On the day after he announced the pardon, the president arrived in Pittsburgh to give a speech and was greeted by demonstrators chanting "Jail Ford, jail Ford." Ford was upset that "even some members of my staff failed to understand my motives." They had described the pardon to the press as "an act of mercy." He blamed himself for not making plain to them and to the public that he wanted Nixon's problems out of the way so he could devote himself fully to "grave economic and foreign policy matters."

But this explanation, even if he had expressed it more clearly, was neither convincing nor satisfying. There was no reason why Ford had to be preoccupied with Nixon's legal problems, which for the most part could have been delegated to his staff. Nor was there conclusive evidence to believe that Nixon's fate would necessarily become a continuing obsession for most of the country. Ford's concern on this point seems to have been, as his long-time aide Robert Hartmann suggested, "a projection of his own personal paralysis within the new parameters of the presidency."

Aside from a small cadre of inveterate Nixon-haters, Americans did not appear to want their former president imprisoned for his sins. But a good many people did want, and certainly had a right to expect, some form of reckoning for what the country had endured under Nixon's leadership. This would have demanded more from Nixon in accepting the pardon than his acknowledgment "that the way I tried to deal with Watergate was the wrong way." And just as important, the country required something more illuminating from Ford than his cryptic reference to Watergate as "an American tragedy in which we all have played a part."

Ford was not obliged to condemn Nixon personally. But since he had chosen to excuse him from further punishment, the new president did have a responsibility to explain his own actions, as well as Nixon's behavior, in terms of the fundamental weaknesses of the political system which had contributed to Nixon's downfall. This would by no means have justified Nixon's conduct. But such an explanation might have added to public understanding of the flaws and frustrations of the presidency, and perhaps even have been a first step toward meaningful reform. By failing even to attempt this, Ford deprived the long confrontation with Nixon of much of its meaning, increased cynicism toward politics and government, and crippled his presidency.

As an unelected president, Ford had only whatever public good will he could muster by his performance in office to buttress him against the Congress. A week after the pardon, Ford's standing in the Gallup Poll dropped more than twenty points. The new president's support was shattered, and his partisan and institutional adversaries in the legislature were quick to take advantage.

The Democratic-controlled Congress had been in an aggressive mood even before Ford took office, in delayed reaction to the presidential overreaching of Johnson and Nixon. Madison's principle of ambition counteracting ambition was put into practice with, literally, a vengeance in international affairs, where both Johnson and Nixon had staked out broad claims for the unhindered exercise of presidential power. In 1973, as Nixon struggled to deal with Watergate, the newly aroused legislators cut off funds for further bombing of Indochina and adopted the war-powers resolution. This required congressional consultation before U.S. troops were committed and congressional approval for any venture lasting more than sixty days. In the wake of the pardon, the congressional offensive was renewed against Ford. Congress slashed Ford's proposal for aid to South Vietnam and imposed an embargo on arms shipments to Turkey because of the Turkish invasion of Cyprus.

Ford protested bitterly, but he lacked the public support to control the Congress. Besides, he had his hands full on the domestic front. At first inflation seemed the principal problem. But even as Ford struggled to cope with rising prices, they were overshadowed by soaring unemployment, presaging the worst economic decline since the Great Depression.

In the 1974 congressional elections—with Watergate, the Nixon pardon, and the economy on the voters' minds —the Republicans lost forty-six seats in the House, one short of the big gain they had made in 1966, and four seats in the Senate. Despite the size of the new Democratic majorities in both houses, they were not quite sufficient to assure the "veto proof" Congress that some party leaders had called for. The veto became the major weapon of Ford's presidency, used mostly to hold down federal spending. He rejected legislation at a greater rate than any chief executive since Harry Truman, who had to contend with the much maligned Republican-controlled 80th Congress. Ford's sixty-six vetoes, of which only twelve were overridden, throttled Democratic policy-making efforts on a broad range of issues. The Democrats retaliated by rejecting or revising most of Ford's major initiatives. The great national problems of energy, the cities, the welfare system and the tax system went untended as the government languished in deadlock.

The shift in power away from the presidency was dramatized in the spring of 1975, two years after the U.S.

military withdrawal from Indochina, when North Vietnam launched a major offensive and South Vietnamese resistance crumbled. Ford pleaded with Congress to increase aid for the regime that the United States had tried to preserve for the better part of two decades. But the leaders of his own party defied him. "I will give you large sums for evacuation but not one nickel for military aid," Jacob Javits of New York, senior Republican on the Senate Foreign Relations Committee, told Ford. The president had no choice but to pull out the remaining Americans in the country, along with a few thousand Vietnamese, and watch Nixon's "peace with honor" disintegrate into defeat.

But even Watergate and Vietnam could not alter the political system's artificial values or prevent the consequent misuses of power. The events that followed the seizure of the American merchant ship S.S. *Mayagüez* in May 1975 demonstrated that in an international crisis the public still rallied around the flag and the president, even if the president had helped to create the crisis.

The capture of the *Mayagüez* by Cambodian patrol boats gave Ford an opportunity to respond to the problems of declining U.S. prestige abroad and his own sagging standing at home. The ship was taken in what the United States regarded as international waters, although the Cambodians claimed jurisdiction. At any rate, Ford told Kissinger to try to get the ship and its forty-man crew back through diplomatic channels. Meanwhile, though, Kissinger argued that unless the United States responded firmly to the challenge, "it would be a serious blow to our prestige around the world." Without waiting to learn the outcome of the diplomatic overtures or to determine the motives or intentions of the Cambodians, Ford ordered a series of air strikes against the Cambodian mainland and a Marine assault on an offshore island where it was incorrectly believed the *Mayagüez* crew was imprisoned. While the Marines were still battling stiff Cambodian resistance, the *Mayagüez* was recovered at sea and her crew turned up on a fishing vessel, safe and sound. The incident cost the lives of thirty-eight Marines.

A study by the General Accounting Office, which the Ford administration tried to suppress, later pointed out that the Cambodians had decided to release the ship and her crew before Ford sent in the bombers and the Marines. Ford had acted with undue haste, the report concluded, and used excessive force.

But at the time of the event, Ford and his associates regarded it as the high point of his presidency. To Ford it seemed as if "all of a sudden the gloomy national mood began to fade. Many people's faith in their country was restored and my standing in the polls shot up 11 points." Hartmann felt that "for the first time since the pardon," Ford "was perceived as the kind of President people wanted." In the judgment of Senator Goldwater, seasoned by years of political trial and error, "It was the kind of decision it takes a strong man to make. This one act of Ford could be the act that elects him."

Indeed, the *Mayagüez* episode might have been politically decisive if the presidential election had been held in June of 1975. But the ship's return itself could not maintain Ford's new prestige for long, particularly in the face of the bleak economic figures. Tension and frustration with the Congress continued. And along with the opposition of the Democrats on Capitol Hill, Ford had to face a serious threat within his own party.

Early in 1975, Republican conservatives began rallying around Ronald Reagan and planning to challenge Ford for the nomination. Right-wing leaders had been restless under Nixon, whose decisions to impose wage and price controls and improve relations with the Communist regime in China they regarded as heresies. To demonstrate the conservative discontent, Ohio congressman John Ashbrook entered the 1972 primaries, but never became a serious challenger.

But Nixon had been an elected incumbent. Ford was only an appointee, and his presidency was floundering. Moreover, the dissidents were spurred on by changes in the nominating system. The 1972 GOP convention had approved a package of reforms proposed by the party's Delegate and Organizations Committee, including a ban on automatic appointment of party leaders and office holders as delegates. But the most significant factor was the continued proliferation of primaries. Though this increase in part resulted from Democratic pressure on state legislatures, Republicans generally had no choice but to adjust. The thirty primaries in 1976 would select about two-thirds of the delegates to the Republican National Convention, offering the prospect of a more open competition than any in the recent Republican past. As John Sears, the former Nixon strategist whom Reagan had retained as an adviser, told me in the fall of 1975: "There are going to be an awful lot of delegates up for grabs next year."

To fire up their troops for the battle, conservatives assembled a list of grievances against the president. He had signed the Helsinki Accords recognizing Soviet control of Eastern Europe. He was negotiating a treaty giving control of the Panama Canal Zone to Panama. He had selected the *bête noire* of the right wing, Nelson Rockefeller, as his vice-president. And his wife, Betty, had indicated in a television interview that she would not find it intolerable if her eighteen-year-old daughter, Susan, decided to have an affair.

More important, though, than any or all of these complaints was the personal appeal of the conservative champion, Ronald Reagan. Not since Goldwater had any politician been able to arouse conservative emotions to such a fever pitch. In February 1975, when some con-

servatives were talking of deserting the GOP in favor of
starting a right-wing third party, Reagan told them that
what was needed, instead of a third party, was "a new
and revitalized second party, raising a banner of no pale
pastels but bold colors which makes it unmistakably clear
where we stand on all of the issues troubling the people."

But once he had announced his candidacy, in November 1975, Reagan had trouble making clear the distinction between where he stood and where Ford stood. The
problem was that the actual differences were slight.
While Reagan reminded conservatives of Goldwater, it
was difficult for him to make Ford, who all his life had
been the epitome of Midwestern conservatism, appear
like Rockefeller. Reagan's first effort to distinguish his
views from the president's turned into a fiasco. Without
considering its implications beforehand, he unveiled a
plan for turning back $90 billion worth of federal pro-
grams to the states. Then during the New Hampshire
primary campaign, he was forced continually to try to
explain how the states could afford these services without
raising taxes.

In fact, for all of Reagan's brave talk about bold colors, the decisive factors in the Republican campaign for
the nomination, as in the Democratic contest, were unrelated to issues. Instead, the battle between Reagan and
Ford turned on personality, tactics, and the power of
Ford's incumbency.

Reagan strategists had calculated that Ford could not
command the loyalty traditionally accorded to an incumbent. But they failed to take into account the prestige a president possesses by virtue of his office, regardless of how he gained it. Right after Ford, with all his
presidential regalia, had campaigned in Florida, David
Keene, Reagan's manager in that primary state, told me:
"We've just been bombed out by *Air Force One*. Ford
was all over the front page and we couldn't get a word in
the paper for our guy."

As Ford himself later acknowledged, he could not match Reagan's rhetoric. "I could, however," he added, "use my incumbency and on a trip to Florida, February 13, I decided to take full advantage of it." And so he did, at every stop on his itinerary. Orlando, he announced, would be the site of the 1978 International Chamber of Commerce Convention, bringing $1 million into the local economy. His new budget proposals would bring Florida an additional $1.25 billion in revenue sharing, he promised. And the city of Big Pines would get a new Veterans Administration hospital with modern facilities and three hundred more beds.

After losing the opening primaries in New Hampshire, Florida, and Illinois to Ford, Reagan tried to salvage his candidacy by accusing the president of letting the Russians push him around. The reason for the foreign-policy attack, besides diverting attention from Reagan's $90 billion misunderstanding, was to highlight what Reagan's pollster, Richard Wirthlin, called "the issue of Ford's leadership style" and to depict Reagan as "stronger, more competent and more decisive."

Having served the purpose of sustaining Reagan's candidacy through the primaries, the foreign-policy issue was subordinated at the Republican convention in Kansas City. Instead of mounting an ideological challenge to the president, Reagan's strategists pinned their hopes for the nomination on a gimmick. Shortly before the convention, Reagan had announced that if nominated he would choose Pennsylvania senator Richard Schweiker, a leading Republican liberal, as his running mate. The move was intended to throw Ford's forces off balance and to demonstrate that Reagan was pragmatic and electable; instead, it simply enraged many of Reagan's conservative admirers. Nevertheless, Reagan's strategists tried to persuade the convention delegates to adopt a new rule that would have forced Ford also to declare his preference for a running mate in advance of the roll call for the presidential nomination. The divided condition of the party and the weakness of Ford's support were reflected in the judgment shared by Ford and Reagan strategists that whoever the president selected would cost him backing for his nomination.

As it turned out, though, Ford's supporters defeated the proposed rule change and that ended Reagan's second bid for the presidency. Ford ultimately chose Senator Robert Dole of Kansas, the former Republican national chairman, as his running mate, mainly because Reagan did not object to him.

The choice of Dole for vice-president did not significantly lessen the resentment of Ford by conservative Republicans, which weakened his chances of retaining the presidency. Moreover, after eight years of Republican rule, the country showed every sign of wanting a change. Nevertheless, Ford's strategists, after analyzing their voter-opinion surveys, concluded they had reason for hope. Carter's advantage seemed not to be based on anything substantive that Ford had done, or that Carter had pledged to do, but rather on contrasting impressions of the two candidates' characters. Robert Teeter, Ford's pollster, "could not find one issue that was statistically significant in predicting the Presidential vote of any large group of voters; it was almost entirely a candidate perception election." Perceptions of personality can be altered more readily than concerns about issues, Ford's planners reasoned. Moreover, they knew that in a competition based on image, a president usually enjoys an advantage simply because he is president.

Accordingly, it was decided that Ford should stick close to the Oval Office and the White House Rose Garden. Polls taken during the primaries convinced Teeter that "the President simply did better in communicating with the voters when he was perceived as the President, not as a candidate for President."

Besides allowing Ford to exploit the prestige of his office and helping to protect him from damaging himself, the "Rose Garden strategy" offered the advantage of focusing attention on his challenger. Once Carter had become the candidate of the Democratic Party, many voters were no longer satisfied with the hazy impressions of good intentions that had helped carry Carter to the nomination. Carter was regarded as a more decisive leader than Ford, according to Carter's pollster Patrick Caddell. But, Caddell said, "The problem was that people weren't sure what he would lead toward."

Nor, for that matter, was Carter himself. He seemed caught in a series of dilemmas between conflicting political imperatives and his own still unresolved view of himself as a candidate and a president. Sensitive to the need for support of blacks, labor and other traditional Democratic constituencies, he had given them a liberal platform at the convention, even if he did not entirely endorse it himself, and also given them Mondale as his running mate. Hoping to revive the traditional New Deal coalition, he had formally launched his campaign against Ford from FDR's old retreat in Warm Springs, Georgia. And everywhere he went he invoked the names of Roosevelt, Truman, Kennedy and Johnson.

But Carter, as Caddell noted, "had a hard time assimilating the traditional Northern Democratic rhetoric, whether it was about the economy or about the party." And the candidate worried that intoning the old liberal battle cries would cost him support among conservatives in the South and elsewhere. By mid-September, as I traveled with Carter through the Deep South, he sounded to me less like FDR's legatee and more like Ford or even Reagan. Warmly introduced by George Wallace to a gathering of Birmingham business leaders, Carter sought to assure them of his dedication to fiscal prudence. "I know what it means to meet a payroll," he said. "I never had known an unbalanced budget in my business or my farm or as governor of Georgia." He could hardly praise the businessmen enough. They were, he said, "just as honest as any farmer, probably as any preacher. It's a cheap shot for elected public officials to blame the business community for the economic, social and political problems of our country."

As the campaign continued, so did Carter's public contortions. For a while he hammered away at Ford for vetoing too many bills passed by the Democratic Congress. Then he dropped that argument because, he concluded, it would not do well for an outsider like himself to be perceived as a defender of the Congress. "Because people kept saying that no one knew who Carter was," his press secretary, Jody Powell, observed, "there were repeated and painful attempts by us to explain who this man really was, sometimes to the point of absurdity."

His clumsiest and most bizarre effort at self-definition was his interview with *Playboy* in which he sought to alleviate apprehensions about his fundamentalist religious beliefs. To prove that he was a regular fellow, Carter volunteered the information that "I've looked on a lot of women with lust. I've committed adultery in my heart many times," and added: "But I don't think I would ever take on the frame of mind that Nixon or Johnson did, lying, cheating or distorting the truth."

The publication of the interview in September, while Carter was in the midst of trying to reconcile his liberal supporters with his conservative inclinations, prompted a stream of mildly prurient wisecracks and obliged Carter to apologize to Lady Bird Johnson for defaming her husband. More important, though, the nature of Carter's gratuitous remarks, and the racy magazine he had chosen as a forum, added to misgivings about his character and judgment.

With Carter's lead in the polls dwindling as he thrashed about, Ford came to his rescue. During the second of three televised debates between the two candidates, the president, trying to defend the Helsinki agreement, contended: "There is no Soviet domination of Eastern Europe and there never will be under a Ford Administration."

This was a preposterous statement, which Ford knew as well as anyone, having visited Eastern Europe. The president meant to say he did not *want* the Soviets to dominate Eastern Europe. But it took Ford five days to admit he had misspoken. Meanwhile, his gaffe remained the focus of public attention and of Carter's rhetoric. "It's time we had a President who understands the facts about Eastern Europe and who will speak up for freedom throughout the world," the challenger declared.

No one believed that Ford's comments on Eastern Europe really reflected his view of Soviet power, any more than Carter's ramblings on God and lust were thought to indicate his attitude toward the separation of church and state. Both took on significance because of the preoccupation of the public and the press with personality. The campaign had become a sort of ink blot test in which the responses of the candidates were analyzed for clues to their character and thus supposedly to their ability to govern. The questions that seemed to overshadow all else that fall were whether Carter was shifty or simply weird, and whether Ford, as Lyndon Johnson had suggested, suffered from the effects of playing football without a helmet.

This Rorschach effect was heightened by the candidates' superficial treatment of issues. Carter called the tax system and also the welfare system "a disgrace to the human race" but did not explain how he would reform either of them and keep his promise to balance the budget, too. Though he repeatedly vowed to reduce the size of the bureaucracy, the challenger declined to say which agencies he would dispense with.

Ford, like Carter, was dead set against inflation and unemployment. But he did not say how he would create more jobs and keep *his* promise to balance the budget.

And in pledging to curb the rise in the cost of living, neither Ford nor Carter referred to the reality of soaring oil prices imposed by OPEC.

The quality of the campaign became a butt for comedians. Johnny Carson quipped that the country faced a choice between "fear of the known and fear of the unknown." In the end, the voters decided to take a chance on the unknown, but not by much. Carter's big lead in the polls had boiled down to a 3 percent advantage in the popular vote. His own Southland pulled him through. He carried ten of the eleven states of the Old Confederacy— all but Virginia—the broadest Southern sweep of any Democratic nominee since Roosevelt. But elsewhere he managed to gain only pieces of the support that had once made up the old New Deal coalition. And voter turnout declined once again, to 54.3 percent from 55.5 percent in 1972 and 62.8 percent in 1960.

His satisfaction with his victory diminished somewhat by the disappointing margin, Carter blamed the closeness of the result on his own failings as a candidate and promised his supporters: "I'll make up for that as President." But he did not elaborate on what he thought his shortcomings had been. Nor did he seem any more prepared to account to his party and to the public as president than he had been as a candidate.

CHAPTER EIGHT

1980

1. "No Strings on Me"

Jimmy Carter thought of the government which the voters had entrusted to his leadership for four years mainly as a mechanical apparatus composed of agencies and procedures. Defects could be remedied, he believed, by rearranging the machinery. Convinced of his own leadership abilities, he regarded Vietnam and Watergate as aberrations, attributable mainly to the deficiencies of Richard Nixon and Lyndon Johnson, to their "lying, cheating or distorting the truth."

However, the public had been badly shaken by these events and did not share Carter's confidence. "Americans have no real expectation that government is willing or able to solve the country's problems," Patrick Caddell warned him a few weeks before his inauguration, in a lengthy memorandum on the public mood and political strategy. "Voters are no longer willing to grant authority to leadership; no longer are willing to follow merely because the government suggests they do so."

Mindful of Carter's distaste for the give and take of politics, and his faith in procedural reforms, Caddell called attention to the tendency of reformers to try to establish " 'good government' by divorcing government and politics. The result of this divorce," Caddell wrote, "is too often that the voters perceive that they unfortunately got a different person from the man they elected," a perception which "leads to disappointing the voters and eventual political disaster."

But this advice had little impact on Carter, for his presidency had been produced by the gap between politics and government. He regarded politics and government as separate fields of endeavor, related only in the fact that the former was the means of gaining access to the latter. By electing him president, Carter believed the voters had made him trustee over their affairs. It was true that many groups had contributed to his success and felt they had a stake in his presidency, but Carter took a limited view of the principle of accountability. "I feel deeply obligated to people but I'll do what I think is best for the country," he said right after his election. "There are no strings on me."

Carter's values and beliefs had been shaped mainly by his training as an engineer and his success in business, and he approached the presidency as if it were a large-scale construction project or commercial enterprise. He believed that the key to success lay in the firm application of the disciplines of good management. "Many state and local governments have devised clear and simple organizational structures, effective and incisive budgeting techniques, comprehensive planning procedures and ready access to the core of government by its own private citizens," he had written in *Why Not the Best?* These procedures, he insisted, "can and will work in Washington."

In Carter's judgment the major goals he had set for his presidency—establishing an energy policy, reforming the tax and welfare systems—could all be attained with the aid of such methodical guidelines. During the campaign, he spoke glowingly of the economies that would result from zero-based budgeting and the efficiencies that would be achieved from long-range planning. Foreign-policy disputes also would be ironed out, he predicted, by "my normal, careful, methodical scientific or planning approach to longer-range policies."

But the problem with the framework of procedures upon which Carter rested such high hopes was that it lacked any ideological foundation. Carter had claimed during the campaign to have forged a unique covenant with the electorate, "a very intense and very personal and very intimate thing." But this special relationship was not based on a mutually understood set of goals and commitments. Rather it derived from Carter's faith in his own wisdom and integrity and his confidence that the citizenry, able to discern these virtues, would follow his lead in whatever course he decided to take.

As his former speech writer, James Fallows, wrote in an incisive memoir in *The Atlantic*, Carter did not provide "an object for loyalty larger than himself." What interested the president most, Fallows came to realize, was "not what he proposed to do, but who he was. Like Marshal Pétain after the fall of France, he had offered his person to the nation."

In personalizing his presidency, Carter was following what we have seen to be the pattern of his predecessors, and he tried to use the prestige of his office in some of the same ways they had to command attention and support. But his own makeup limited his effectiveness.

Carter lacked the compelling manner and appearance which had helped John Kennedy carve out the presidency in his own image. Nor could he even come close to matching Kennedy as an orator. Carter's voice was weak, his cadences irregular and distracting, and his taste for rhetoric ran to bare and bloodless phrases. After Carter's first year in the White House, Milton Gwirtzman, who had written campaign speeches for him and for other prominent Democrats, told me in exasperation: "If Carter had given FDR's 'the only thing we have to fear is fear itself' speech, the Depression would still be going on."

Lyndon Johnson, no spellbinder as a public speaker himself, had built support for his personal goals by dealing with leaders of interest groups, alternately persuading and bullying, but always ready to strike a bargain. Carter, however, scorned interest groups and their leaders. During his campaign he liked to boast: "I owe the special interests nothing, I owe the people everything," and his attitude did not change when he became president.

To gain the support of the people, or at least their attention, Carter relied heavily during the first months of his presidency on gestures and symbols. The imagery was intended to demonstrate that Carter was an open and unpretentious man, whose election marked a break with the Washington establishment he had campaigned against. On Inauguration Day, after delivering a lackluster address, Carter walked home from the Capitol to the White House, hand in hand with the First Lady and their daughter, Amy, to the delight of the crowds lining Pennsylvania Avenue. He deprived his senior aides of the chauffeured limousines which had long been a perquisite of their positions and stripped their offices of television sets. He was photographed lounging in the White House in blue jeans and delivered his first televised address to the nation wearing a cardigan sweater instead of a suit coat.

The leveling approach extended to the rest of the executive branch, too. Cabinet officers were firmly instructed to fly coach instead of first-class. To cut down on government regulations, and to clear up their meaning, Carter decreed that each new ruling would have to be signed by its author and read word for word by the head of the agency which promulgated it.

Inevitably, the heavy dose of imagery provoked criticism that Carter was relying on style rather than substance. Caddell had advised him not to worry about such complaints. The symbolism was needed, Caddell maintained, to "buy time" with an uneasy public until substantial progress could be made in dealing with energy, the economy and other pressing concerns.

But advances on these fronts would have to depend on the cooperation of Congress, the traditional institutional adversary of the chief executive, and here Carter ran into serious difficulties. Some were not of his making. The combative mood of the lawmakers, which had manifested itself under Nixon and Ford, continued with Carter's arrival, and in a way the friction was increased by the presence of a Democrat in the White House. A backlog of legislative proposals had built up as a result of Ford's vetoes. Now the Democratic lawmakers were impatient for action. Moreover, the Democrats in Congress were not used to giving the chief executive a helping hand. "For eight years the Democratic Party in Congress has been the Democratic Party of the nation," an aide to one Democratic senator reminded me. "Its position has been one of reflex opposition. Now suddenly the Democrats are forced to operate as the majority party."

The adjustment process was complicated by a number of recent reforms in the procedures of the House of Representatives which weakened the traditional authority of the party leadership and the committee chairmen. These changes undermined the already weak party discipline and made it harder than ever to assemble dependable majorities for administration programs.

And Carter added to the problem. From the start Congress had been suspicious of him because of his antiestablishment rhetoric as a candidate and his implied threats to go over their heads to their constituents if they balked at his initiatives. Carter had made plain his distaste for compromise and for bargaining. "I've always been inclined on a matter of principle or importance not to compromise unless it's absolutely necessary," he said during the campaign. Nor was he inclined "to twist arms or force people to vote different from what they thought." But he added pointedly: "There is a final forum that even transcends the inclination of the legislative body. That's the people themselves."

Lawmakers soon found confirmation for their misgivings about the new president in his seeming unconcern with their political needs and prerogatives. Some of Carter's offenses were relatively minor. The legislators grumbled that the White House often failed to consult or sometimes even inform them about federal appointments in their states and districts. More serious was Carter's abrupt announcement, a month after his inauguration, that he planned to eliminate about $5 billion in funding for federal water projects scattered around the country. The president considered these projects to be expensive boondoggles which offended his sense of order and economy. But to the legislators whose constituents would benefit from the dams and reservoirs, they represented the fruits of years of strenuous haggling with the bureaucracy and their own colleagues.

The congressional resentment of Carter's action reflected the fact that the political system works against the development of common policy goals for the legislature and the president. This was particularly true under President Carter because of his studied remoteness from his party. Since there was little to hold the Democratic lawmakers and the Democratic president together, it did not take much to drive them apart.

Once again, under Madison's grand design, ambition counteracted ambition. The outraged sponsors of the projects subtly and not so subtly threatened to take revenge on Carter's other legislative measures, and the president was ultimately forced to compromise. But the furor left a residue of hard feelings which added to the obstacles confronting the broader proposals of Carter's legislative program.

That program was destined for trouble in any case. It had been assembled around the vague and sometimes contradictory promises Carter had made during the campaign, as he tried to appeal to an ill-assorted group of constituencies. The package of promises, like his candidacy, lacked definition and cohesion. But the president, convinced of the correctness of his goals and impatient to make his mark against the Washington establishment, was determined to press ahead on all fronts.

Energy was his first priority. But the nature of the problem dictated that any serious attempt at a solution would demand considerable sacrifices. The public, still skeptical about the reality of the energy crisis, had to be convinced of the need for sacrifice and persuaded that the hardships would be distributed equitably. Moreover, the plans for energy had to be tailored to match the administration's overall economic policy. All this would have required time and widespread consultation in the government and among the interest groups concerned.

But one of the characteristics of the personalized presidency is the failure to take into account the significance of political forces and institutions beyond the Oval Office. Carter arbitrarily established a deadline ninety days from his inauguration for the launching of his energy program, a timetable which offered little opportunity for the necessary groundwork. Moreover, on Carter's instructions, his energy adviser, James Schlesinger, drafted the program in strictest secrecy, without informing or consulting the public, the Congress or other high officials in the administration.

Schlesinger met Carter's deadline. But the program inevitably came under attack from all sides and found few supporters outside the White House. By the time Congress finished trimming back Carter's far-reaching plans for tax increases and tax credits, they were hard to recognize as the ambitious blueprint which Carter had earnestly introduced, in a phrase borrowed from William James, as "the moral equivalent of war."

The fate of Carter's hopes for welfare reform illustrated the difficulties of reconciling Carter's campaign promises with each other, as well as with political realities. Welfare reform had been one of the strongest commitments Carter had made as a candidate. But he had been just as vehement on the stump in pledging to balance the federal budget. Carter, who had never spelled out his welfare reform proposals in the campaign, instructed Joseph Califano, the former aide to Lyndon Johnson who had become the Secretary of Health, Education, and Welfare, to create an entirely new program. He added the caveat that the new plan should cost no more than the existing system. But after weeks of study Califano reported back that no significant reform could be implemented without spending billions more than the current outlays.

Carter rapidly lost enthusiasm for the idea. "We don't have $5 to $10 billion to put in a new system," he told Califano. "Why don't we just say the hell with it?" Ultimately the administration did submit a watered-down version of welfare reform to the Congress. But lacking strong backing from the White House, the proposal succumbed to the inevitable crossfire from interest groups, the bureaucracy and the legislators.

Tax reform, another major promise in Carter's standard campaign speech, was another victim of the internal contradictions and overlap of Carter's program. By the time the president submitted his long-heralded plan to eliminate such loopholes and preferences as entertainment deductions and the favorable rate for capital gains, he had already irritated lawmakers handling tax legislation by first promoting and then abruptly withdrawing a proposal for a fifty-dollar tax rebate to spur the economy. Moreover, Carter had blurred the argument against tax loopholes, which were the main target of his tax reform plan. His own energy program had proposed new loopholes in the form of tax credits and rebates to encourage conservation and ease economic burdens. Under pressure from business lobbyists, Congress brushed aside Carter's proposals for basic tax reform and approved a tax cut skewed to favor upper-income taxpayers. Instead of eliminating the loophole for capital gains, the new law enlarged it.

Paralleling and contributing to Carter's difficulties with Congress were the president's problems with traditional Democratic constituency groups. Like the Democrats in Congress, many leaders of these groups had been dubious about Carter during the campaign. But they had submerged their doubts in wishful interpretations of his rhetoric as a candidate. Now they found it hard to live with his performance as president.

The discontent ran across the Democratic board. Labor leaders grumbled about the inadequacy of his minimum-wage proposals. Jews worried that the administration's "evenhanded" Middle East policies would injure Israel. Blacks complained about Carter's lack of enthusiasm for spending on social programs.

But Carter, with his mind fixed on achieving his own goals by his own means, had no patience with such criticism. In July 1977 Vernon Jordan, director of the Urban League, publicly chided the administration for sluggishness in aiding the cities and the unemployed. Carter shot back that he had "no apologies to make." More ominously, he warned that criticism of his policies was "damaging to the hopes and aspirations of poor people."

In his political strategy memo, Caddell had predicted that the president would run into such difficulties with Democratic interest groups, many of whom, he noted, had mixed feelings about the new president. To offset their anticipated opposition, Caddell recommended that the president form a new coalition, based on an ideological approach that would attract "better educated white collar people" to the Democratic fold, while still preserving the loyalty of traditional party supporters.

But Carter did not think in terms of ideology and coalitions. After he had been president for a hundred days, I had the chance to talk to him in the White House and ask him about Caddell's prescription.

"I have a coalition of what might generically be called consumers," Carter said. "When it comes down to a choice between what's good for consumers and good for manufacturers, my natural inclination is to favor what's good for customers."

Since the category of consumers took in nearly everyone in the country, I asked Carter what new ideology he had in mind to attract such a wide range of voters.

The president referred me to his speeches, a collection of which was about to be published. "There's an amazing consistency in my speeches, in what I emphasize as being important. I'd say basic morality is there—not that I'm better than other people. It's hard for me to describe," he added, "because it's part of my consciousness."

The closest Carter came to defining his beliefs during our hour-long conversation in his office was his reference to "basic morality." For Carter moralism was a substitute for ideology. This was a president who viewed the political struggle not as a competition between groups with varying claims on public policy, but as a conflict between good and evil in which he rarely, if ever, doubted on which side he was positioned. That a president could come to power with nothing more substantive as an intellectual touchstone testified to the barrenness of the political system.

"Not that I'm better than other people," Carter had made a point of interjecting during our talk. In fact, an important part of his appeal, first as a candidate and then in his early days as president, derived from the impression, which he fostered, that he was a good deal better, in his fealty to truth and rectitude, than other politicians,

218 / NONE OF THE ABOVE

particularly some of his recent predecessors in the White House. But this reputation for morality, and the favorable aura it created, proved to be perishable.

It did not survive Carter's response to the disclosures during the first summer of his presidency of the financial finagling of Bert Lance, his close friend and former banker and his director of the Office of Management and Budget. "Bert, I'm proud of you," Carter publicly declared, despite the overdrafts and other irregularities that studded Lance's record as a freewheeling Georgia banker. His support for Lance was impossible to square with the president's populist denunciations of "big shots" and his pious pledges to elevate ethical behavior in public life. When Lance was forced to quit, his friends in the White House complained that he had been judged by an artificial standard. Whether this was true or not, it was a standard that Carter himself had established.

With Lance's resignation in September 1977—he was later indicted but ultimately acquitted on criminal charges—the public controversy over his affairs subsided. But the damage to Carter was enduring. Democratic pollster Peter Hart told me at the time that the Lance case was "the turning point in Carter's Presidency." Vice-President Mondale privately agreed. "It made people realize that we were no different than anyone else," he later acknowledged to a group of reporters.

The impact of the Lance case demonstrated how greatly Carter leaned on the shaky pillars of character and symbolism. If he was no different from anyone else, as the Lance case made it seem, then the public would judge him like anyone else in the White House, on his ability to deal with the nation's problems. This would have been a tough test for anyone, and it was particularly difficult for Carter because he had made great claims about what he could accomplish and was unwilling to rearrange his goals to adjust to political realities.

As his proposals on energy, welfare, taxes, and other issues were being chopped up on Capitol Hill, Carter's approval rating in the public opinion polls went into decline. In his frustrations with domestic problems he concentrated more of his time and energies on foreign affairs —his crusade for human rights, strategic arms negotiations with the Soviets, ratification of the Panama Canal treaty, and, particularly, the tensions in the Middle East. His success in helping to bring about a peace treaty between Israel and Egypt after the Camp David meetings in the fall of 1978 was hailed on all sides and for a time lifted his prestige.

But his standings in the polls soon began falling again under the steady pressure of inflation and energy shortages. Carter's enthusiasm for dealing with these problems had long since faded. As he met with his advisers to discuss inflation solutions late in 1978, James Fallows wrote, Carter appeared "bored and impatient" with the subject and "plainly eager to return to shaping international history."

But he could not escape domestic problems for long. The president was in Tokyo for an economic summit conference in the summer of 1979 when a severe gasoline shortage, in the midst of skyrocketing inflation, aggravated the public's discontent. The president's chief domestic policy adviser, Stuart Eizenstat, sent Carter a grim memorandum: "In many respects this would appear to be the worst of times. I do not need to detail for you the political damage we are suffering."

Returning to Washington, Carter announced plans for an address on energy, then changed his mind in favor of a broader theme. After conferring for six days at Camp David with about a hundred prominent citizens, Carter made his broader speech. He told Americans they were suffering "a crisis of confidence" and "a malaise of the spirit" and said: "I realize more than ever that as President I need your help." He also declared that "The gap between our citizens and our government has never been so wide." This had been a familiar theme of his campaign but, as critics were quick to point out, after three years as president, Carter could no longer escape blame for this estrangement.

Whatever benefits Carter might have gained from this melodramatic moment were wiped out when immediately after the speech he demanded the resignation of all the high officials in his administration and then fired four cabinet members for not being sufficiently loyal. Instead of using the opportunity of the energy crisis to focus attention on the nation's problems, Carter had called attention to his own difficulties and his own weaknesses. His words and actions made clear that the management techniques he had relied on had failed, that his personal bond with the voters had withered and that he was vulnerable to a challenge for the office he held.

2. "Against the Wind"

On a fine October day in 1978, Edward Kennedy flew to West Virginia to campaign for his Democratic Senate colleague Jennings Randolph, who was being hard pressed for reelection. Kennedy was riding high in the public opinion polls then, and though he insisted he had no plans to seek the presidency in 1980, this did not deter speculation that ultimately he would do just that.

His trip culminated that evening in a torchlight parade and an open-air rally. In a rousing speech, Kennedy heaped praise upon the venerable Randolph and recalled his brother John's momentous victory in the 1960 West Virginia primary. "No member of my family has ever felt a stranger in the hills and the hollows, the mines and the cities of West Virginia," Kennedy declared. "My brothers came here, so did my sisters and my mother. It's good to be home again."

The West Virginians shouted their approval, and after the senator was finished they surged around the speaker's platform. Kennedy worked the crowd for a while and then, with a grin, urged me to help him out. "It's easy," he said. "All you have to do is shake their hands and wave at them and they elect you president."

But as Kennedy would learn a year later, the road to the White House was by no means that easy. His challenge to President Carter was engulfed in a campaign which, because of a combination of tactics and circumstances, demonstrated the distortions of the political system at very nearly their worst.

In part this was Kennedy's own fault. He failed, until it was too late, to offer the Democratic electorate a clear set of alternatives to Carter's policies, choosing instead to rely on his personal strengths as a leader. As it turned out, though, Kennedy had serious liabilities in a contest of personalities; recollections of the ten-year-old tragedy at Chappaquiddick raised questions about his character which he could not put to rest.

Even more damaging to Kennedy, and to the quality of the campaign, were events abroad and the public response. The hostage seizure in Iran and the Soviet invasion of Afghanistan stirred a wave of patriotic fervor, which Carter exploited. The emotional response to these crises for a time overshadowed dissatisfactions with Carter's presidency and allowed him to avoid defending his policies.

As the campaign dragged on, Carter and Kennedy came to resemble two characters in a Greek tragedy, each able to injure the other more than he could help himself. But the real victims were the voters, who were denied a reasoned debate on the national condition. It was painfully appropriate that the contest ended in a cynical debate over the reforms in Democratic Party rules, whose failure to remedy the irrelevance of the political process had once again been demonstrated.

From the earliest days of Carter's presidency, his political advisers had anticipated that he would face a challenge for the nomination in 1980, an expectation that reflected their awareness that the president's hold on his party was shaky at best. The president's advisers could only guess at how many opponents they might face and who they would be. But they considered their most likely rival to be California governor Jerry Brown. In his 1976 strategy memorandum, Caddell labeled Brown as one of the party's "Young Turks," whose willingness to challenge and criticize traditional Democratic liberal orthodoxy "represents the coming generation of power." In January 1979 Hamilton Jordan wrote the president that Brown was "the single candidate who is sure to run and sure to announce early." Brown had to be taken seriously, Jordan argued, not only because of his success against Carter in the 1976 primaries, but also because of his "adept handling" of the vote on Proposition 13. That ballot initiative, which drastically reduced the property tax rate in California, had been approved by a landslide margin in June 1978.

Though the California voters were reacting to a specific problem, an unusually onerous tax burden, their vote was widely interpreted as confirmation of a national swing to the right and the start of what was heralded as a taxpayers' revolution. Its passage spurred nervous lawmakers in state legislatures and the Congress to introduce a flock of proposals to cut taxes and spending. After first opposing Proposition 13, Brown later claimed that its adoption confirmed his own "era-of-limits" credo. He ultimately became a leading advocate for the drive to amend the federal Constitution to require a balanced budget, an endeavor that won him considerable national attention but irritated and perplexed potential supporters.

Brown's motives reflected his own view of the forthcoming campaign—and also the general overriding concern in presidential politics with tactics rather than substance. In early 1979, around the same time that Jordan was warning Carter that Brown would seek the presidency, Brown came to the conclusion that Edward Kennedy, too, would challenge Carter. Brown announced his support for the balanced-budget amendment in large part because, as his campaign manager, Tom Quinn, said later, the governor felt "he had to do something to distinguish himself from Kennedy."

But if Brown believed he knew what Kennedy would do, the senator's intentions at that point remained unclear, even to his closest aides. He had been the early favorite for the party's nomination in 1972 and 1976. But he held back each time, in large part because of the lingering shadow of Chappaquiddick. The prevailing opinion in the Carter camp was that Kennedy would let the 1980 campaign pass, too, and wait four years until he would not have to compete against an incumbent president.

Judging by his words and actions, Kennedy's own feelings about making the race were ambivalent. He had backed most of the Carter administration's positions in the Senate. He repeatedly said that he expected the president to be renominated and that he intended to support him. When I asked Kennedy about his presidential ambitions as we flew back to Washington from his visit to West Virginia, he said: "I have the luxury of time. I can afford to wait." All of this evidence argued that he would not run.

But there were arguments on the other side, too. Kennedy, his staff, and his liberal supporters in the party were becoming increasingly critical of Carter's efforts to slash spending for social programs. The senator was especially disturbed by the president's unwillingness to support Kennedy's full-scale approach to national health insurance, the most important program on Kennedy's own legislative agenda. And in general Kennedy felt that Carter failed to appreciate and utilize the full powers of his office. When I reminded Kennedy of Carter's assertion in his 1979 State of the Union address that "government cannot solve our problems," the senator's face hardened. "What does he want to be president for?" he asked.

A few weeks after the West Virginia trip, during a panel discussion on health insurance at the Democratic Party midterm conference in Memphis, Kennedy made his boldest public attack yet on Carter's policy priorities. "Sometimes a party must sail against the wind," Kennedy told a wildly cheering group of conference delegates. "We cannot afford to drift or lie at anchor. We cannot afford to heed the call of those who say it is time to furl the sail."

In addition to his policy differences with Carter, another and more pragmatic factor pushed Kennedy toward running. Carter's weakness created a vacuum of leadership in the party, and someone was bound to fill it. Largely because of the personal legend woven around his brothers, Kennedy was considered the strongest prospect. But if he failed to challenge the president, he would disappoint the liberals who looked to him for leadership and run the risk of Brown or some other rival defeating Carter and taking control of the party for the next four or perhaps even eight years.

So Carter's political standing was the key to Kennedy's decision. And all through 1979, while Kennedy watched from the Senate, Carter's strength ebbed away. The climax came in midsummer with the "malaise" speech and the cabinet firings. Carter's dismal ratings in the polls dropped even lower, sinking in the Harris Poll to a score of 74 percent negative and only 25 percent positive, which Harris described as "the worst standing for any President in modern times."

In early September Kennedy let it be known that he intended to run. He was leading Carter in the polls by a margin of two to one, and few Democrats outside the Carter White House believed that he could be denied the nomination. Many of his partisans seemed to believe that to win he had little more to do for the voters than "shake their hands and wave at them."

But in reality Kennedy owed his advantage in the polls mainly to a combination of dissatisfaction with Carter and the sentimental memories of his brothers. Most voters who gave their advance approval to the idea of his candidacy had no clear idea of his positions on the issues which troubled the country and the Carter presidency. Some whom I interviewed during the period when Kennedy's ratings were at a peak gave reasons for supporting him that had little connection with Kennedy's liberal record in the Senate or his inclinations as a political figure.

In West Virginia, where local Democratic politicians guessed in the fall of 1978 that Kennedy could defeat Carter in the state's primary by a margin approaching ten to one, Angelo Moschella, a highway worker, said he wanted Kennedy to be president because "he'd run the country right and get the communists out of the government." In Minneapolis a truck driver attending a Republican tax-cut rally volunteered: "The Republicans are way behind on this issue. Right now, Ted Kennedy and the Democrats lead the bandwagon."

As Kennedy knew, once he became an actual candidate instead of just a hypothetical prospect, his views would be subjected to much tougher scrutiny by the press and the public. And this led to one of the first serious problems of his candidacy. Despite his rhetoric about sailing against the wind, Kennedy concluded that it would be more prudent for him to tack before the prevailing conservative gusts. As he tried to define his views as a candidate, he was far more specific about separating himself from the tenets of traditional liberalism than in explaining his plans for the future. "We reject the idea that government knows best across the board, that public planning is inherently superior or more effective than private action," he told a group of investment advisers. "We do not ask to bring back the New Deal or restore the New Frontier to life. Instead we seek to generate once again the 'can do' attitude that always has been the hallmark of America at its best."

But Jimmy Carter also could have endorsed the "can do attitude"—whatever that phrase meant. And Carter also would have no difficulty supporting the broad goals Kennedy laid down in the speech formally announcing his candidacy on November 7, 1979—equal opportunity for women and minorities, "progress for the poor and helpless," "a fair and prosperous economy," and an energy policy that concentrated on conservation and development of new sources of power.

In attempting to distinguish himself from the president he was challenging, Kennedy relied not on differences in specific ends or means, but rather on a contrast in "competence" and "leadership." "He believes in this system and he thinks he can make it work better than President Carter," Stephen Smith, Kennedy's campaign manager and brother-in-law, told me in outlining the premise for Kennedy's candidacy. "I question no man's intentions," Kennedy declared in his announcement speech. "But I have a different view of the highest office in the land—a view of a forceful, effective Presidency, in the thick of the action, at the center of all the great concerns our people share."

Kennedy was trying to build his candidacy around subjective judgments and hazy perceptions. In effect, he was calling on voters to examine and compare his personal traits with Jimmy Carter's, and this was bound to cause him difficulty. The Kennedy family mystique, which had contributed so much to his initial support, and which Kennedy liked to evoke in his speeches, as he had done in West Virginia, now contributed to his problems as a candidate. The press and the public tended to judge Kennedy against their own remembrances, or more often, what they thought they remembered of John and Robert Kennedy. And Edward Kennedy inevitably suffered by comparison with these romanticized recollections.

After his first weeks as a candidate, it was generally decided that EMK was not as commanding as JFK or as passionate as RFK. At the conclusion of a question-and-answer session at Vanderbilt University early in Kennedy's campaign, I overheard one student grumble to another, "Bobby Kennedy would never have been that wishy-washy." The disappointed student could not have been more than ten years old when Robert Kennedy was slain in 1968.

But it was the unresolved circumstances surrounding Chappaquiddick that prompted the harshest personal judgments on Kennedy. Though he had known that he would be confronted with questions about the tragedy, Kennedy was poorly prepared to deal with them. The gist of his answers was that there was nothing more to say. He had had ten years to reflect on the drowning of Mary Jo Kopechne and his own delay in reporting the accident, but he was unable during the campaign to put these circumstances in the perspective of the rest of his life and career, to convince voters that he was conscious of the character flaws the episode revealed, and that he had overcome them.

The misgivings about his behavior at Chappaquiddick were compounded by the well-publicized difficulties of his marriage. Though his wife, Joan, gamely accompanied him on some of his campaign tours, her fragile presence did not allay the impression that Kennedy's personal life was not as disciplined and upstanding as a presidential candidate's should be.

This was an impression the president's television advertising sought to underline by contrast. One Carter commercial boasted: "Husband, Father, President—he's doing all three jobs with distinction." Another television "spot" pointedly asserted: "A man brings two things to a Presidential ballot. He brings his record and he brings himself. Who he is is frequently more important than what he's done."

As Kennedy struggled to deal with these problems, events abroad overshadowed his candidacy and the entire campaign and greatly benefited Carter. When the American hostages were seized at the U.S. embassy in Teheran on November 4, three days before Kennedy formally announced his candidacy, the incident seemed likely at first to be another blow to Carter's prestige. It was Carter, yielding to pressure from influential friends of the Shah, who had made the controversial decision to allow Iran's deposed ruler to come to the United States for medical treatment, thus providing the militant Iranians with a motive for storming the embassy. Moreover, although the embassy had been seized briefly once before, a few months earlier, security precautions had not been significantly increased, nor had embassy employees been evacuated.

But these facts were generally overlooked. Out of concern for the hostages and indignation against their captors, Americans rallied behind the president. Carter played his role of beleaguered leader to the hilt. Although in fact, once he had forsaken the use of force, his range of actions was limited, he dedicated his presidency to dealing with the hostage crisis. He withdrew from a scheduled debate with Kennedy in Iowa, contending that he could not spare the time for this or any other campaign activities. As the holiday season approached, the president even ordered that the national Christmas tree go unlighted until the hostages were freed.

While church bells tolled around the country to demonstrate the nation's support for the captives in Iran, and the hostages dominated the network news and the nation's attention, Carter's standing in the polls soared. A month after the hostage seizure, the president had moved in front of Kennedy.

Kennedy walked a narrow line, trying to avoid discussing the impasse in Iran on which the nation's attention was centered. On this issue, he said repeatedly, Americans should "speak with one voice and that voice should be that of the President." As Tom Quinn, Brown's campaign manager, said later: "The feeling was that it was unpatriotic to criticize the President at that point. No matter how accurate or cogent or persuasive your arguments, the President was cloaked in the flag very effectively."

In actuality, Carter's immunity extended beyond his handling of the hostage situation. For Kennedy it was awkward to deliver his obligatory statement of support for the president in his confrontation with the Ayatollah Khomeini and then go on to accuse Carter of incompetence in managing the economy. As the crisis dragged on, Kennedy's frustration increased. Finally, during a television interview in December, he denounced the Shah for having run "one of the most violent regimes in the history of mankind" and he rejected the suggestion which had been made by Ronald Reagan that the Shah should be allowed to stay in the United States permanently.

Though Kennedy had not criticized the president or his handling of the hostage situation, Carter's forces assaulted him. The State Department said Kennedy's comments would make "delicate negotiations more difficult." Robert Strauss, the president's campaign chairman, said:

"It is an error to inject anything in the campaign that could in any way endanger the lives of the people over there."

Kennedy was badly hurt. As he campaigned in Iowa for support in the January precinct caucuses, he was put on the defensive and forced to continually reiterate his concern for the hostages. In New Hampshire, site of the first presidential primary in February, his campaign workers were physically assaulted. Joanne Symons, Kennedy's New Hampshire manager, said the reaction to Kennedy's remarks about the Shah "was the single most devastating thing that happened to our campaign."

Public concern with international tensions was increased late in December when the Soviet Union invaded Afghanistan. This was another situation, like the hostage seizure, about which the president could do little of practical consequence. But he added to the aura of crisis by calling the Soviet action "the most serious threat to world peace since World War II" and imposing an embargo on sales of grain to the Russians. When Kennedy, campaigning in Iowa farm country, called the embargo ineffective and unfair to farmers, Vice-President Mondale in effect questioned Kennedy's patriotism. Kennedy should decide, Mondale said, "whether to do the political thing or the thing that best serves this nation."

Meanwhile, though Carter had confined himself to the White House, he managed to make good use of the prestige and power of his incumbency. He spent hours on the phone calling hundreds of influential Democrats in Iowa and other battleground states asking for their support. Some were invited to Washington for "consultations" on inflation and other policy questions. And the president and his cabinet secretaries tried to arrange the award of federal grants when and where they would do Carter's candidacy the most good. When Mayor Richard Fulton of Nashville, who had endorsed Kennedy, asked whether the people of Nashville would be punished for his action by the withholding of federal funds, Jack Watson, Carter's liaison to state and local governments, replied. "We will not punish the people of any city. But having said that, when there is discretion in the use of federal funds on how the President can help the people, we will go to our friends."

Carter gained steadily while Kennedy floundered. Not until a week after Kennedy's two-to-one defeat in the January 21 Iowa caucuses, which the senator had called the first real test of the campaign, did he finally announce a substantive basis for his challenge to the president. In a speech at Georgetown University he proposed the rationing of gasoline to deal with the energy shortage and the imposition of mandatory economic controls—on profits, dividends, interest rates and rent as well as on prices and wages—to cope with inflation. Moreover, Kennedy called for a national debate on the Carter administration's foreign policy. "If the Vietnam War taught us anything, it is precisely that when we do *not* debate our foreign policy, we may drift into deeper trouble."

This was too little and too late to save Kennedy. Carter defeated him in a string of primaries in New Hampshire, in the South, and then in Illinois, which made the president's renomination all but inevitable. However, Kennedy's belated program solidified his support among committed liberals. Moreover, as Kennedy's chances for getting nominated dwindled, voters began to look at him less as a potential president with character flaws than as an instrument for registering their own objections to the Carter administration. This shift, demonstrated by Kennedy's substantial victory in the New York primary in March, gave him justification for continuing his campaign, even while Carter was steadily accumulating the delegates he needed for a majority.

By late April, Brown had dropped out of the race. His

balanced-budget gambit had failed as voter interest in the idea was diminished by the dramatic events overseas. And Brown was unable to find any other way to call attention to his candidacy. But Kennedy continued to pound away at Carter, whose standing in the country was once again declining as a result of the onset of a recession and a sharp rise in unemployment.

Carter remained sequestered in the White House, refusing Kennedy's repeated challenges to debate. In a sense, Carter had made himself a hostage to events in Iran. His advisers thought the president could help himself politically by campaigning. But they worried about how to justify such a change unless there was a break in the hostage crisis. "We had painted ourselves into a corner," Caddell said later, "and the problem was how to get out of it."

No really good solution ever presented itself. But after the failure of an attempt to rescue the hostages in April, the president announced, without explaining why, that the nation's problems had now become "manageable" enough so that he felt free to campaign. But he still refused to debate Kennedy. Carter made his only official political trip of the campaign to Ohio, where he won the June primary while Kennedy was defeating him in California and New Jersey.

By now Carter had won more than the 1,665 delegates he needed for a majority at the convention. But the Kennedy forces devised one last desperate stratagem to change the arithmetic by changing the rules. According to the rules governing delegate selection, a product of more than a decade of reform, delegates were obliged to cast their ballots at the convention for the presidential candidate they had been elected to support.

This had clearly been the rule all through the campaign, but the convention itself still needed to ratify the procedure to impose it upon the delegates. Kennedy supporters, many of whom had fought for years to ensure that the convention's decision would represent the preference of the voters, now contended that binding the delegates infringed on their right to change their minds and converted the convention into a collection of robots.

In July, the month before the Democratic convention met in New York, the delegate-binding rule came under attack from another quarter. A group of unaligned congressmen and old-line party regulars, fearing that Carter's nomination would mean certain defeat for the Democrats, banded together to support "an open convention," which would be free to nominate someone other than Kennedy or Carter.

The Carter forces denounced the open-convention drive as an attempt to violate a sacred pledge between the party and the voters. Underlying the hypocritical allusions to principle on both sides was the simple reality that adoption of the rule would ensure Carter's nomination while its defeat would allow the convention to make another choice.

Another reality was that the open-convention forces, who were unwilling to back Kennedy, could not agree on another alternative to Carter. The time-worn names most frequently mentioned, Henry Jackson and Edmund Muskie, pointed up the bankruptcy of leadership in the party.

Carter's victory on the rule-change vote at the convention in New York guaranteed his nomination and led to Kennedy's withdrawal from the contest. But even in Carter's moment of triumph the divisions between him and his party were emphasized. Just before the convention the Democratic National Committee had surveyed the delegates' views on issues to be covered by the party's platform. "If you read the questionnaires coming back from the delegates," said Robert Keefe, an adviser to the president's campaign, "clearly the Carter delegates agreed with Kennedy's posture on the issues a helluva lot more than they did with Carter's."

The most significant differences were on the platform's economic plank. When these came up for a vote, after an electrifying address by Kennedy, the delegates gave Kennedy most of what he wanted, including a $12 billion antirecession program for public service jobs. The revised platform demonstrated not only the weakness of Carter's hold on his own delegates but contradicted a major new economic program the White House was prepared to use in its campaign against the Republican nominee, Ronald Reagan.

In his acceptance speech to the delegates at Madison Square Garden, Carter recalled his nomination four years before in the same hall and declared: "I am wiser tonight than I was four years ago." But now that claim would be tested by his Republican opponent, and by the voters.

3. "A Leap of Faith"

Though he may not have realized it, Ronald Reagan had some fundamental things in common with Jimmy Carter. The careers of the Republican challenger and the Democratic incumbent had similar origins and relied on similar premises. Both men exploited and contributed to public mistrust of politics and government. In fact, Reagan's election was a natural, almost inevitable sequel to Carter's presidency.

Like Carter, Reagan started out as an antipolitician. He entered politics relatively late in life when his personality and beliefs had already been shaped, and like Carter, he pitted himself against the political establishment. Campaigning for governor of California in 1966, he styled himself a "citizen politician" and declared: "They've been in power so long, these professional politicians, that we're beginning to see a degeneration of moral standards."

Later on, as his ambitions turned toward the presidency,

Reagan made the government in Washington the focus of his attacks. Running against Ford in 1976, Reagan pledged to "dismantle" the federal bureaucracy and occasionally even suggested that the best service that the national government could perform for its citizens would be simply to shut itself down.

Though this rhetoric may have sounded extreme in 1976, it seemed less so in 1980. During the preceding four years Americans had heard Jimmy Carter blame the problems of the country and the frustrations of his presidency on the deficiencies of the governing system he headed, and in which he had expressed great confidence as a candidate.

"All the legislation in the world can't fix what is wrong with America," Carter declared in his 1979 "malaise" speech. "What you see too often in Washington and elsewhere around the country is a system of government that seems incapable of action." Adding to the impact of Carter's attack on government, and helping to make Reagan's own continuing assaults more plausible and respectable, was that Carter was speaking as the head of the political party which for nearly half a century had made the ability of government to deal with the nation's problems an article of faith. But it was not just Carter's rhetoric which strengthened Reagan's case against government. Of greater weight were the problems themselves, at home and abroad—from the check-out line at the supermarket to the embassy compound in Teheran—which defied government solution and which had proliferated and worsened during Carter's presidency.

Carter tried to suggest that these conditions could be blamed on the system, while his critics denounced his performance in office. Actually, the fault lay with both the flaws of the system and Carter's response to them. At any rate, the record was bad enough so that Carter was unwilling to defend it or to depend upon it to gain him support. Nor could he count on much help from his own party, which had grown weaker during his presidency and from which he had estranged himself. In something close to desperation, he placed his hopes for reelection on an effort to portray Reagan as a threat to peace and a purveyor of hate and divisiveness. This strategy wrecked whatever chance there might have been for a serious discussion of issues during the campaign, and it also backfired on Carter. The combination of his performance as a candidate and his record as president overshadowed the voters' misgivings about Reagan and allowed Reagan to win a landslide victory.

Like his predecessors, President Reagan was confronted by a mixed public mood of hope, anxiety and skepticism, which had been conditioned by the cycles of expectation and disillusionment resulting from the gap between politics and government. In his first months in office Reagan demonstrated far more skill than Carter in imposing his will on Congress and his early accomplishments recalled the tumultuous days of Lyndon Johnson.

But the manner in which Reagan achieved his success also served as a reminder of Johnson's ultimate failure. In his haste to exploit his impressive victory at the polls and his considerable personal appeal, Reagan, like Johnson, claimed a mandate that he had not established during the campaign. Moreover, the disarray and divisions among the Democrats prevented genuine debate on the far-reaching economic measures Reagan rammed through the Congress.

As Reagan's policies, once in effect, produced serious economic and social dislocations, his supporters tried to quell protests by claiming that here at last was a president who kept his promises. But this was a hollow defense. It was true that Reagan, like Carter before him, tried to carry out some of the commitments he had made as a candidate. But it was also true, as it had been for Carter, that many of these pledges had never been clearly articulated and that some contradicted each other. The consequent confusion and tension were ill omens for the future of his presidency.

On a February afternoon in 1980, campaigning in the Massachusetts primary, Reagan halted his motorcade to inspect Plymouth Rock, a traditional stop for any candidate. After the ritual was duly recorded for television, Reagan returned to the campaign bus, which at the moment contained only three occupants, myself included, and then provided a brief glimpse into his personality and into his reasons for his domination of the contest for the Republican nomination.

Just before he took his seat, he faced his fellow passengers and delivered a brief declaration about the import of the Pilgrim Fathers' voyage more than three centuries ago. "If they could come all that way in that little boat," Reagan said, "how can we dare be afraid of anything?"

The logic of that proposition does not necessarily stand close scrutiny. But the words had a nice ring to them and Reagan rendered them with fervor. Although the setting was unusual and the audience sparse, it was a typical Reagan performance. His ability to express his reverence for such icons as the Pilgrims, the flag, free enterprise, church and family, in catchy phrases and with unquestionable conviction, had over the years inspired the admiration and allegiance of legions of conservative Republicans. Thus he had developed an ardent personal following. And in a time of weak parties and splintered interest groups, this hard core of support gave him a substantial advantage over his rivals.

Two other personal qualities made Reagan, despite his age—he turned sixty-nine that February—an ideal candidate for the modern era of presidential politics ushered in by John Kennedy in 1960.

First, his acting experience had made him a master of television—the key to the hearts and minds of voters.

"Ronald Reagan was the best electronic media candidate in American history," claimed Richard Wirthlin, his campaign pollster and chief strategist.

Secondly, Reagan wanted badly to be president—badly enough that he was willing to submit himself to the ordeal of the modern selection system. In fact, he had been running for the presidency on and off since 1968, all the while absorbing techniques and building support which would stand him in good stead in 1980.

Reagan's personality dominated the campaign for the Republican nomination. On issues and ideology, voters had little to choose between Reagan and his half-dozen rivals, with the exception of Congressman John Anderson of Illinois, a vigorous advocate of civil rights and gun control. Anderson's distinctive views and his eloquence on the stump gained him a respectable amount of support among moderate voters in New England and a disproportionate measure of national attention from the media. But the steady rightward shift of the GOP since Goldwater's nomination in 1964 left little toleration for Anderson's heresies. He soon abandoned the Republican competition and began making preparations for an independent presidential candidacy in the fall.

The susceptibility of the nominating process to simple hard work, which Jimmy Carter had demonstrated in 1976, was shown again by George Bush's victory in the Iowa caucuses. Bush expended vast amounts of time and energy in the state while Reagan visited there only a few times. Bush had respectable credentials in politics and diplomacy. But when the spotlight shifted to him after Iowa, he had little to say to distinguish himself from Reagan. Their match-up in New Hampshire was made memorable chiefly by Bush's public sulking during a row over the rules governing a televised campaign debate. After Reagan's big victory in that primary, the outcome of the campaign was no longer in doubt.

Bush's only noteworthy attempt to air a substantive

disagreement with Reagan came after his decisive New Hampshire defeat, when he denounced Reagan's proposal for slashing income tax rates as "voodoo economics." But with his candidacy sinking fast, his arguments had little impact.

Reagan finished where he started, in front. Though he had promised not only to cut taxes but also to increase defense spending and balance the budget at the same time, he was not forced during the campaign to explain how he would accomplish this. Instead of testing his policy proposals, the campaign served mainly to prove that in his seventieth year he was able to withstand the physical challenge of the primaries.

Spared the frictions of prolonged competition, Reagan emerged from the Republican convention in Detroit, with his running mate Bush, who had recanted his "voodoo" criticism of the tax cut, at the head of a united and confident party. The optimism in the Republican camp derived largely from the divisions among the Democrats, after the bitter struggle between Kennedy and Carter for the nomination, and the evident weaknesses of the president.

Inflation was rampant, unemployment was high and frustration over the hostages in Iran was increasing. The Carter campaign's own surveys in the last round of primary states in June showed that even among hard-core Democrats, the majority judgment was that Carter was not up to the challenges of the presidency. "The fact is," Carter's campaign chairman Robert Strauss confided to a fellow Democrat after Carter's renomination, "I don't know a single person who really wants Jimmy Carter re-elected."

When Carter's advisers met to plan their strategy for the fall they were confronted with polls that, recalled Patrick Caddell later, "showed that by two to one the American people did not want Jimmy Carter to be President. And so we had to find them a reason why they would be forced to keep him." The best argument they could devise for that purpose amounted to saying that as bad as Carter might seem, Ronald Reagan in the White House would be horrendous. In effect, Carter's old campaign slogan of "Why not the best?" was transformed into "At least not the worst."

The president's advisers resolved, as Jack Nelson reported in the *Los Angeles Times*, to make Ronald Reagan the issue of the campaign and to depict him as "a saber rattling, inexperienced ideologue who lacks the judgment and compassion needed to be President." This strategy was a natural outgrowth of the president's conduct of his campaign for renomination. By restricting himself to the White House and refusing to debate Kennedy, Carter had avoided having to directly defend his record. And thanks to the public's preoccupation with the hostages and its negative reaction to Kennedy, both of which Carter fostered, the president prevailed.

But even as he was winning renomination, Carter was losing public support. And Carter's record would not disappear from the public consciousness simply because he preferred to talk about Reagan's purported deficiencies. By saving himself from dealing with difficult questions about his handling of the nation's problems, Carter also cost himself the chance to put his performance in a more favorable perspective than the view generally taken; he might have explained his decisions, pointed out his accomplishments and focused attention on his goals for the future.

Largely because of Carter's negative strategy, the campaign came to be dominated by low blows, cheap shots and false alarms. Opinion polls indicated that both major party candidates were held in low esteem by the public, and criticism from the press was biting.

"There is no way given the nature of the two prime contenders for the office that the country is going to elect a President in November who is especially gifted in or suited to the conduct of the office," the *Washington Post* declared.

The *New York Times* was even more acerbic: "Someone chases a voter down an alley, points a gun to his head and demands an answer: 'Carter or Reagan?' After thinking for a moment the voter replied, 'Shoot.' " That joke, the *Times* editorialized, "turns out to be not merely a joke, but the story of the 1980 campaign."

With its concentration on personality and negativism, the campaign seemed to be a culmination of twenty years and six quadrennials of irrelevance in presidential campaigning, which had become dominated by thirty-second commercials and the frenetic competition of the primaries, and of unaccountability in government, symbolized by Vietnam, Watergate, the Nixon pardon, and Carter's unkept and conflicting promises.

Reagan was certainly not blameless for the mindlessness of the 1980 campaign. Early in the contest he demonstrated a propensity for gratuitous and distracting remarks. Seeking to establish support among religious fundamentalists, he expressed doubts about Darwin's theories of evolution and suggested the biblical story of creation should be given equal time in the schools. More maliciously, he described the Alabama town where Carter had opened his campaign as the birthplace of the Ku Klux Klan, an assertion which, besides being inaccurate, offended a good many Southerners.

But Reagan's lapses were drowned out by the vehemence of Carter's calculated demagoguery. With minimal justification he accused Reagan of reviving "the stirrings of hate" between the races and claimed that a Reagan victory would divide the nation "black from white, Jew from Christian, North from South." And trying to exploit Reagan's tough talk about nuclear arms negotiations with the Soviets, Carter asserted that the outcome of the election would decide nothing less than "whether we have war or peace," making clear that he himself was for peace.

His own staff quickly conceded that this comment was "overstated" and Carter felt obliged to offer a form of apology in a television interview. He did not really believe that Reagan was a warmonger, the president said, and he promised to be more restrained in the future.

The upshot of these assaults, whatever doubts they might have raised about Reagan, was to deflect public attention to Carter and his tactics. A hue and cry developed in the press about what came to be called Carter's "meanness." The president was forced on the defensive and he lost credibility. And the furor obscured genuine public misgiving about Reagan's inexperience, his judgment, his conservative beliefs, and his proposals for taxing and spending.

"Carter had a better record than his campaign," Richard Wirthlin told me after the election. "People may have been very angry at him. But many of them, especially Democrats who had voted the party ticket all their lives, would have listened if he had said: 'Look, I've made some mistakes, but don't throw it all away.' " Instead, as Wirthlin put it, Carter tried to "demonize" Reagan. Reagan responded more in sorrow than in anger, and Wirthlin's polls showed that voters began to view the challenger as more presidential than the president.

The negative outlook of the Carter campaign also shaped the president's strategy toward his other challenger, John Anderson. Anderson's candidacy was the most serious independent effort since George Wallace's in 1968. But he was handicapped from the start because, unlike past third-party candidates—George Wallace in 1968, Henry Wallace and Strom Thurmond in 1948, and Robert La Follette in 1924—he lacked a distinctive geographical or ideological base of support. Instead, his candidacy sought to appeal to a generalized discontent with the nominees of the two major parties. This attitude was widespread enough so that early in the campaign the Gallup Poll showed Anderson having the support of 25 percent of the nation's voters.

Anderson was drawing support from both parties. But Carter strategists concluded that he was a bigger threat to the president than to Reagan and set out to wreck his campaign. In a number of states Democrats made it their business to obstruct Anderson's efforts to get on the ballot. Although Anderson's National Unity Party ultimately succeeded in getting his name before the voters in all fifty states, the Democratic opposition added to the cost of this effort, draining away funds that would have otherwise been used for television advertising Anderson badly needed.

More important was Carter's refusal to take part in a presidential debate if Anderson was included, on the grounds that it would be unfair for him to have to confront two Republicans. But this strategy ultimately hurt Carter by bringing about a joint televised debate between Anderson and Reagan. Although Carter's absence damaged Anderson's efforts to make himself appear as a credible alternative, Reagan benefited from the chance to perform on his best medium before a huge audience.

The collapse of Anderson's candidacy after the debate was inevitable. Without a party structure or an ideological or regional underpinning, he could not organize his supporters. And without sufficient exposure in the media he could not define his candidacy and its purposes.

Anderson's decline in the polls cleared the way for the debate between Carter and Reagan that sealed Carter's defeat. Carter sought to use the debate to bolster his contention that a Reagan presidency would threaten peace abroad and stability at home. Had the debate been an academic exercise, he might have won on points. But most voters viewed the confrontation as a clash of personalities. The president's tense, acerbic manner hurt him by contrast with the relaxed, benign impression which

Reagan created, and which seemed to belie the ominous inferences Carter asked voters to draw from Reagan's rhetoric.

If the debate was the climax of the campaign, developments in Iran provided the anticlimax. In the final days before the election, action by the Iranian parliament raised hopes for release of the hostages. But when these hopes were not fulfilled, the episode served mainly to remind voters of Carter's inability to deal with the long captivity, and also of how the president had made political capital of the crisis.

The reaction reinforced a trend that had begun running against the president since his debate with Reagan. On election day Carter was prepared to lose and Reagan to win. But neither anticipated the magnitude of the voters' disenchantment with the president. They gave Reagan 51 percent of the vote to 41 percent for Carter, who carried only six states and the District of Columbia. The Republican landslide shook the Congress, too, giving the GOP control of the Senate for the first time since 1954 and a gain of thirty-four seats in the House. For the fifth consecutive election the turnout declined, to 53.9 percent of the eligible voters, the lowest figure since 1948.

The president-elect had promised to get off to a running start in office, and he was as good as his word. Within six months of his inauguration he gained approval of a program of deep budget cuts and even deeper tax reductions which was hailed as a dramatic comeback for the presidency after years of frustration and deadlock.

But Reagan's success did not narrow the gap between politics and government; it only demonstrated the ability of a president under favorable conditions to exploit the imbalances of the system. Reagan had won a big personal victory at the polls in November, far more decisive than any of his predecessors in the past twenty years except for Nixon in 1972 and Johnson in 1964. But Nixon, after his reelection landslide over McGovern, faced determined Democratic opposition in both houses of Congress and the crisis of Watergate. Johnson, on the other hand, like Reagan, had a clear field and he used the impetus from his landslide to push the Congress into adoption of the Great Society program, a good part of which Reagan now intended to undo.

Also contributing to Reagan's achievements was his well-honed talent for dramatizing his personality and arguments on television. Only John Kennedy among recent presidents had possessed a comparable flair. But Kennedy's concern about his narrow election victory in 1960 and the divisions within his party made him reluctant to commit his personal prestige in his legislative goals.

Reagan had no such reservations, and he was determined to move swiftly before the November glow of victory faded. To arouse the public and prod the Congress, he resorted to a favorite presidential tactic, creating a crisis atmosphere. In his first postinaugural address he declared, "We are in the worst economic mess since the Great Depression," and warned Americans that they were threatened by "an economic calamity of enormous proportions."

In point of fact, though conditions were bad, they were not all that bad, and they were certainly not comparable to the horrors of the Depression. The unemployment rate, which stood at 7.4 percent when Reagan spoke, averaged 8.5 percent in 1975, and by some measurements inflation had been worse in that year, too. Moreover, during the months Reagan was hurrying his program through Congress, the inflation rate actually declined, due to a drop in oil and food prices, and the economy otherwise showed resiliency which contradicted Reagan's forecasts of catastrophe. But the continuing alarms sounded by the president and his economic policy-makers helped to subdue criticism and parry questions about Reagan's proposals.

Even more dubious was the reiterated claim by the president and his advisers that the voters had given their program a mandate. "The mandate for change expressed by the American people was not my mandate, it was our mandate," Reagan sternly told the Congress when he submitted his budget proposals in March. In June, as Congress was debating the budget cuts he demanded, the president pushed the mandate button again. "Last November," he declared, "the American people gave their elected representatives in Washington an overwhelming mandate to rescue the economy from high inflation and high unemployment."

But exactly what had the voters mandated? It could not have been the major reductions in federal programs that Reagan insisted upon, because he had not advocated them during the campaign. Instead, in his major economic policy statements he promised that he could save "billions of taxpayer dollars" by eliminating "waste, extravagance, abuse and outright fraud." The $35 billion in budget cuts that Congress obediently granted, mostly in economic and social programs for low-income families, were a postelection afterthought, designed by Reagan to help offset the revenues that would be lost by his proposed tax cuts.

The tax cut was supposedly the other half of Reagan's mandate. But the tax legislation that Congress, under heavy presidential pressure, ultimately passed in July 1981, with its provisions for permanent indexing of tax rates and its generous benefits for big corporations and wealthy individuals, went well beyond the program Reagan had advocated during the campaign. For that matter, surveys conducted by the University of Michigan indicated that fewer than half the people who voted for

Reagan approved of the tax-cut remedy the candidate actually had advocated.

The electorate's opinion of Reagan's economic proposals "was not that clear," Reagan's own pollster, Richard Wirthlin, acknowledged after the election. "The mandate was really made up of two things," Wirthlin told me. "One was the feeling of a need for change. And secondly, there was a leap of faith that a lot of voters took that Reagan would be able to accomplish the task of reducing inflation, keeping unemployment at the same levels and turning the economy around."

Reagan's conversion of that leap of faith into the drastic realities of his economic program was made easier by the failure of the Democrats to provide a responsible opposition. Though they had lost the Senate to the Republicans, the Democrats still controlled the House by a margin of fifty seats. Theoretically, that should have given them an influential voice in the economic policy debate.

But in fact there was not much of a debate and the Democrats failed to raise significant challenges or propose significant alternatives as their leaders thrashed about in indecision. The lack of party discipline and the fragmentation of constituencies which have always hindered congressional leadership were exacerbated by Reagan's victory at the polls. Democrats with liberal records were shaken by the November vote results. Their conservative party colleagues, mostly from the South, saw in the election returns additional justification for their traditional tendency to side with the Republicans on economic issues.

Lacking substantial new ideas of their own to offer as economic remedies and fearful of conservative defections, the Democratic leadership passively accepted the two basic premises of the president's program—that government was the main cause of inflation and that generous tax cuts for the wealthy and for business would revive the economy. As Reagan's proposals moved forward, the Democratic high command maneuvered to shift the impact of the budget cut from some programs to others and to give lower-income groups more benefit from the tax cuts. But these differences with the president were over questions of detail and degree; the Democrats had no distinctive program to rally public support. Their meager counterproposals were designed mainly to gain the support of conservative members of their party so that the leaders could claim some form of victory to boost their sagging prestige. But as it turned out, this strategy failed and the conservatives defected to Reagan en masse on the showdown votes. When the struggle was over, the Democratic leadership had little to comfort themselves with except the thought that if Reagan's program failed, as they confidently predicted it would, the president would suffer all the blame.

No one really knew, though, how Reagan's program would fare because of the haste with which it was enacted, the untested assumptions of supply-side economics upon which it rested, and the complex and contradictory components it contained: the huge tax cuts intended to encourage economic expansion conflicted with the administration's tight money policy, which curbed borrowing and investment. On the one hand, the president promised a revival of federalism, but on the other, his budget cuts slashed federal aid to the states. And the most evident contradiction was between the tax cuts enacted in July 1981 and Reagan's promise to balance the budget by 1984. That pledge was soon washed out by a tide of red ink. And with even bigger deficits looming ahead, it appeared that Reagan, to avoid economic calamity in the long run, would be forced to seek political support for additional and even more painful budget cuts, or for new forms of taxation, or for both.

What made that prospect doubtful, apart from the

frustrating experiences of Reagan's predecessors, was the misleading rhetoric Reagan had used to advertise his remedies for the economy. Jimmy Carter had asserted that government could not solve the country's problems. Reagan went beyond that in his inaugural address: "In the present crisis," he said, "government is not the solution, it is the problem." But that is as meaningless as saying that people are the problem. Government in and of itself, of course, is neither a solution nor a problem. It is simply an instrument for creating one or the other, usually a combination of both. It is certainly true that government policies have contributed to the nation's economic problems. But it is equally true that without the effective and responsible use of government there can be no solutions.

With similar illogic Reagan told the Congress that the taxing power should only be used to raise revenue. "It must not be used to regulate the economy or bring about social change," he declared. But the revenue needs of the government are necessarily so immense that they inevitably dominate our economy and our society. In establishing tax policy, the question is not whether there will be regulation or change, but what kind and for whose benefit. Reagan's 1981 economic program answered those questions in one way, a way that most directly benefits the economically advantaged. The majority of Americans have until 1984 to decide whether they are satisfied with that answer.

In the meanwhile, the new president faces a long and difficult road toward the economic improvement he promised. And his initial dissembling is likely to make it harder for him to persuade voters, when he needs their support, to make another leap of faith.

CHAPTER NINE

The Counter-Reformers

When Richard Nixon first heard that agents of his 1972 reelection campaign had broken into Democratic Party headquarters at the Watergate he claimed to be genuinely surprised. "The whole thing made so little sense," Nixon wrote later. "Why of all places, the DNC? Anyone who knew anything about politics would know that a national committee headquarters was a useless place to go for inside information on a Presidential campaign."

As warped as Nixon's view of the political process was, he had a keen eye for the arrangement of power. He assumed, correctly as it turned out, that the Democratic National Committee was as ill-informed about the inner workings of George McGovern's candidacy as he knew the Republican National Committee to be about Nixon's own campaign.

This situation was not the result of inadvertence. Rather it reflected the dominant reality of the modern political age—the diminishing role of political parties in both politics and government, widening the gap between the two.

Some years ago V. O. Key, a revered figure in American political science, divided our parties into three parts; first, the party organization, the state and county chairmen and national committees; second, officials elected under the party label; and finally, the voters who pay some degree of allegiance to the party. At its best, in the past, this arrangement provided a rough way for the electorate to keep in touch with and make claims upon the government. It provided only limited satisfaction, but inertial forces held it together.

Under the pressures of the crises and upheavals of the past twenty years, however, the system has been falling apart. The party of the first part, the organization, and the party of the second part, the elected officials, have been losing touch with each other, and the parties have been losing their hold on the voters. The result has been instability in politics and government, exaggerated expectations and excessive responses from the presidency and a deepening cynicism among the voters.

The decline of parties is evident at every level and branch of government. Candidates for the House and Senate, most of whom once depended heavily on party support, have learned to set up their own organizations, to use television and direct mail techniques and to cultivate special interest groups for their backing. "In recent years," Thomas E. Mann points out in *The New Congress*, "more and more groups with a Washington legislative agenda have developed grass roots organizations that can be mobilized for or against House and Senate candidates." The net result is that "the substance of the campaign as presented to the voters revolves around the candidate, not the party."

But the dominance of personality over party is most conspicuous, and most significant, in presidential politics. As we have seen, it did not start with Richard Nixon and Watergate; its origins can be traced back to the early postwar years, and the trend was accelerated by the candidacy of John Kennedy. After gaining the presidential nomination in 1960, despite the misgivings and in some cases the resistance of the established party leadership, Kennedy carried over his entrepreneurial style into the management of his general election campaign. Robert Kennedy, as his brother's proconsul, took over the Democratic National Committee and converted it into a Kennedy fiefdom. Mistrustful of state and local organizations, he dispatched his own handpicked operators to coordinate the Kennedy campaign effort around the country.

The future attorney general demonstrated his disdain for party affairs and concerns when he dressed down a group of New York reformers, among them the state's distinguished U.S. senator and former governor, Herbert Lehman, for feuding with the regular party organization. "I don't give a damn if the state and county organizations survive after November," Kennedy told them. "I don't give a damn if *you* survive. I want to elect John F. Kennedy."

Subsequent presidential candidates in both parties have paid even less attention to their party organizations, as reflected by Nixon's observation on Watergate. Starting in 1976, the isolation of parties from presidential campaigning was reinforced by the establishment of federal campaign subsidies paid directly to the candidate which leave the parties only an ancillary role in campaign financing. These rules encourage the tendency of presidential nominees to operate their own political shops. Though he had bitterly denounced Nixon's 1972 CREEP organization and its role in the Watergate scandal, and urged that the Republican National Committee run future GOP presidential campaigns, Gerald Ford chose to rely on his own President Ford Committee when he ran against Carter in 1976.

The subordination of the party's role in presidential campaigning has inevitably been reflected by lessened party influence in the White House. Presidents used to feel obliged to take into account the wishes and judgments of party leaders who had helped place them in the Oval Office. These leaders, or bosses, were of course interested in personal favors and prerogatives. But if they were effective in their roles they also had broader concerns. "These men do not operate as individuals," James Rowe, Jr., an old New Dealer once advised Hubert Humphrey. "They are essentially catalysts—catalysts who remain in power by reflecting accurately the moods and desires of their constituents. Their constituents happen to be minor organization politicians, but these in turn often reflect accurately the mood of the voters." But there are no such catalysts today in either party; thus presidents make decisions with little or no regard for the impact of their actions on their parties.

One measure of the present relationship between the president and the party is the status of the party's national chairman. Although theoretically the chairman is elected by the party's national committee, he or she has in fact always been chosen by the president and served at the president's pleasure. Nevertheless, at times in the past, if only because of his own personal prestige, the chairman enjoyed significant influence with the president as, for instance, James J. Farley did for a time with Franklin Roosevelt. But the chairmanship has since been downgraded to a job whose overriding requisite is unquestioning loyalty to the White House.

When George Bush was Republican national chairman, during the darkest days of Watergate, he doggedly defended the president and protested his innocence of any wrongdoing, while the GOP was being devastated by the scandal. When the Democrats returned to power in 1977, Kenneth Curtis, the former Maine governor whom Jimmy Carter had chosen to be national chairman, was forced to resign because he was incautious enough to disagree with the White House on some minor matters.

Curtis's replacement, John White, a longtime party functionary in Texas, made certain he would not suffer a similar fate. After Carter's confidant Bert Lance resigned the directorship of the Office of Management and Budget in disgrace, having shattered many of the early illusions about the Carter presidency, White publicly praised

Lance as "a folk hero." Later, when Carter was challenged for renomination in 1980, Chairman White backed the president vigorously, in violation of the spirit if not the letter of the federal campaign law's provisions intended to ensure the neutrality of the committee in nomination contests.

Ronald Reagan's White House has made plain its disregard for the views of Richard Richards, whom Reagan chose to head the Republican National Committee. Though an ardent conservative, Richards had criticized the operations of conservative political action committees which operate independently of political parties because, he complained, "they create mischief" and are responsible neither to candidates nor to parties. But Reagan's political director at the White House, Lyn Nofziger, and Nofziger's replacement, Edward J. Rollins, brushed aside Richards's criticism and praised the efforts of the groups which mainly finance negative advertising campaigns against Democratic candidates. Despite Richards's contention that such groups are a threat to both political parties, Rollins proclaimed them to be "the wave of the future."

Competition for funds and voter support among these independent political action committees, with their disparate goals and undisciplined methods, was only one of a host of problems that confronted both parties in the wake of the 1980 election. The setbacks suffered by the Democrats made their difficulties more evident, but what was bad news for the Democratic Party was not necessarily good news for the GOP.

The 1980 returns made it harder than ever for the Democrats to support their longtime claim of being the majority party. Not only have Democrats been unable to do better than an even split in the last six presidential elections, but they also were outvoted in the cumulative totals by a margin of more than nine million. It is true that the Democrats have controlled the Congress most of the time since 1932, and they did retain a majority in the House following Reagan's victory. But their majorities have been inflated by their century-old dominance in the South, an advantage which has been steadily diminishing.

In 1961 all twenty-two senators from the eleven states of the Old Confederacy were Democrats, as were ninety-nine of this region's 106 House members. But in 1981 these same states were represented in the Senate by eleven Democrats, ten Republicans and one independent, Sen. Harry F. Byrd, Jr., of Virginia. Their House delegations were made up of seventy Democrats and thirty-eight Republicans. Moreover, a significant number of Southern Democrats have frequently voted with the opposition on critical issues, as many of them did on Reagan's major economic proposals in 1981.

The support for Reagan from self-styled Southern "boll weevils" and some other Democratic House members infuriated some party leaders. "We will not forget those who chose to abandon the principles of the Democratic Party," said Richard Hatcher, the vice-chairman of the Democratic National Committee. But in fact the national committee had no power to punish the rebels, and the House Democratic Caucus, which conceivably might have stripped away committee assignments from the conservatives, let them off with a scolding and a vague warning that future defections could bring retributions.

Even this mild response stirred resentment from the defectors, who have grown accustomed to considering themselves as totally free agents. Two conservative House Democrats, Bob Stump of Arizona and Eugene Atkinson of Pennsylvania, who announced they would formally leave their party to become Republicans, said the caucus pronouncement had influenced their decisions.

Republicans greeted the news of these conversions

with loud cheers. But my conversations with Stump and Atkinson indicated that they are not likely to be any more reliable as Republicans than they were as Democrats. A political party's main function, Stump said, "is selecting the best candidate for office. Partisanship should be put aside after the election." The idea of party discipline on issues, Atkinson said, "went out with high-button shoes."

For their part, Republicans exulted in the Democratic reverses of 1980 and gave their new president unusually solid support in the Congress in the first months of 1981. But by the fall of the year the self-interest of legislators once again asserted itself against the claim of party loyalty, and Republican "gypsy moth" congressmen deserted Reagan when his proposed budget cuts threatened trouble for them in their own districts.

In the wake of Reagan's impressive victory, Republicans pinned their hopes for the future on what they perceived to be a conservative trend and on expectations of continued popular support for Reagan. But conservatism appeared to be more appealing as an abstract label than as a bulwark for specific programs or for building party support. A Harris poll of 16,000 voters during the closing days of the 1980 campaign showed that conservatives enjoyed a slight numerical edge over middle-of-the-roaders and a considerable advantage over liberals. But the same poll also showed that a big majority of those surveyed opposed such conservative goals as a constitutional amendment banning abortion, while supporting handgun registration and the Equal Rights Amendment, both opposed by conservatives.

In a later Harris poll a majority regarded "big government" as the biggest threat to the country. But even larger majorities believed that government has "deep responsibility" for taking care of the poor, that government should handle "the most important issues," such as curbing inflation and avoiding recession, and that government regulators should make certain that private industry does not "take advantage of the public."

The Republican reliance on Reagan to give the party a long-term lift is also dubious. Reagan's personal standing, like that of his predecessors, has been subject to sharp swings. His Gallup rating at the end of his first year in the White House was lower than that of any elected president since Gallup began polling in the 1930s. Moreover, even Dwight Eisenhower, who maintained an unusually high level of popularity throughout his White House tenure, had difficulty transferring his personal appeal to his party.

Demographic breakdowns of the 1980 returns showed that while the old Democratic coalition continued to deteriorate, no new Republican coalition of distinctive social or economic groups emerged. Voting differences blurred between groups that have been traditionally aligned with one party or another, and Reagan benefited from the discontent with Carter's record among such once reliable Democratic constituencies as blue-collar workers and Catholics.

Reagan himself highlighted the extent to which his candidacy was oriented toward generalized dissatisfaction with Carter when, in his peroration during the televised presidential campaign debate, he asked voters to ask themselves: "Are you better off than you were four years ago?" A CBS survey showed that more than half the voters who believed themselves to be better off than in 1976 cast ballots for Carter. But nearly two-thirds of those who felt they were worse off voted for Reagan.

That judgment carried Reagan to victory but left his political future, and his party's, hostage to the unpredictable and often uncontrollable fluctuations of the economic indices. This is a shaky foundation for building a new political alignment.

But the Democrats had nothing more constructive to offer. To be sure, following their 1980 defeat, some

Democratic leaders talked earnestly about the need for their party to establish a new identity and find a new ideology. "When you say 'I'm a Democrat' now, people don't know what you stand for," Harold Ickes, Jr., son of the New Deal curmudgeon and a Kennedy campaign strategist, told me. "The Democratic party has to develop a new core of ideas." But the national party officially took no action in this area, beyond establishing a so-called strategy council designed so that it would confine itself mainly to mounting periodic attacks on Reagan and the Republicans.

In fact, most Democrats I talked to after the election seemed resigned to staking their party's future on their ability to capitalize on Reagan's anticipated mistakes and misfortunes. "Sure we need a new umbrella," said Anne Wexler, a White House political adviser under Carter. "But Reagan has got to be the handle. For the short term we are going to have to rally around issues created by what he does as president." For the long term the Democrats had no strategy except to wait until 1984, when their next presidential nominee might help them redefine themselves, at least temporarily.

For each party "the center of gravity," in V. O. Key's phrase, remains roughly what it has been for nearly a century. As their 1980 national platforms testify, the Democrats remain more eager advocates of federal intervention in domestic problems, the Republicans more determined to rely on the private sector.

Yet neither party possesses the intellectual and political discipline to convert these general tendencies into realistic and effective policy alternatives. Democrats jeered, not without reason, that Reagan won the presidency by promising gains without pains. But when Reagan's budgetary policies damaged the economy, Democrats could not agree on a remedy. Each party continues to get intermittent injections of strength from the other's failures, but neither seems able to establish a consistent appeal to a significant coalition. And so the political pendulum swings back and forth, and voter disaffection increases.

The enfeebled condition of both parties, once decried mainly by academics or insurgents outside the party organizations, is now acknowledged by insiders and higher-ups. "The parties today are really more or less impotent," no less a regular than Gerald Ford wrote on the eve of the 1980 election, "and if you do not have party responsibility, the system does not work."

What can the parties do to make themselves more potent and more relevant? The answer, under the existing strictures of the Constitution, is nothing much. In its 1950 report, the American Political Science Association's committee on political parties recommended creation of a party council, composed of the president or presidential nominee, congressional leaders, constituency group representatives, and others with a substantial stake in party affairs. The council would be expected to supervise party management, draft a proposed platform and generally harmonize relations between the president and his party's members in Congress in order "to cultivate the idea that the party in power itself, rather than particular individuals at either end of Pennsylvania Avenue, is responsible for its record of legislative and executive action."

But the deep-rooted institutional rivalries between executive and legislature, and between both and the party, which the report sought to heal, doomed this proposal from the start. Its nearest actual counterpart was the Democratic Advisory Council, set up after the 1956 election by Democratic National Chairman Paul Butler to develop alternatives to the programs of the Eisenhower administration so that the Democrats could fulfill "the true role of an opposition party." But the top Democratic congressional leaders, Sam Rayburn and

Lyndon Johnson, did not choose to be advised on such matters by anyone outside their own legislative hierarchies. They refused to join the council and resolutely ignored its recommendations. When John Kennedy regained the White House for the Democrats in 1960, he saw to it that the council was abolished.

After the 1980 election, Democratic National Chairman Charles Manatt tried to establish a roughly similar entity for propounding policy proposals. But the suspicious Democratic congressional leadership agreed to participate only if the group's activities were limited and the word "policy" was not even used in its name. This was why the Democrats came to establish a party strategy council instead of a policy council.

Unable to deal effectively themselves with their isolation from issues and the inherent causes of their difficulties, party leaders once again turned their attention to the familiar subject of procedural reform. Within a few months of the 1980 election, the Republican National Committee and the Democratic National Committee each established commissions to review and to revise the mechanical framework for nominating presidential candidates. Their efforts were launched against a background of criticism, widely expressed by office holders and the press, to the general effect that the present system is too lengthy and too disjointed and unable to present the voters with suitable choices for national leadership.

Even before they began their deliberations, the counterreformers placed most of the blame on the proliferation of primaries. There is no doubt that primaries have increased in importance. The number has climbed steadily from seventeen in 1968 to twenty-three in 1972 to thirty in 1976 to thirty-seven in 1980.* Moreover in 1980 about

---

* The 1980 total of primaries included Puerto Rico and the District of Columbia, as well as thirty-five states. Not all jurisdictions had primaries for both parties; for the Democrats there were thirty-five, for the Republicans, thirty-six.

75 percent of the delegates to both conventions came from primary states, compared with about 40 percent in 1968. But what remained in doubt was what could be done to lessen the impact of the primaries and, more importantly, what benefit such changes would bring to the system of politics and government.

One frequently heard proposal was to bunch the primaries together, either by region or by some other method, and schedule them all on four or five dates instead of allowing them to be spread out over seventeen weeks as they were in 1980. Such a change, its advocates contend, would shorten the campaign and diminish the heavy influence on the outcome of scattered early contests, such as the Iowa caucus and the New Hampshire primary.

But the length of the campaign is mainly a function of the demands of modern politics, not the primary calendar. Kennedy's candidacy in 1960, Goldwater's in 1964, and Nixon's in 1968 all demonstrated the advantages of an early start even in the prereform era, when only a relatively few primaries were seriously contested or given much attention. Because of weak political parties, the volatile electorate, and fragmented interest groups, unless a presidential candidate happens to be an incumbent, he is forced out to the hustings early and often to build support, and of course to offset the efforts of his competitors.

Moreover, bunching the primaries together would provide a substantial advantage to candidates who are already well known, well established and well financed and make it harder than ever for outsiders to succeed. The Democratic Party's experiences with George McGovern and Jimmy Carter may have given outsiders a bad name. But on the other hand, Richard Nixon was an insider. His performance and the record of other insiders in both parties in recent years are good reasons for doubting that a system designed to help insiders at the expense of outsiders will necessarily provide better candidates or better governance.

Regional primaries might permit candidates to save travel time, but there is no reason to believe that their time would be put to any better use than it is now. The real problem with the nominating process is not its length, but its irrelevance. Simply compressing the schedule, while leaving untouched the inherent weaknesses in the relationships between politics and government, would do nothing to shift the focus of the campaign from personalities and slogans to serious debate over issues and program alternatives.

A more significant and more hotly debated remedy advanced for the ills of the nominating system is to strengthen the influence of elected officials and party leaders by making a substantial number of them automatic delegates to the national convention, free to support whichever candidate they favor regardless of the outcome of the primaries and caucuses. In other words, they would be designated in advance as kingmakers in the event of a deadlock, which they would presumably seek to bring about.

When the latest in a succession of Democratic Party delegate selection commissions, chaired by North Carolina Governor James Hunt, met in Washington in the fall of 1981, it was confronted with a formal request from the AFL-CIO that up to 30 percent of the convention delegates should be made up of elected and party officials, officially unpledged to any candidate.* And Rep. Gillis Long of Louisiana, chairman of the House Democratic Caucus, proposed that this contingent should in-

---

* A version of this proposal, adopted by the Democratic National Committee in 1982, provides that about 15 percent of the delegates to the 1984 national convention will be unpledged party and elected officials, including three-fifths of the Democratic members of the House and Senate.

clude two-thirds of all the Democratic members of the
House, who would be selected by their own colleagues.
In justification, Long told the commission members:

> One of the unanticipated, and I believe, unfortu-
> nate consequences of the reform movement in the
> Democratic Party has been the exclusion of elected
> officials from the convention process. We have paid
> a terrible price for that. Most elected officials are
> attuned to mainstream concerns. For the health and
> vigor of our party, they need to be involved in the
> party process. They know the political waters. They
> know the shoals and prevailing currents. Our party
> cannot afford to carry on without this knowledge.

Long's argument deserves examination because it ex-
poses some widely held misconceptions about the impact
of reform and the workings of the political system. To
begin with, there was no shortage of professional politicians at the 1980 Democratic convention. According to a
CBS survey, about two-thirds of the 3,381 delegates were
elected officials or party officials or both. No fewer than
twenty-one out of twenty-nine Democratic governors
were present and accounted for.

It is true that only eight senators and thirty-five representatives were in attendance as fully accredited delegates. Many others were on hand at the convention
under a special provision of the party rules which granted
members of Congress access to the convention floor
and all other significant delegate privileges except the
right to vote. But other members of Congress were not
excluded, as Long and others suggested. All they had to
do to become delegates was to go through the regular
selection process and take their chances with other delegate candidates. Conceivably they could have run as uncommitted delegates, but as a practical matter they
would have had a better chance if they pledged themselves to a presidential candidate.

A good many of the stay-at-homes explained that they did not want to get involved in the friction of the campaign, which might have damaged them among their own constituents. But the campaign was where the action was, where the voters were deciding about the Democratic Party's future, and where there was an opportunity for elected officials to exercise leadership. By passing up that opportunity, the Democratic House and Senate members demonstrated a sense of isolation from their party which will take more than the granting of convention voting privileges to overcome.

The rationale for encouraging their participation at the convention, as Long contended, is that "they know the political waters" and are thus endowed with a superior insight which enables them to recognize the candidate most qualified to govern, or at least most likely to succeed on election day in their own bailiwicks. Once that may have been true. But recent experience makes this assumption dubious.

When the 1972 campaign started, the all but unanimous judgment of the Democratic Party's most prominent office holders was that Edmund Muskie would be their party's strongest candidate for the presidency. They rushed to endorse him and to pledge themselves as convention delegates in support of his nomination As a result many of them were absent from the national convention that year after Muskie's candidacy turned into what his own managers acknowledged to be one of the worst fiascos of modern politics.

Consider also the example of Mayor Richard Daley of Chicago, regarded as the most puissant and pragmatic professional politician of his day. Daley's haste to anoint Jimmy Carter as the party's standard-bearer in 1976 precluded any further effort by Carter's rivals to carry the contest for the nomination to the convention floor. The mayor had already passed on to his reward when his former colleagues in the party were condemning the reforms and the reformers for bringing down upon them the blight of Carter's presidency. But he was still among us on election night in 1976 when Carter, running against the man who had pardoned Richard Nixon and presided over the worst recession since the 1930s, was unable to carry Daley's own state of Illinois.

In sum, the record in recent years offers little evidence that giving elected officials a special status at the convention would improve the nominating process. If a candidate won a majority, or close to it, of the delegates in the preconvention competition, as has been the case in both parties since 1960, elected officials would be unlikely to put themselves in the position of thwarting the will of the voters by opposing their favorite. If, on the other hand, the nomination was still in doubt at the convention, the elected officials could hold the balance of power. But it is unlikely that they would wield this power in the deliberative and statesmanlike fashion envisaged for them because they would be under intense pressure from their own supporters, and most particularly their financial contributors, to vote for one candidate or another.

This largely explains the enthusiasm of organized labor for making elected officials automatic delegates. The determination of the unions to implement this change is a commentary on both the labor movement and the political process. Individual union leaders have had a hard time persuading their rank-and-file members to vote for candidates they endorse. As a result they have been frustrated by the dominance of primaries and their influence in the Democratic Party's nominating process has faded. But as the biggest single source of campaign funds and organization support for Democratic candidates, the unions still carry considerable weight with elected officials. And so an enhanced role for elected officials at the convention offers labor leaders a back-door opportunity to regain power in the picking of a president.

Along with unions and other interest groups, another potential source of pressure on elected officials is an incumbent president, whose control over federal funding and appointments has a strong tendency to influence judgment. Thus, in 1980, about 80 percent of the Democratic office holders in New York State endorsed Carter before the state's presidential primary, in which Senator Kennedy defeated the president by nearly 400,000 votes.

The power of an incumbent president, even when he is not an active candidate, was earlier demonstrated at the 1968 Democratic convention, which included a substantial contingent of senators and representatives among its delegations. That convention refused to allow the party platform to deviate from Lyndon Johnson's policy on the Vietnam War despite the pleas of its own nominee, Hubert Humphrey.

Desperate for support of the antiwar forces in his campaign against Nixon, Humphrey favored a compromise plank on Vietnam, which was supported by the Kennedy and McCarthy delegates, but which Johnson opposed. The chairman of the convention platform committee was the late Hale Boggs, a longtime Louisiana congressman and a longtime ally and confidant of Lyndon Johnson. "The Congressman's position was clear and also immovable," Humphrey later wrote of his encounter with Boggs. "If the President would not accept the plank, then he, as chairman of the platform committee, would resist it, send out the word that the plank was unacceptable." The compromise died and Humphrey was forced to spend much of his campaign trying to win the backing of the opponents to the war.

The behavior of elected officials at conventions is part of the syndrome that afflicts their party, the presidency, and the entire political system. "We have become a disconnected party," Glenn Watts, president of the Communications Workers of America, warned members of the Hunt Commission. He added, in words that could be applied to the Republicans as well as the Democrats: "If the White House, the Congressional Democrats, the State Parties and the DNC continue to go their separate ways, we would question whether the word Party is the appropriate descriptive term."

Arguing for a broader role for elected officials at the convention, Watts declared: "Let us be honest about the problem. The elected officials aren't grabbing for power, they're running for cover. We ought not allow them to avoid responsibility for selecting a nominee, writing a platform and organizing a party. We must bind their fate to ours in a common undertaking."

Watts defined part of the problem. But its solution demands change more fundamental than the alteration of national convention procedures.

CHAPTER TEN

Bridging
the Gap

In searching for a way to bridge the gap between politics
and government one needs first to look back at James
Madison's view of human nature which helped mold the
Constitution. Determined to ensure that the separate
branches of government would restrain each other, Madison devised a system that made checking and balancing
an imperative of individual self-interest, and that created
a perennial clash of ambitions which has been heightened
significantly by the social and economic dynamics of the
past twenty years.

If the legislature, the executive and the party are to
agree to bind their fates in common, as Glenn Watts envisaged, a comparably powerful incentive of self-interest
must be provided. This common self-interest is what
our system of politics and government notably lacks. At
present, what is right for the national party, and for the
national government, is often not what is most important
for the self-interest of the congressman. A host of other
factors, apart from the political fortunes of his party's
president or presidential candidate, control the careers of
a member of Congress. With his own constituencies to
satisfy, and his own opposition to face every two years,
the congressman's political priorities only occasionally
coincide with those of the president. Most of the time
the congressman follows the general rule, in Lloyd Cutler's phrase, of "every man for theirself."

In a pinch, a president can sometimes gain a congressman's vote by expediting a grant or an appointment, or promising some other concession. But the dominant ethic then becomes, as that pillar of the New York Democracy, Monroe Goldwater, put it: "What have you done for me lately?" This is not a satisfactory formula for creating consistent support for public policies, nor is it likely to constructively influence the congressman's judgment of competing candidates for his party's presidential nomination.

To provide a reliable incentive of common self-interest for the different parts of the system, changes need to be made in government as well as in politics. Before politics can become more relevant, and political parties healthier, some of the constitutional structures of government that work against these goals must be revised. Over the years, scholars and politicians have offered a number of proposals for this purpose. Here are some worth considering:

Combining presidential and congressional elections. The point of this idea is to encourage the linkage of presidential and congressional campaigns and to give both branches more reason for cooperation in government. The Johnson administration introduced a proposed constitutional amendment to extend the terms of House members to four years so that House elections would coincide with presidential elections. A more far-reaching version of this plan would put a party's candidates for president, House and Senate on the same slot on the ballot, obliging voters to support all or none of them. This would mean reducing the terms of all senators to four years. As long as the president continues to be chosen by electoral votes, this change would not guarantee that the same party would control the presidency and both chambers of the legislature. Under this arrangement, Democrats John Kennedy in 1960 and Jimmy Carter in

1976 would have faced a Senate controlled by the Republican party since Kennedy and Carter won fewer states than their presidential opponents—unless, of course, the appeal of Democratic senatorial candidates would have been strong enough to reverse the results in some of the states Kennedy and Carter lost. But it would at least make more likely one-party control of the presidency and the House of Representatives. In any event, it would strengthen the ties between the president and his party in Congress and make it easier for voters to hold them accountable when they were in control.

Electing at-large members of the House of Representatives. Professor Charles Hardin of the University of California has devised a scheme that would assure one-party control of the presidency and the House and at the same time make the House more sensitive to concerns of the national electorate as opposed to local issues. As outlined in Hardin's book *Presidential Power and Accountability*, each party would nominate one hundred House members to run at large, in addition to their regular candidates in the 435 congressional districts. The party winning the presidential election would automatically elect its entire at-large slate. The losing party would be awarded a maximum number of fifty at-large seats, less whatever number would be needed to give the winning party a majority in the House.

This would still leave open the possibility of the Senate being controlled by the minority party, although Hardin would offset that problem by reducing the powers of the Senate. Another problem is that voters would face a mind-boggling task in trying to assess the competing slates of one hundred at-large candidates.

Lifting the ban on members of Congress serving in the cabinet. This is another approach to fostering cooperation between the branches. According to various versions of this idea, the president would be allowed or required to select some or all of his cabinet from sitting members of the House and Senate. This would give the legislature a direct role in shaping executive policy and offer the executive a reliable sounding board in the legislature. Some lawmakers might have difficulty serving their own constituents while carrying out their cabinet duties, but this problem could be avoided by selecting cabinet members from among at-large legislators.

Allowing intraterm elections. Either the president or the Congress would be allowed to issue a call for a new national election once during the regular four-year term, as a means of resolving deadlocks and crises in government leadership. The fact that by invoking this power the president and the lawmakers would be putting their own offices at risk would presumably prevent its abuse.

Eliminating the vice-presidency. This would remove from the political system an element of fortuitousness and unaccountability and a source of confusion and derisive humor. Twice during the past six quadrennials, presidents have been replaced by vice-presidents who most people believed could not have gained the White House on their own. In the event of presidential death or disability, the Speaker of the House could serve as acting president pending a special election to choose a new chief executive.

Such alterations in the separation of powers, by making the government more cohesive, more accountable, and more responsive, could pave the way for parties to help make politics more relevant. Among the steps that then could be taken, by changes in party rules or by acts of Congress:

Creating a coordinating party council. This council could carry out a coordinating role along the lines suggested in the American Political Science Association's committee report, but it could go even further because the parties would be strengthened by constitutional changes the report did not contemplate. The council could turn party platforms into a significant force in the real political world, and thus shift the emphasis in campaigns from personalities to issues. The council could be empowered to reject party candidates who did not pledge to support the platform and to discipline them if they did not fulfill these pledges in office. The new constitutional ties between the president and the Congress would make these sanctions reasonable.

Nominating by party caucus. With the establishment of clear party policy goals and tight party discipline, presidential candidates could be chosen by a caucus of elected officials, expanded perhaps to include representatives of major constituency groups. One possibility would be for the top choices of the caucus to compete in a single, federally funded national primary. But that sort of personalized competition could be avoided by making the first choice of the caucus the candidate of the party.

Institutionalizing the opposition party. Leaders of the losing party in the general election could be given special status as leaders of the opposition. They would be afforded access to information from executive-branch agencies, equal time on television to respond to majority party statements and regular opportunities to question cabinet secretaries before the Congress.

As I have indicated, all the foregoing proposals present mechanical and other problems that require extensive examination and discussion. But their overall thrust offers potential benefits of large significance. The fostering of cooperation between the two political branches of government and the stressing of joint policy aims would help to create a climate in which party coalitions could flourish. Candidates would be encouraged to construct alliances around clear alternatives, spelled out in the party platform, and to develop corresponding policies once in office.

The multitude of interest groups in our society will

always be a problem for politics and government. But a more cohesive system would be better able to establish and to achieve broad goals which would transcend some of the competing concerns of special constituencies. One of the supposed virtues of the present system is that the parties resist extremism and strive for compromise on conflicts between competing interests. But in reality these so-called compromises are often achieved by making unrealistic promises to both sides. If the parties can be made accountable for their pledges, they will be forced to seek genuine compromises by reconciling differences and advocating attainable bargains.

Party politics would be less divisive and more substantive. State primaries and caucuses could be dispensed with. Candidates for the presidency would no longer need to establish elaborate personal campaign organizations or to rely on the technology of polling, television advertising and fund raising. Since contenders for leadership would be appealing to a constituency of only a few hundred members of Congress, and perhaps other party leaders, campaigns would be short, simple and inexpensive. Decisions by the party caucus would be based mainly on the politics advocated by the candidate and the candidate's ability to carry them out rather than on personality factors which dominate campaigning in the primaries. The members of the party caucus would certainly not be infallible. But they would be powerfully motivated to exercise their best judgment by their own self-interest in the party's success in appealing to the voters at large and in governing the country. And by depersonalizing the presidency, and strengthening the party, the disproportionate influence of the incumbency on nominating campaigns would be curbed.

And at the base of the system the voters would have a better chance of understanding their real stakes in national policy, of influencing ultimate decisions and of assessing responsibility for success or failure. They would be given the opportunity to make real choices between values and goals, and thus gain a measure of control over public policy and their own lives.

One way to gauge the potential impact of these changes on the political future is to reflect on how they might have altered the history of the past twenty years.

With a disciplined majority party behind him in the Congress, John Kennedy would not have had to struggle vainly for approval of his legislative program and might have been less inclined to indulge in excessive rhetoric and provocative international ventures.

Lyndon Johnson, had he been elected to succeed Kennedy, would not have been pressured to race against the clock to create the Great Society. But his own party, and the opposition, would have been more strongly positioned to force him to justify his escalation of the war in Vietnam.

Richard Nixon might have been spared the burden of trying to lead a divided government. At any rate, his party and the opposition could have monitored his use of executive power and probably prevented the abuses of Watergate. If Watergate had occurred, Congress could have forced a special national election which would have produced a new government, avoiding the two years of stalemate and division of the Ford presidency.

Jimmy Carter would probably not have been nominated for the presidency in 1976, because it is unlikely that a party caucus would select a candidate so unfamiliar with the national government and so alien from his own party. If Carter had gained office, he probably would have been forced to call a special election when he proclaimed that the nation was suffering a crisis of confidence and then shook up his cabinet.

As for Ronald Reagan, his polished nonchalance and skill as a television performer would not have been decisive in a campaign focused on issues. If he had been elected, his economic policies would have been subjected to more careful scrutiny by his own party and a more effective challenge from the opposition than he had to face.

What would it take to bring about the sort of fundamental changes in the system I have described? The same elements that are required for the success of any political enterprise—financial backing, intellectual energy, grassroots organizing, and committed and imaginative leadership. So far, though, the cause of reforming the separation of powers has not attracted this combination of resources.

Not that the present system has lacked critics. The Constitution is nearly two centuries old and for at least half that time the impediments to responsive government created by the separation of powers have come under fire. Many of the early critics, of whom Woodrow Wilson was the most prominent, were chiefly troubled by the resistance of Congress to the president. The clashes between FDR and the Congresses of the later New Deal era stimulated similar critiques.

In the wake of Vietnam and Watergate, constitutional critics such as Charles Hardin proposed amendments mainly to prevent further abuses of presidential power. With the Carter presidency, the focus shifted from the excesses of the presidency back to the friction between the presidency and Congress, a concern that continued with the Reagan Administration.

But for all the varied evidence of shortcomings, no single issue has yet emerged to set in motion a sustained effort at reform. James Sundquist, one of the more cogent scholars of politics and government, doubts that any such catalytic cause will develop. "However grave the structural weaknesses of the American government," Sundquist writes, "those that are embedded in the Constitution are quite beyond the reach of reformers—barring some governmental breakdown more catastrophic than any so far experienced."

It remains to be seen what sort of a catastrophe is needed to energize reform. Just before Thanksgiving in 1981, Ronald Reagan, in the midst of a budget dispute with the Congress, ordered a shutdown of all but the essential services of government for the better part of a day. The action was widely derided as a piece of political theater by a president determined to depict himself as the taxpayer's best friend. It certainly was theatrical, but it could also have been a harbinger of events to come—if not during Reagan's tenure, then during the stewardship of a successor. It may be that it will not require a catastrophe itself, but simply the threat of a catastrophe, to rouse the forces of reform into action.

Clearly the impetus for change must come from outside the political establishment, although there are sympathizers within. Democratic Congressman Henry Reuss, in a newsletter to his Wisconsin constituents drafted in the fall of 1981, noted that the twentieth century had posed problems for government undreamed of by the Founding Fathers. "Increasingly in this century," Reuss wrote, "we have to ask ourselves whether the competition between the President and the Congress helps create an effective government or makes it impossible."

A constituency for change does already exist—among businessmen, labor leaders, and other segments of the public—as a result of disaffection with the present system. A Gallup poll after the 1980 election showed that two-thirds of those surveyed wanted campaigns conducted differently. Among the ideas mentioned were shortening the campaign, putting more focus on issues, and imposing lower ceilings on campaign spending. Other polls show that the public is sympathetic toward some constitutional revisions. A majority favor lengthening the term of House members to four years and eliminating the electoral college. Significantly, though, the idea of limiting presidents to one six-year term, which has been applauded by some previous presidents, but which would make chief executives even less accountable than they are now, was rejected by a margin of two to one.

The threshold question about closing the separation of powers is not whether it can be done, but whether it can be done in such a way that the benefits will outweigh the disadvantages. Even beginning to find an answer will require some form of national commission, composed of elected officials, party leaders, scholars, and representatives of interest groups, which would spend an extensive period on research and evaluation, and supplement these activities with public hearings and educational programs. The task of the commission would be to consider the desirability of modifying the separation of powers and to draft alternative proposals. Congress could then lay down the guidelines for a constitutional convention, which would be needed if broad changes are being considered.

Meanwhile, though, it is worth considering briefly some of the objections that have been traditionally raised to modifying the separation of powers. The most frequently expressed concern is that any such change would make the government too powerful. As Laurence H. Silberman, a scholarly lawyer who has served two Republican presidents, puts it: "The separation of powers among the three branches of government makes it very difficult for the government to accrue power and it is as desirable today as it was 200 years ago to make it difficult for government to accrue power, because that is a potential threat to the well-being of citizens."

But the record of the past two decades—and indeed the past two centuries—shows that the separation of powers has not prevented government from accruing power. The changes in our own society and in the world have made the steady growth of government power inevitable. What the separation of powers has done is to make it difficult for either the executive or legislative branch of government to exercise power responsibly, and this is the most serious threat to the citizenry.

The threat of government intrusion on individual rights is always with us and always to be guarded against. But the best protection we have is in the Bill of Rights, in the Fourteenth Amendment to the Constitution, and in the Supreme Court's role as their institutional guardian. None of the proposals for making the political branches of the government more coordinated and more accountable need in any way diminish these bulwarks against the weight of government.

Other defenders of the status quo claim that American society is too variegated to support a party system which offers distinct choices on policy to the voters. James Q. Wilson, Harvard professor of government, describes the American public as "a collection of separate publics that have discovered, or would readily admit if it were pointed out, that if they have to vote yes or no on a Party's cohesive performance or comprehensive set of policies, they cannot do so. They are torn with too many internal contradictions."

Professor Wilson did not offer any samples of comprehensive policies that had been submitted to the public and it would be a challenge to think of any during the past twenty years. No one could disagree that the public is fragmented and torn. Indeed, the evil of faction, which the Founding Fathers so abhorred, is rampant today in the form of dozens of special interest groups. If anything, the separation of powers has contributed to this problem by debilitating political parties. The increasing fragmentation of the electorate is a compelling argument for change—which could help parties establish cohesive programs and coalitions, which in turn could provide us with a badly missing sense of purpose and direction as a country.

Still other opponents of change worry that significant revision of the Constitution would lead to a massive unraveling of the American system and destroy the relative stability which is one of its virtues. Such alarms ignore the fact that the separation of powers can be modified while still preserving the integrity of state governments and the existence of the Senate, which could continue to express the principles of federalism. Moreover, the perpetuation of single-member districts in the House of Representatives, as opposed to some form of proportional representation, and the winner-take-all formula for awarding a state's electoral votes in presidential elections, as opposed to election by a nationwide popular vote, along with the force of habit and of tradition are all likely to ensure the continuance of the two-party system as a stabilizing force. Indeed, the present threat to stability is not from the specter of some third or fourth or fifth party but from the difficulties the two parties have maintaining themselves as credible forces.

The final objection to constitutional change comes from those who point out in effect that "nobody's perfect." All sorts of defects are prevalent in our society and how can government be expected to rise above these human shortcomings? Or so the argument goes. Madison touched on this point, more elegantly, in *Federalist* No. 51, when he asked: "But what is government itself but the greatest reflection of all on human nature?" The answer is that human nature has many sides, some better than others, and these differing facets express themselves in the values of our society. Through government we can pick and choose which values should be encouraged and affirmed. Government cannot change human nature. But we can try to change our government so that it responds to the needs of our citizens, appeals to their reasoned self-interest, encourages their higher aspirations, and, ultimately, brings out the best in human nature.

Certainly, no change, no matter how far-reaching, will be a panacea that by itself can cure the problems that confront us on a broad range of fronts. The most that can be expected from any constitutional reform is that it would allow the political and governing system to respond more quickly and rationally to these problems. But that would represent a critical improvement.

The approach of the bicentennial of the Constitution serves as a reminder of the unique circumstances attending the birth and development of the United States, which, however much they have altered since 1787, still offer reason for hope about our ability to adjust to and benefit from constitutional change. Daniel Bell has described the old-fashioned faith in "American exceptionalism," a concept based on the special advantages offered by our political tradition of liberty, egalitarianism, and free expression, our abundant natural resources, and our heterogeneous pool of human talent. The self-confidence derived from these conditions helped Americans to endure, and generally to prevail against a host of difficulties, including the deficiencies of their political machinery.

In recent years, as Bell points out, some of these old advantages have lost their luster and the old confidence has been jolted. Nevertheless, compared with other nations, the United States is still relatively strong in body and spirit, strong enough to risk a fundamental change in its Constitution. The greater risk is in avoiding change and allowing the present system to undermine our heritage and our hopes for the future.

A Note on Sources

This book would not have been possible without the profusion of literature dealing with the past six quadrennials. The volume of material contrasts with the scarcity of contemporary chronicles of pre-1960 elections and reflects our mounting absorption with the presidency. As a result of this bounty, I have been able to rely, in addition to my own notes and recollections, almost entirely on firsthand accounts by the participants in the quadrennials and the journalists who recorded them. I have listed some works as sources which are not cited in the notes because I found them valuable as background and I believe others will, too.

My debt to two books listed here—*The Deadlock of Democracy* by James MacGregor Burns and *The Party's Over* by David S. Broder—is much greater than indicated by the citations. Both works were essential in helping me develop my structure and theme, although of course neither author bears any responsibility for my conclusions.

To avoid cluttering the source list and notes I have for the most part not given specific citations for speeches and other public statements which were widely reported.

Published Sources

I. General

Beard, Charles A., and Beard, Mary R. *The Rise of American Civilization*. 2 vols. Rev. ed. New York: Macmillan, 1945.

Bensman, Joseph, and Rosenberg, Bernard. "Mass Media and Mass Culture." In Philip Olson, ed., *America as a Mass Society*. New York: The Free Press, 1963.

Bode, Kenneth H., and Casey, Carol F. "Party Reform: Revisionism Revised." In Robert A. Goldwin, ed., *Political Parties in the Eighties*. Washington, D.C.: American Enterprise Institute, 1980.

Bowen, Catherine Drinker. *Miracle at Philadelphia*. Boston: Atlantic–Little, Brown, 1966.

Bryce, James. *The American Commonwealth*. Vol. 1. 2d ed. New York: Commonwealth, 1908.

Burns, James MacGregor. *The Deadlock of Democracy*. Rev. ed. Englewood Cliffs, N.J.: Prentice-Hall, 1963.

Citrin, Jack. "The Changing American Electorate." In Arnold J. Meltsner, ed. *Politics and the Oval Office*. San Francisco: Institute for Contemporary Studies, 1981.

Committee on Political Parties, American Political Science Association. "Toward a More Responsible Two-Party System." Supplement to *The American Political Science Review*, September 1950. New York: Johnson Reprint Corp., 1969.

Cronin, Thomas E. *The State of the Presidency*. 2d ed. Boston: Little, Brown, 1980.

Cutler, Lloyd. "To Form a Government." *Foreign Affairs,* Fall 1980.

Davis, James W. *Springboard to the White House.* New York: Thomas Y. Crowell, 1967.

De Vries, Walter, and Tarrance, V. Lance. *The Ticket-Splitter.* Grand Rapids, Mich.: William B. Eerdmans, 1972.

Fairfield, Roy P., ed. *The Federalist Papers.* 2d ed. Garden City, N.Y.: Anchor, 1966.

Ford, Gerald R. "Imperiled, Not Imperial." *Time,* November 10, 1980.

Goldman, Peter. "The Presidency: Can Anyone Do the Job?" *Newsweek,* January 26, 1981.

Goodman, William. *The Two Party System in the United States.* 3d ed. Princeton, N.J.: Van Nostrand, 1964.

Grob, Gerald N., and Billias, George Athan, eds. *Interpretations of American History.* Vol 1. 3d ed. New York: The Free Press, 1978.

Hardin, Charles M. *Presidential Power and Accountability.* Chicago: University of Chicago Press, 1974.

Hofstadter, Richard. *The Idea of a Party System.* Berkeley: University of California Press, 1969.

Huntington, Samuel P. *American Politics: The Promise of Disharmony.* Cambridge, Mass.: Belknap Press of Harvard University Press, 1981.

Janowitz, Morris. *The Last Half-Century.* Chicago: University of Chicago Press, 1978.

Key, V. O., Jr. *Politics, Parties and Pressure Groups.* 5th ed. New York: Thomas Y. Crowell, 1964.

King, Anthony. "How Not to Select Presidential Candidates." In Austin Ranney, ed., *The American Elections of 1980.* Washington, D.C.: American Enterprise Institute, 1981.

Koch, Adrienne. *Jefferson and Madison: The Great Collaboration.* New York: Alfred A. Knopf, 1950.

Krammick, Isaac. "Tom Paine: Radical Democrat." *Democracy,* January 1981.

Ladd, Everett Carll, Jr. "The Brittle Mandate." *Political Science Quarterly,* Spring 1981.

———. "Political Parties and Governance in the 1980s." In Arnold J. Meltsner, ed., *Politics and the Oval Office.* San Francisco: Institute for Contemporary Studies, 1981.

————. "205 and Going Strong." *Public Opinion*, June/July 1981.

Ladd, Everett Carll, Jr. "The Brittle Mandate." *Political tions of the American Party System*. New York: W. W. Norton, 1975.

Leuchtenburg, William E. *Franklin D. Roosevelt and the New Deal*. New York: Harper Colophon Books, 1963.

Mann, Thomas E. "Elections and Change in Congress." In Thomas E. Mann and Norman J. Ornstein, eds., *The New Congress*. Washington, D.C.: American Enterprise Institute, 1981.

Mitofsky, Warren, and Plissner, Martin. "The Making of the Delegates, 1968–1980." *Public Opinion*, October/November 1980.

Moos, Malcolm. *The Republicans: A History of Their Party*. New York: Random House, 1956.

Neustadt, Richard E. *Presidential Power*. Rev. ed. New York: John Wiley, 1980.

Penniman, Howard R. *Sait's American Parties and Elections*. 5th ed. New York: Appleton-Century-Crofts, 1948.

"President vs. Congress" (An AEI Forum.) Washington, D.C.: American Enterprise Institute, 1980.

"The Presidential Nominating Process: Can It Be Improved?" (A roundtable discussion.) Washington, D.C.: American Enterprise Institute, 1980.

"The Presidential Nominating System: A Primer." Institute of Politics, John F. Kennedy School of Government, Harvard University, Cambridge, Mass.: 1979.

Ranney, Austin. "The Political Parties: Reform and Decline." In Anthony King, ed., *The New American Political System*. Washington, D.C.: American Enterprise Institute, 1978.

Rose, Richard. "Government Against Sub-Governments." In Richard Rose and Ezra N. Suleiman, eds. *Presidents and Prime Ministers*. Washington, D.C.: American Enterprise Institute, 1980.

Sanford, Terry. *A Danger of Democracy: The Presidential Nominating Process*. Boulder, Col.: Westview Press, 1981.

Schlesinger, Arthur M., Jr. *The Politics of Upheaval*. Boston: Houghton Mifflin, 1960.

Sundquist, James L. *The Decline and Resurgence of Congress.* Washington, D.C.: Brookings Institution, 1981.

Vance, Cyrus. "Reforming the Electoral Reforms." *New York Times Magazine*, February 22, 1981.

Ver Steeg, Clarence L. "The Constitution of the United States of America, 1787: The Preamble." In Daniel J. Boorstin, ed., *An American Primer.* New York: New American Library, 1968.

Walker, Jack. "Presidential Campaigns: Reforming the Reforms." *The Wilson Quarterly*, Autumn 1981.

II. The Quadrennials

Sources used for more than one quadrennial are marked with an asterisk.

1960

* Broder, David S. *The Party's Over.* New York: Harper & Row, 1972.

* Eisele, Albert. *Almost to the Presidency.* Blue Earth, Minn.: Piper, 1972.

Fairlie, Henry. *The Kennedy Promise.* Garden City, N.Y.: Doubleday, 1973.

Kennedy, John F. "The Speeches, Remarks, Press Conferences and Statements of Senator John F. Kennedy, August 1 through November 7, 1960." In *Freedom of Communications: Part I.* Washington, D.C.: U.S. Senate Commerce Committee, 1961. (Referred to in notes as Kennedy Speeches.)

Mailer, Norman. "Superman Comes to the Supermarket." *Esquire*, November 1960.

Nixon, Richard M. "The Speeches, Remarks, Press Conferences, and Study Papers of Vice President Richard M. Nixon, August 1 through November 7, 1960." In *Freedom of Communications: Part II.* Washington, D.C.: U.S. Senate Commerce Committee, 1961. (Referred to in notes as Nixon Speeches.)

* O'Brien, Lawrence F. *No Final Victories*. Garden City, N.Y.: Doubleday, 1974.

Schlesinger, Arthur M., Jr. *Kennedy or Nixon: Does It Make Any Difference?* New York: Macmillan, 1960.

―――. *A Thousand Days*. Boston: Houghton Mifflin, 1965.

Sorensen, Theodore C. *Kennedy*. New York: Harper & Row, 1965.

Whalen, Richard J. *The Founding Father*. New York: New American Library, 1964.

White, Theodore H. *In Search of History*. New York: Warner, 1979.

―――. *The Making of the President: 1960*. New York: Atheneum, 1961.

1964

*Evans, Rowland, and Novak, Robert. *Lyndon B. Johnson: The Exercise of Power*. New York: New American Library, 1966.

Goldwater, Barry M. *With No Apologies*. New York: William Morrow, 1979.

Gilder, George F., and Chapman, Bruce K. *The Party That Lost Its Head*. New York: Alfred A. Knopf, 1966.

Johnson, Lyndon Baines. *The Vantage Point*. New York: Holt, Rinehart and Winston, 1971.

Mohr, Charles. "Requiem for a Lightweight." *Esquire*, August 1965.

Novak, Robert D. *The Agony of the GOP*. New York: Macmillan, 1965.

Shadegg, Stephen. *What Happened to Goldwater*. New York: Holt, Rinehart and Winston, 1965.

* White, F. Clifton, with William J. Gill. *Suite 3505*. New Rochelle, N.Y.: Arlington House, 1967.

White, Theodore H. *The Making of the President: 1964*. New York: Atheneum, 1965.

1968

Chester, Lewis; Hodgson, Godfrey; and Bruce Page. *An American Melodrama*. New York: Viking Press, 1969.

Commission on the Democratic Selection of Presidential Nominees, Harold Hughes, Chairman. "The Democratic Choice." Adopted by the 1968 Democratic National Convention. Reprinted in the *Congressional Record*, October 15, 1968, vol. 114, pt. 23, 31544–60. (Referred to in notes as "The Democratic Choice.")

* Commission on Party Structure and Delegate Selection, George McGovern, Chairman. "Mandate for Reform." Washington: The Democratic National Committee, 1970. (Referred to in notes as "Mandate for Reform.")

Greenhaw, Wayne. *Watch Out for George Wallace*. Englewood Cliffs, N.J.: Prentice-Hall, 1976.

Humphrey, Hubert H. *The Education of a Public Man*. Garden City, N.Y.: Doubleday, 1976.

McGinnis, Joe. *The Selling of the President: 1968*. New York: Trident Press, 1969.

Newfield, Jack. *Robert Kennedy: A Memoir*. New York: Bantam, 1970.

Nixon, Richard M. *Six Crises*. Garden City, N.Y.: Doubleday, 1962.

———. *Nixon on the Issues*. (Positions taken during the 1968 campaign.) New York: Nixon-Agnew Campaign Committee, 1968.

———. *Nixon Speaks Out*. (Speeches and statements during the 1968 campaign.) New York: Nixon-Agnew Campaign Committee, 1968.

* ———. *RN: The Memoirs of Richard Nixon*. New York: Grosset and Dunlap, 1978.

Phillips, Kevin P. *The Emerging Republican Majority*. New Rochelle, N.Y.: Arlington House, 1969.

* Safire, William. *Before the Fall*. Garden City, N.Y.: Doubleday, 1975.

Whalen, Richard J. *Catch the Falling Flag*. Boston: Houghton Mifflin, 1972.

White, Theodore H. *The Making of the President: 1968*. New York: Atheneum, 1969.

Witcover, Jules. *85 Days: The Last Campaign of Robert Kennedy*. New York: G. P. Putnam's, 1969.

———. *The Resurrection of Richard Nixon*. New York: G. P. Putnam's, 1970.

1972

Dougherty, Richard. *Goodbye, Mr. Christian: A Personal Account of McGovern's Rise and Fall*. New York: Doubleday, 1973.

Evans, Rowland, Jr., and Novak, Robert D. *Nixon in the White House*. New York: Random House, 1971.

Glass, Andrew, and Cottlin, Jonathan. "Democratic Reform Drive Falters." *National Journal*. June 19, 1971.

Hart, Gary Warren. *Right from the Start*. New York: Quadrangle, 1973.

McGovern, George. *An American Journey*. (Campaign speeches.) New York: Random House, 1974.

———. *Grassroots*. (Autobiography.) New York: Random House, 1977.

May, Ernest R., and Fraser, Janet, eds. *Campaign '72: The Managers Speak*. Cambridge: Harvard University Press, 1973.

Reich, Charles A. *The Greening of America*. New York: Random House, 1970.

Scammon, Richard M., and Wattenberg, Ben J. *The Real Majority*. New York: Coward-McCann & Geoghegan, 1971.

* Schlesinger, Arthur M., Jr. *The Imperial Presidency*. Boston: Houghton Mifflin, 1973.

* ———. *Robert Kennedy and His Times*. Boston: Houghton Mifflin, 1978.

Thompson, Hunter S. *Fear and Loathing on the Campaign Trail: '72*. San Francisco: Straight Arrow Books, 1973.

Watts, William, and Free, Lloyd, eds. *State of the Nation*. New York: Potomac Associates, Universe Books, 1973.

Weil, Gordon L. *The Long Shot*. New York: Norton, 1973.

White, Theodore H. *The Making of the President: 1972*. New York: Atheneum, 1973.

1976

Caddell, Patrick, and Shrum, Robert. "White Horse, Pale Rider." *Rolling Stone*, October 24, 1974.

Carter, Jimmy. "The View from the Top of the Carter Campaign." (Interview.) *National Journal*, July 17, 1976.

Commission on Delegate Selection and Party Structure, Barbara Mikulski, chairwoman. "Final Report." Washington, D.C.: Democratic National Committee, 1973.

Ford, Gerald R. *A Time to Heal*. New York: Harper & Row, 1979.

Hartmann, Robert T. *Palace Politics*. New York: McGraw-Hill, 1980.

Knott, Jack, and Wildavsky, Aaron. "Jimmy Carter's Theory of Governing." *The Wilson Quarterly*, Winter 1977.

Moore, Jonathan, and Fraser, Janet, eds. *Campaign for President: The Managers Look at '76*. Cambridge, Mass.: Ballinger, 1977.

Reichley, A. James. *Conservatives in an Age of Change: The Nixon and Ford Administrations*. Washington, D.C.: Brookings Institution, 1981.

Scheer, Robert, and Golson, Barry. "Jimmy Carter: A Candid Conversation." *Playboy*, November 1976.

Schram, Martin. *Running for President 1976: The Carter Campaign*. New York: Stein and Day, 1977.

Witcover, Jules. *Marathon*. New York: Viking Press, 1977.

1980

Boyarsky, Bill. *The Rise of Ronald Reagan*. New York: Random House, 1968.

Broder, David, *et al. The Pursuit of the Presidency 1980*. New York: Washington Post-Berkley, 1980.

Caddell, Patrick, and Wirthlin, Richard. "Face Off: A Conversation with the Presidents' Pollsters." *Public Opinion*, December/January 1981.

Califano, Joseph A., Jr. *Governing America*. New York: Simon and Schuster, 1981.

Carter, Jimmy. *Why Not the Best?* New York: Bantam, 1976.

Commission on Presidential Nomination and Party Structure, Morley A. Winograd, Chairman. "Openness, Participation and Party Building." Washington, D.C.: Democratic National Committee, 1978. (Referred to in notes as Winograd Commission.)

Fallows, James. "The Passionless Presidency." *Atlantic*, May 1979.

Germond, Jack and Witcover, Jules. *Blue Smoke & Mirrors.*
New York: Viking Press, 1981.
Kuttner, Robert. *Revolt of the Haves: Tax Rebellions and
Hard Times.* New York: Simon and Schuster, 1980.
Ladd, Everett Carll, Jr. "The 1980 Presidential Election."
Public Affairs Review, vol. 2 (1981).
Miller, Arthur H. "What Mandate? What Realignment?"
Washington Post Outlook, June 28, 1981.
Moore, Jonathan, ed. *The Campaign for President: 1980 in
Retrospect.* Cambridge, Mass.: Ballinger, 1981.
Shogan, Robert. *Promises to Keep: Carter's First 100 Days.*
New York: Thomas Y. Crowell, 1977.
Wirthlin, Richard; Breglio, Vincent; and Richard Beal.
"Campaign Chronicle." *Public Opinion,* February/March
1981.

Reference Notes

The following abbreviations are used in the notes: *NYT*
for the *New York Times,* *WP* for the *Washington Post* and
LAT for the *Los Angeles Times.*

CHAPTER ONE

Page 1

"Why not the best?": the question also served as the
title of Carter's campaign autobiography. Carter, *Why
Not the Best?,* 58–65, 179.
John Marshall's view: from *M'Culloch v. Maryland,*
quoted by Ver Steeg.
"Why Great Men Are Not Chosen": Bryce, 84–92.
Bryce wrote: "It would seem that the natural selection
of the English parliamentary system, even as modified

by the aristocratic habits of that country, has more tendency to bring the highest gifts to the highest place than the more artificial selection of America."

Disarticulation: Janowitz, 15–26, *et seq.*

Interest-group involvement: Gallup Poll, August 16, 1981.

Wirthlin's campaign role: Wirthlin, Breglio, and Beal.

Viguerie's fund raising: *LAT*, December 19, 1977.

"No way to run a railroad": *NYT*, November 23, 1981.

"No member of that majority": Cutler.

"Rise of individualism": Sundquist, 475.

"The only power I have": Goldman.

"I sit here all day": Neustadt, 9.

Assassination attempt and Reagan's ratings: *WP*, April 1 and April 2, 1981.

"We all know what he looks like": *NYT*, September 20, 1974.

Iowa caucus campaign: *LAT*, January 20, 1981.

Disenchantment with parties: CBS-*NYT* poll, May 3, 1981, De Vries and Tarrance, 19–38; Ladd, "The Brittle Mandate"; Citrin.

CHAPTER TWO

Page 27

"The only no-no": *NYT*, January 8, 1981; also *Washington Star* editorial, "Presidents and Politics," January 10, 1981.

"An albatross around my neck": *NYT*, March 19, 1981. Carter used the metaphor in a question-and-answer session with Princeton University students.

"Today's politicians": *WP*, September 4, 1981.

The Framers' dilemmas: Burns, 16–20; also Grob and Billias, 145–59.

Congress "unhinged": Burns, 43.

"I've never seen": Evans and Novak, *Lyndon B. Johnson*, 490.

"Every man wishes": Krammick.

The "poison" of faction: Fairfield, 34.

"If I could not go": Burns, 27.

Contradictory partisanship: Hofstadter, 17–18.

"Now is the time": Burns, 47.

Demise of King Caucus: *ibid.*, 52–56; also Penniman, 258–71.

Calhoun's second thoughts: Penniman, 262.

Flaws in the convention system: *ibid.*, 262–77.

"The pot house politician": Herman E. von Holst, *The Constitutional and Political History of the United States*, quoted in Grob and Billias, 222.

The "irrepressible conflict": Beard, Vol. II, 1–51.

"I was always Erie": Penniman, 275.

Conflicts between parties on issues: Key, 217.

"Only one life": Burns, 99.

Impetus for primaries: Penniman, 282–94.

The rise and fall of primaries: Davis, 25–30.

FDR not prepossessing: Leuchtenburg, 32, refers to the feeling among "sober observers" that Roosevelt "was an immature politician with little sense of the seriousness of the tasks that lay ahead." He also quotes Walter Lippman's celebrated appraisal of FDR as "a pleasant man who, without any important qualifications for the office, would very much like to be President."

"Deny you ever made it": Schlesinger, *Politics of Upheaval*, 621.

"The right kind of people": Burns, 159.

"Met their match": Schlesinger, *Politics of Upheaval*, 639.

Roosevelt's coalition: Ladd, with Hadley, provides statistical analysis of voting alignments during the New Deal era.

CHAPTER THREE

Page 45

Truman's pointed question: *Facts on File*, 1960, 230. Truman had his own candidate for the nomination, fellow Missourian Stuart Symington.

"These party barons": Neustadt, 175.

Postwar changes: The data are from the *Statistical Abstract of the United States: 1980*. Ladd, with Hadley, analyzes the impact of these changes on voting patterns.
"The visitor from Mars": Samuel Lubell, "Who Elected Eisenhower," *Saturday Evening Post*, January 10, 1953, quoted in Moos, 485.
"Made divided government work": Evans and Novak, *Lyndon B. Johnson*, 195.
Muted party differences: Key, 217.
Johnson grumbled. Schlesinger, *A Thousand Days*, 20. The remark is from a conversation Johnson had with Schlesinger in January 1960.
"The romantic dream": Mailer.
JFK's first race: Whalen, *The Founding Father*, 393–399.
"Holdovers from another era": Burns, 308.
"Feigns an ignorance": Whalen, *The Founding Father*, 402.
JFK and McCarthy: *ibid.*, 437.
JFK and the liberals, his self-description: Sorensen, 17–22.
Strategy against Lodge: O'Brien, 29; Whalen, *The Founding Father*, 424.
JFK and the regulars: O'Brien, 28.
"Man of destiny": *ibid.*, 50.
The pros' view of JFK: Sorensen, 124.
JFK's early travels: *ibid.*, 101.
JFK's primary strategy: *ibid.*, 122–53.
Humphrey's campaign tactics: Eisele, 135–46.
"And if he breaks that oath": Theodore White, *1960*, 107–8.
"There is no contest": Kennedy Speeches, 170.
"Prepared for apathy": Schlesinger, *A Thousand Days*, 66.
Kennedy on sacrifices: Kennedy Speeches, 183.
The missile gap: *ibid.*, 427.
Contest for the GOP nomination: Theodore White, *1960*, 159–77, 180–208.
"I'm tired of hearing": Nixon Speeches, 745.

"Nothing else but America": *ibid.*, 619.
"No new proposals": Sorensen, 181.
"Packaged products": Schlesinger, *A Thousand Days*, 64–65.
"Nixon lacks taste": Schlesinger, *Kennedy or Nixon*, 13.
"A bookish man": *ibid.*, 22.
"The America I fought for": Kennedy Speeches, 209.

Voter turnout: the figures on turnout used here and in subsequent chapters are from the Committee for the Study of the American Electorate.

"The center of action": *ibid.*, 951.
"The margin is narrow": Sorensen, 219.
"Slender majorities": Broder, *The Party's Over*, 30.
"Party means damn little": Sorensen, 346.
"Drop the domestic stuff": *ibid.*, 242.
"All my life": Sorensen, 309.
"No difference *in fact*": *ibid.*, 678.
The symbolism of space: *ibid.*, 523–29.
"We couldn't survive": *ibid.*, 325.
Krock's complaint: Fairlie, 216.
"A golden interlude": Schlesinger, *A Thousand Days*, 207.
"The wrong president" and "Didn't he show the Irish?": Sorensen, 449, 458.
"My style is harder": Theodore White, *In Search of History*, 461.
"The worse I do": Schlesinger, *A Thousand Days*, 292.
"Let's win this one": O'Brien, 107.
Cuba as a GOP issue: F. Clifton White, 80–82.

CHAPTER FOUR

Page 78

The Chicago Meeting: F. Clifton White, 36–42.
"A whole new dimension": *ibid.*, 151.
"Ripe for revolt": *ibid.*, 50.
"Not such a bad fellow": Novak, 74.

Reaction to the remarriage: *ibid.*, 146–48.
Rockefeller avoided involvement: Gilder and Chapman, 117–25.
The Southern tilt: F. Clifton White, 174–75, 213; Novak, 188–201.
Reversed strategy: F. Clifton White, 253; Novak, 252.
New stress on primaries: F. Clifton White, 261.
New Hampshire campaign: *ibid.*, 280–98; Novak, 301–30.
Rockefeller's armory show: Gilder and Chapman, 131.
"It's up to you": Novak, 396n.

"What needed to be done": Johnson, 28.
Texas party politics: Broder, 65–74.
Johnson's Senate tactics: Evans and Novak, *Lyndon B. Johnson*, 81–118.
"You know I will": Johnson, 29.
"Doubts and reservations": *ibid.*, 92–98.
The Kennedy problem: Evans and Novak, *Lyndon B. Johnson*, 435–43.
"As easy as possible": Johnson, 103.
"The President seemed relieved": Goldwater, 192–93.
Goldwater later noted that "LBJ campaigners" exploited the charges his Republican rivals had made against him on the issues of war and race. Nevertheless, he chose to hold Johnson himself blameless: "I don't recall a single statement from the President or the White House which could be regarded as in violation of that private agreement."
Won't send American boys: Evans and Novak, *Lyndon B. Johnson*, 532.
"Talked about it all the time": Mohr, "Requiem for a Lightweight."
"Against mighty few": Theodore White, *1964*, 347.
"Able to get by": The story, from the *Washington Star*, is quoted in Broder, 46.
"Look at that damn woman": Mardian told me the story several years after the event, when he was serving in the Nixon administration.

"The biggest popular margin": Evans and Novak,
Lyndon B. Johnson, 490. Actually, Johnson won by
nearly 16 million votes. But in any event his concerns
proved to be justified.
Califano's new phone: O'Brien, 182.
Eighty-four out of eighty-seven: *ibid.*
"Is that *our* Billy?" Johnson, 210.
"A healthy two-party system": Broder, 64.

CHAPTER FIVE

Page 107
Shifting alignments on Vietnam: Ladd, with Hadley,
232–46.
"When a President is wrong": Chester, Hodgson, and
Page, 58.
"It will be Lyndon Johnson": *ibid.,* 395.
"I can't run": Newfield, 207.
"Badly defeated": O'Brien, 229.
"A large share of the money": Humphrey, 375.
Incongruities of primaries: Bode and Casey.
One-third already selected: "Mandate for Reform."
Nonexistent rules: *ibid.*
The Indiana caucuses: "The Democratic Choice."
The unit rule and proxy voting: "Mandate for Reform."
"What have you done for me lately?": "The Demo-
cratic Choice."
"A revolution on my hands": *ibid.*

"The wisdom of Lincoln": the comment, from the
preface to the 1968 edition of *Six Crises,* is quoted in
Nixon Speaks Out, 273.
"Throw them in the Potomac": Greenhaw, 300.
"Undercuts our whole policy": Humphrey, 389.
"Too much on substance": Nixon, *Six Crises,* 422.
Nixon's appraisal of Romney: Safire, 46.
"A package deal with IBM": Whalen, *Catch the Falling
Flag,* 77.
Nixon's computers: Chester, Hodgson, and Page, 612.

Enemas for elephants: Whalen, *Catch the Falling Flag*, 192.

"The omnipotent eye": Nixon, *Memoirs*, 303.

Nixon's commercials: Witcover, *The Resurrection of Richard Nixon*, 238–39.

"Impression is easier": McGinnis, 36.

Nixon and the Southern delegates: Chester, Hodgson, and Page, 462–63.

Chipped away at the courts: Nixon, *Nixon on the Issues*, 80–87.

"If there's war": Safire, 58.

The new conservative majority: Phillips provides the clearest outline in print of Mitchell's hopes. Appropriately, Phillips served for a time as an aide to Mitchell in the Justice Department, which Mitchell sought to employ as the cutting edge of Nixon's Southern strategy. A tactical triumph: Evans and Novak, *Nixon in the White House*, 341.

CHAPTER SIX

Page 139

The McGovern Commission's work: "Mandate for Reform."

"The greatest goddam change": May and Fraser, *Campaign '72*, 4.

More than twenty-one million: Richard M. Scammon, director of the Elections Research Center, provided this figure in an interview.

Origins of reform: Bode and Casey.

"A regular Democrat": Glass and Cotlin.

"An air of uneasiness": Watts and Free, 20.

"The coming revolution": Reich, 4.

"The unyoung, unblack and unpoor": Scammon and Wattenberg, 45–71.

Opinion on busing: Watts and Free, 100.

White flight: *ibid.*, 91.

Black strategy conference: *ibid.*, 89.

Muskie's shifts: May and Fraser, *Campaign '72*, 42; Hart, 87.

"From the top down": May and Fraser, *Campaign '72*, 92.

"The angry cry": McGovern, *An American Journey*, 181, from a speech given in Milwaukee, March 23, 1972.
Archie Bunker enclaves: Hart, 144; May and Fraser, *Campaign '72*, 110.
McGovern's issue problems: Hart, 204–5; Weil, 96–101.
McGovern's advisers warned: Weil, 77.
"I wish I had never heard": Hart, 190.

Pledge to end the war: McGovern, *An American Journey*, 115.
Cutting defense spending: *ibid.*, 142–48.
New ethical standards: *ibid.*, 46–50.
"Dangerous and useless": Bowen, 272.
As Hart recalled: Hart, 238–45.
A flat no: Dougherty, 157; Weil, 169.
"I have nine kids": Theodore White, *1972*, 203.
Comments from *WP* and *NYT*: quoted in Thompson, 330–36.
Reston's and Kraft's comments: quoted in *Newsweek*, August 14, 1972.
"This wouldn't have happened": Schlesinger, *Robert Kennedy*, 210.
Nixon's selection of Agnew: Whalen, *Catch the Falling Flag*, 202–3.
"We were McGovern in trouble": Dougherty, 213.
Nixon's poll lead: Theodore White, *1972*, 216.
Nixon's campaign role: Nixon, *Memoirs*, 665.
"The most efficient": *ibid.*, 669.
Kissinger's Watergate quip: Safire, 656.

Jefferson's "higher obligation": Koch, 240.
Nixon's reaction: Nixon, *Memoirs*, 628.
Nixon's defense on Cambodia: Schlesinger, *The Imperial Presidency*, 187.
"It would be a signal": Nixon, *Memoirs*, 509.
"Light a fire": *ibid.*, 513.
"The pre-emptive strike": Safire, 315.

Nixon's view of break-in: Nixon, *Memoirs*, 514.
The Carswell controversy: Evans and Novak, *Nixon in the White House*, 166.
Nixon's impoundments: Schlesinger, *The Imperial Presidency*, 237–38.
"New majority momentum": Nixon, *Memoirs*, 669.
"No sacred cows": *ibid.*, 761.
"A completely new beginning": *ibid.*, 768.
Investigation of Strauss: The case was dropped by the Watergate special prosecutor's office because under the statute of limitations, too much time had elapsed since the alleged offense. *LAT*, January 10 and June 14, 1975. Watergate impact not significant: *LAT*, December 8, 1973.
"Parties in disrepute": May and Fraser, *Campaign '72*, 219.

CHAPTER SEVEN
Page 177
Carter's range of identities: *LAT*, May 25, 1975.
The debate on reform: This material is based on my own reporting at the time, and also on interviews with John Quinn, special assistant to Mikulski, and Carol Casey, research coordinator of the commission. See also the Mikulski Commission report cited in the source list for Chapter Seven.

Jordan's August 1974 memo: Witcover, *Marathon*, 134–38.
Analysis of Wallace prospects: Caddell and Shrum, "White Horse, Pale Rider."
"All right on race": Young interview with *LAT* Washington Bureau, June 29, 1976.
Carter's use of Wallace's name: Schram, 48.
Jordan's advice on Wallace: Witcover, *Marathon*, 110–12; Schram, 54.
"Don't bring all the good guys": Young interview.
"If Jimmy wins": Shogan, 44.
"I don't yield to them": *LAT*, May 3, 1976.

"I would rather die": *ibid.*
Carter and the lobbyists: *ibid.*
"What distinguishes me": *LAT*, January 21, 1976.
Daley's position: Witcover, *Marathon*, 369–74.
The *Times's* guess: *NYT*, July 1, 1976.
Harris poll: "Carter: A New Positive National Figure,"
June 17, 1976.

A spirit of amity: Ford, *A Time to Heal*, 135–40.
"An activist pace from the start": *ibid.*, 133.
"Cardiac insufficiency": quoted in Hartmann, 238–39.
Ford brooded: Ford, *A Time to Heal*, 158–75.
Kissinger's advice: *ibid.*, 161.
"The monkey off my back": *ibid.*, 159.
"Jail Ford": *ibid.*, 179.
"His own personal paralysis": Hartmann, 269.
Ford's veto record: Reichley, 322–25.
"Not one nickel": Ford, *A Time to Heal*, 255.
"A serious blow": *ibid.*, 276.
The GAO study: *LAT*, October 6, 1976.
"Faith . . . restored": Ford, *A Time to Heal*, 284.
A "President people wanted": Hartmann, 329.
Goldwater's judgment: *WP*, May 17, 1975.
"No pale pastels": Witcover, *Marathon*, 46.
Using the incumbency: Ford, *A Time to Heal*, 364.
"Ford's leadership style": Moore and Fraser, *Campaign for President*, '76, 47.
Teeter's findings: *ibid.*, 119–20.
Carter's problems: *ibid.*, 135.
"Democratic rhetoric": *ibid.*, 144.
Carter in Birmingham, *LAT*, September 14, 1976.
The veto argument: *NYT*, October 29, 1976.
"To the point of absurdity": Moore and Fraser, *Campaign for President*, '76, 134.
"Adultery in my heart": Scheer and Golson.

CHAPTER EIGHT

Page 208
"I don't have any strings": Shogan, 57.

Management disciplines: Carter, *Why Not the Best?*, 170–71.
Foreign-policy disputes: *NYT*, July 7, 1976, quoted in Knott and Wildavsky.
"Like Marshal Pétain": Fallows, May 1979.
"Inclined . . . not to compromise": Carter, "View from the Top."
Dealing with energy: Shogan, 233–39.
"The hell with it": Califano, 336.
The proposal succumbed: *ibid.*, 364.
Blurred the argument for reform: Kuttner, 246–49.
No apologies: *LAT*, July 26, 1977.
"My natural inclination": Shogan, 278–79.
The Eizenstat memo: *WP*, July 7, 1979.

Brown "sure to run": Broder, *et al.*, *Pursuit of the Presidency*, 94.
"He had to do something": Moore, *1980*, 19.
"The worst standing": Harris Poll, July 31, 1979.
Kennedy announcement: *LAT*, November 8, 1979.
"Unpatriotic to criticize": Moore, *1980*, 19.
Assault on Kennedy: *LAT*, December 4, 1979.
"Most devastating thing": Moore, *1980*, 35.
Kennedy should decide: Germond and Witcover, 142–43.
Carter's use of incumbency: *Wall Street Journal*, January 11, 1980.
"We will go to our friends": *NYT*, December 10, 1979.
Kennedy's Georgetown speech: *NYT*, January 29, 1980.
"Painted ourselves into a corner": Moore, *1980*, 90.
The delegate binding rule: Winograd Commission, rule 11H.
Delegate survey: Moore, *1980*, 91.

Moral degeneration: Boyarsky, 178.
"The best electronic media candidate": Caddell and Wirthlin.
Strauss's comment: *LAT*, November 15, 1980.
"By two to one": Moore, *1980*, 199.

"A saber rattling ideologue": *LAT*, August 15, 1980.
"There is no way": quoted in King, 305.
The *New York Times*'s joke: *NYT*, October 26, 1980.
"The worst economic mess": *NYT*, February 6, 1981.
Comparison with the Depression: Leonard Silk, "A Look at Reagan Economics 'Lesson,'" *NYT*, February 7, 1981.
"It was our mandate": *NYT*, March 11, 1981.
"An overwhelming mandate": *NYT*, June 17, 1981.
Reagan's economic statements: fact sheet and text issued by Reagan-Bush campaign, September 9, 1980.
University of Michigan surveys: Miller. Also Arthur H. Miller and Martin P. Wattenberg, "Policy and Performance Voting in the 1980 Election," paper delivered at the 1981 meeting of the American Political Science Association.

CHAPTER NINE

Page 250

"Why of all places?": Nixon, *Memoirs*, 629.
The three parts of parties: Key, 163–65.
JFK's entrepreneurial style: Sorensen, 171–72; O'Brien, 91–92.
"I don't give a damn": Schlesinger, *Robert F. Kennedy*, 212.
"Essentially catalysts": Eisele, 139–40.
Bush's defense of Nixon: *LAT*, February 4, 1974; "GOP Chairman Undaunted by Watergate," *LAT*, July 25, 1973. "Nixon Officials Were Bugged in 1960, Bush Says." Bush complained that it was "a gross distortion to microscopically analyze" the 1972 Nixon campaign.
Curtis forced out: *Washington Star*, December 7, 1977; *LAT*, December 8, 1977.
Lance "a folk hero": *LAT*, March 21, 1978.
White's backing for Carter: *Facts on File*, 1980, 366.
Richards and the controversy over independent spending: *WP*, November 17 and November 24, 1981.
"We will not forget": *WP*, June 15, 1981.

A vague warning: *WP*, September 17, 1981.

Mixed views of conservatism: Harris polls of November 11, 1980, and March 23, 1981.

Blurred distinctions: Ladd, "The 1980 Presidential Elections"; Gallup Poll, December 21, 1980.

"Are you better off": CBS-*NYT* poll, November 4, 1980, cited in Ladd, "The 1980 Presidential Elections." The Gallup Poll, December 7, 1980, measured aspects of the "anti-Carter" vote.

"More or less impotent": Ford, "Imperiled, Not Imperial."

Democratic Advisory Council: Sundquist, 473–74.

Focus on procedural reform: for typical criticism of present system, see Sanford; Vance; and *NYT*, March 27, 1981, "4 Election Studies Focus on Presidency," by Adam Clymen.

Rescheduling primaries: Among those offering such proposals were Senator Robert Packwood (R.-Ore.) and Rep. Morris Udall (D.-Ariz.).

No shortage of professionals: Mitofsky and Plissner.

About 80 percent: *NYT*, February 9, 1980.

Clear and immovable: Humphrey, 389–90.

CHAPTER TEN

Page 268

Proposals for constitutional change: Cutler; Sundquist, 464–67.

"Beyond the reach": Sundquist, 466.

Constituency for change: Gallup polls of November 23 and December 4, 1980, and February 25 and May 14, 1981.

Silberman's views: *President vs. Congress.*

"Separate publics": *ibid.*

"American exceptionalism": Daniel Bell, "The End of American Exceptionalism," *The Public Interest*, Fall 1975, quoted and discussed in Ladd, "205 and Going Strong."

Index